'Love me or kill me'

MANCHESTER
UNIVERSITY PRESS

theory·practice
·performance·

The series will offer a space for those people who practise theatre to have a dialogue with those who think and write about it.

The series has a flexible format that refocuses the analysis and documentation of performance. It provides, presents and represents material which is written by those who make or create performance history, and offers access to theatre documents, different methodologies and approaches to the art of making theatre.

The books in the series are aimed at students, scholars, practitioners, and theatre-visiting readers. They encourage reassessments of periods, companies, and figures in twentieth-century and twenty-first-century theatre history, and provoke and take up discussions of cultural strategies and legacies that recognise the heterogeneity of performance studies.

The series editors, with the advisory board, aim to publish innovative challenging and exploratory texts from practitioners, theorists and critics.

also available

The Paris Jigsaw: Internationalism and the city's stages
DAVID BRADBY and MARIA M. DELGADO (eds)
Negotiating cultures IAN WATSON (ed.)

'Love me or kill me'

Sarah Kane
and the theatre of extremes

GRAHAM SAUNDERS

Manchester University Press
Manchester and New York

distributed exclusively in the USA by Palgrave

Published by Manchester University Press
Oxford Road, Manchester M13 9NR, UK
and Room 400, 175 Fifth Avenue, New York, NY 10010, USA
www.manchesteruniversitypress.co.uk

Distributed exclusively in the USA by
Palgrave, 175 Fifth Avenue, New York, NY 10010, USA

Distributed exclusively in Canada by
UBC Press, University of British Columbia, 2029 West Mall, Vancouver, BC, Canada V6T 1Z2

British Library Cataloguing-in-Publication Data
A catalogue record for this book is available from the British Library

Library of Congress Cataloging-in-Publication Data applied for

ISBN 0 7190 5955 0 *hardback*
     0 7190 5956 9 *paperback*

First published in 2002

10 09 08 07 06 05 04 03 02   10 9 8 7 6 5 4 3 2 1

Typeset by Northern Phototypesetting Co. Ltd, Bolton
Printed in Great Britain by Bell & Bain Ltd, Glasgow

CONTENTS

List of illustrations   *page* vii
Preface   ix
Acknowledgements   xiii

1 Introduction   1

PART I **The plays**

2 'This disgusting feast of filth': *Blasted*   37

3 'If there could have been more moments like this':
   Phaedra's Love   71

4 'This sensible hell': *Cleansed*   86

5 'Only love can save me and love has destroyed me': *Crave*   100

6 'Remember the light and believe in the light': *4.48 Psychosis* 109

PART II **Conversations**

7 Conversation with James Macdonald   121

8 Conversation with Vicky Featherstone   128

 9 Conversation with Nils Tabert   134

10 Conversation with Mel Kenyon   143

11 Conversation with Phyllis Nagy   154

12 Conversation with Kate Ashfield   163

13 Conversation with Daniel Evans   168

14 Conversation with Stuart McQuarrie   180

    Afterword: Sarah Kane and theatre *by Edward Bond*   189

    Select bibliography   193
    Index   199

ILLUSTRATIONS

Sarah Kane and Michael Shannon in rehearsals for *Woyzeck*
(1997)   *title page*

1 Sarah Kane and Michael Shannon (playing the title role) in
   rehearsal for *Woyzeck*, The Gate Theatre, 16 October 1997   *page* 82

2 Sarah Kane at rehearsals for *Woyzeck*   83

3 Sarah Kane and cast members in rehearsal for *Woyzeck*   83

4 Cas Harkins as Hippolytus in *Phaedra's Love*, The Gate Theatre,
   May 1996   84

5 Cas Harkins and Phillipa Williams in *Phaedra's Love*   84

6 Cartoon from the *Independent* newspaper, 31st January 1995   85

7 Paines Plough's production of *Crave*, November 1998   85

Title page illustration and 1, 2, 3, 4 and 5 are reproduced by kind per-
mission of the photographer, Pau Ros; 6 is courtesy of the artist Heath
and the *Independent*; and 7 is courtesy of the photographer, Manuel
Harlan.

PREFACE

Sarah Kane's reputation as a playwright has gone through a series of ambiguous and contradictory changes since her debut *Blasted* premiered at the Royal Court in 1995. In their recent assessment of twentieth-century British theatre, Richard Eyre and Nicholas Wright comment that Kane was a 'profoundly original playwright who ... rewrote the theatrical map'.[1] Yet, *Blasted* at the time of its first British production was almost universally castigated by the critical establishment as 'no more than an artful chamber of horrors designed to shock and nothing more'[2] and 'a lazy, tawdry piece of work without an idea in its head beyond an adolescent desire to shock'.[3]

While from early on Kane established a reputation in France and Germany as an important new dramatist, in Britain she has sat uneasily as the theatrical representation of 'Cool Britannia', and included amongst work ranging from Danny Boyle's film *Trainspotting* (1996) to artists such as Damien Hirst. She has also unwillingly been claimed as one of the leading figures in the emergence of a young group of dramatists in the wake of *Blasted*; these figures included Mark Ravenhill, Rebecca Prichard,

1 Richard Eyre and Nicholas Wright, *Changing Stages: A View of British Theatre in the Twentieth Century* (London, 2000), p. 374.
2 Nick Curtis, 'Random Tour in a Chamber of Horrors', *Evening Standard*, 19 January 1995.
3 Charles Spencer, 'Awful Shock', *Daily Telegraph*, 20 January 1995.

Jez Butterworth and Nick Grosso, who were said to exhibit a shared interest in violence together with an abnegation of morality in their work.

This muddied status changed further after Kane's suicide in February 1999. Her last play, *4.48 Psychosis* (1999; Performed 2000), was reviewed by the majority of British theatre critics as little more than a dramatic suicide note, and the appraisal of previous work given a bio-graphical approach in an attempt to seek connections between her work and life. Those looking for such methodology in this book will be sadly disappointed. David Greig comments in his introduction to Sarah Kane's *Collected Plays* that 'it would be a pity if, in attending to the mythology of the author, we were to miss the explosive theatricality, the lyricism, the emotional power, and the bleak humour that is contained within the plays themselves.'[4]

The aim of this study is to provide an introduction to Sarah Kane's work as a dramatist, exploring principle themes and dramatic structure as well as literary and dramatic sources. Sarah Kane was an eloquent and passionate defender of both her own writing and the importance of theatre itself as both an art form and a tool for living sanely. Bringing together interviews, letters and Kane's own writings about the theatre, I have attempted, as much as possible, to let her own words provide the commentary on her own work. In keeping with the introductory nature of this book I have tried to eschew a particular 'reading' or theoretical approach to the plays, but rather draw attention to, and elaborate upon, particular aspects of Kane's dramatic style, as well as develop comparable parallels to some of the rich dramatic and literary sources that inform the plays.

Of course it is also impossible to remain scrupulously neutral in assessing and criticising the work, and my own prejudices and interests surface on occasions. Mainly this takes the assertion that Sarah Kane's theatre was essentially 'Jacobean' in its imagery, characterisation and phi-losophy. Kane herself draws attention to this in the chapter on *Blasted* with her admission that Shakespeare's *King Lear* was a major influence, and where this aspect occurs in other work (notably *Cleansed*) I do point this out.

The book is divided into two parts. The first section is a chronologi-cal introduction to each of the plays. The first chapter attempts to outline the main dramatic methods and themes employed in Sarah Kane's work, as well as her place within the context of a so-called 'movement' of other young writers with shared concerns who emerged in the British theatre of the mid 1990s. Each chapter thereafter looks in more detail at each play.

---

4   David Greig, Introduction to *Sarah Kane: Complete Plays* (London, 2001), p. ix.

The second section is comprised of interviews with various theatre practitioners who have either worked directly on Sarah Kane's plays or express a particular interest in her work. All the material in the second section is free of commentary. Hopefully these exchanges open up new avenues regarding Sarah Kane's work not discussed in the first section. There is also a reprinted essay by Edward Bond, *Sarah Kane and Theatre,* which was originally written shortly after Kane's death. Bond was one of the earliest and most perceptive commentators on Kane's work,[5] realising from the start both its moral integrity and bold theatrical experimentation. The essay makes a passionate argument, for both Sarah Kane's drama and the crucial human need for theatre itself.

I am aware that a book of this nature contributes to David Greig's fear that the plays will become choked by a colonising critical process, 'interpreting, analysing and decoding ... until eventually, the plays themselves come to seem only palimpsests, barely glimpsed beneath the commentary.'[6]

However, it is hoped that both the first section as well as the 'other voices'[7] in the second, will help to give a chance to those with an interest in Sarah Kane's drama to develop a positive criticism and appreciation of her work, either through scholarship, or more importantly by actual performance of the plays.

A book of this nature will always contain omissions and in keeping with the title I have only made cursory mention of the short film *Skin* Kane wrote in 1995. The script has now been published in the collected edition of the plays, and while it is evident that it shares many of the themes and imagery realised in the theatrical work, I have limited the scope of the book to discussing the stage plays only.

A note on the text

Unless stated otherwise, all quotations from Sarah Kane's work come from *The Complete Plays.* A reference such as (4:53) refers to the scene followed by the page number.

Graham Saunders
Birmingham

5 See Edward Bond, 'A Blast at our Smug Theatre', *Guardian*, 28 January 1995, p. 22.
6 Greig, *Complete Plays*, p. xviii.
7 *Ibid.*

ACKNOWLEDGEMENTS

I would like to thank the following individuals and institutions who gave their time and advice in helping with this study. I particularly want to thank the interviewees Kate Ashfield, Daniel Evans, Vicky Featherstone, Mel Kenyon, James Macdonald, Stuart McQuarrie, Phyllis Nagy and Nils Tabert. Edward Bond generously sent me selections from his own correspondence with Sarah Kane and theatre notebooks relating to her work, as well as reading and offering advice on the manuscript; Ingrid Craigie, Josephine Machon, Dan Rebellato and Aleks Sierz also generously allowed me access to interview material. Greg Hobbs allowed me to see the 1993 Birmingham drafts for *Blasted*; Lesley Gabriel and Simon Glaves transcribed several of the interviews; Caridad Svich kept me up to date with productions in America; Sarah Wolf also pointed me in the direction of several obscure but useful resources. My colleague David Ian Rabey at the University of Aberystwyth provided valuable criticism which contributed greatly to the shaping of the book. I particularly wish to thank Maria Delgado who has constantly offered prompt and practical guidance at all stages of its writing.

1

Introduction

I've only ever written to escape from hell – and it's never worked – but at the other end of it when you sit there and watch something and think that's the most perfect expression of the hell that I felt then maybe it was worth it.
(Sarah Kane, Royal Holloway College, London, 3 November 1998)

On Christmas Eve 1994 the dramatist John Osborne died. This prompted commentators, not surprisingly, to reassess his contribution to post-war British theatre. Most agreed that his debut, *Look Back in Anger* (1956), while not necessarily being his best play, nevertheless 'set off a landmine'[1] and invigorated a British theatre which until then had seemed in a state of genteel decline, 'dominated by ingenious productions of the classics or insipid little comedies assuming that manners [had] really not changed since 1914'.[2]

Osborne's death, together with almost exactly five years remaining to the end of the millennium, gave commentators just the excuse they needed to launch a discussion on the current state of British theatre. Bold new writing in the vein of Osborne's early work was felt to be lacking: Benedict Nightingale, surveying 1990s' drama, alludes to this poverty through the somewhat backhanded compliment that Stephen Daldry's

---

1 Alan Stiltoe, 'An Osborne Symposium', in John Russell Taylor (ed.), *Look Back in Anger: A Casebook* (London, 1978), p. 185.
2 *Ibid.*, p. 183.

1992 revival and reinterpretation of J. B. Priestley's *An Inspector Calls* (1947) 'seemed the most contemporary play in London'.[3] The dramatist David Hare also saw the 1990s as a time that marked a breach in the continuity of a process that had evolved since *Look Back in Anger*. 'When Stoppard and Pinter looked behind their backs they saw us coming up ... when Howard [Brenton] or I look back we see no one – no young writers coming up to challenge what we stood for'.[4]

While these commentators might have been looking back to a dimly realised golden-age of radical yet populist drama, they appeared to represent a consensus who believed the raw energy of *Look Back in Anger* was unlikely to happen again. This debate had been intermittently revived since the decade began; indeed a month before Osborne's death, eighty-seven prominent British playwrights signed a joint letter to the *Guardian* newspaper complaining about the lack of new drama on the country's main stages. The theatre critic Michael Billington pointed out that if allowed to continue this policy would turn British theatre into 'a dusty museum rather than a turbulent forum where society carries on a continuous debate with itself'. Billington felt this to be symptomatic of an equally worrying cultural trend whereby, 'It is as if we, as a society, are becoming increasingly wary of work that confronts the nature of the times or that deals head on with big issues.[5]

It was during this atmosphere of nostalgia for another *Look Back in Anger* that less than three weeks after Osborne's death, on 12 January 1995, a new play called *Blasted* would premiere at the Royal Court's Theatre Upstairs by an unknown 23-year-old woman that would share some striking similarities with *Look Back in Anger*. Some commentators, such as Richard Morrison writing in *The Times*, saw this connection between the two plays very early on: 'Three weeks ago, after John Osborne's death, I deplored the lack of danger in the British theatre at present. How they must have giggled at the Royal Court when they heard that! For they knew what I did not.[6]

Wendy Lesser believes that at the time of Osborne's death, Stephen Daldry, then Artistic Director of the Royal Court, was looking back to the period of Osborne in order to find a strategy for its role in the future. Hence Daldry's directorial debut in February 1994 was a revival of Arnold Wesker's *The Kitchen* (1959), and Jez Butterworth's new play *Mojo* (1996)

---

3 Benedict Nightingale, *The Future of Theatre* (London, 1998), p. 27.
4 Peter Ansorge, *From Liverpool to Los Angeles: On Writing for Theatre, Film and Television* (London, 1997), p. 4.
5 Michael Billington, '87 Deadly Sins', *Observer*, 22 November 1994, p. 5.
6 Richard Morrison. 'Radical Chic Better than FBI Cheat', *The Times*, 21 January 1995, p. 5.

would be his 'talismanic'[7] version of *Look Back in Anger*. Lesser also believes 'If Macdonald's [Sarah Kane's *Blasted* and Sam Shepard's *Simpatico*] and Rickson's [*Mojo*] turned out to be the hottest plays in the Royal Court's 1994-5 season, that was in part because Daldry used all his charm, connections and theatrical clout to make them hot'.[8] Despite headlines that greeted its reception such as, 'Rape Play Girl in Hiding',[9] and 'Cash Fury at Vilest Ever Play',[10] Kane herself seemed sceptical about a carefully constructed master-plan by the Royal Court to unleash a new generation of controversial young dramatists in the wake of *Blasted*. In fact Kane maintained that everything possible was done *not* to promote her play: 'The Court had programmed the play into a dead spot. They didn't really know what to do with it. A lot of the people in the building didn't want to do it – they were a bit embarrassed by it so they put it into a spot just after Christmas when no one was going to the theatre and hopefully nobody would notice'.[11]

Moreover, some commentators, writing after Kane's death, felt at the time there was also an element of mischief-making in some of the expressions of outrage that greeted the play. Paul Taylor in the *Independent* observed:

> I was present straight after the first-night performance when two of my colleagues on other papers led the charge by deciding to cook up this play as a news item. My informed guess is that: a) neither of them had been profoundly offended by the play, and b), their subsequent behaviour was not motivated by malice, but by an almost childish sense of journalistic fun – they thought that it would be a wheeze to drag the theatre out of the ghetto of the theatre pages and into mainstream public attention.[12]

The irony concerning *Blasted* is that despite starting out on a trajectory of mock outrage, time has given it a far more favourable assessment, and while it might be an exaggeration to claim that *Blasted* caught the *Zeitgeist* in quite the same way as *Look Back in Anger*, or galvanised a new generation of young writers in the theatre (although some commentators, as we shall see, have made such claims for it), its director James

7   Wendy Lesser, *A Director Calls: Stephen Daldry and the Theatre* (London, 1997), p. 114. Also see Aleks Sierz, *In-yer-face Theatre: British Drama Today* (London, 2000), pp. 38–9, 234–5.
8   Lesser, *A Director Calls*, p. 98.
9   *Daily Express*, 20 January 1995.
10 *Daily Mirror*, 20 January 1995.
11 Dan Rebellato, 'Brief Encounter Platform', public interview with Sarah Kane, Royal Holloway College, London, 3 November 1998. See Mel Kenyon's comments about the Royal Court's scheduling of *Blasted*, p. 146.
12 Paul Taylor, 'Obituary' *Independent*, 23 February 1999.

Macdonald is probably right when he calls *Blasted* 'perhaps the least seen and most talked about play in recent memory'.[13]

'F****** and Chopping': the New Brutalists

Another notable effect of *Blasted* was that it came to be seen, in much the same way as *Look Back in Anger* over thirty years previously, as a catalyst in restoring the fortunes of new writing to the British stage. The impact and notoriety of the play *seemed* to spawn and bring to prominence a group of young dramatists whose work, like those who followed Osborne such as John Arden and Arnold Wesker, came to be seen – rightly or wrongly – as sharing similar themes and styles. Certainly, *Blasted* was considered by some commentators to be the precursor 'that put critics on their toes about a new strain of writing and a new kind of audience'.[14] These so-called writers of 'smack and sodomy plays'[15] included Jez Butterworth, Nick Grosso, Joe Penhall, Rebecca Prichard and Michael Wynne. Probably the other most prominent figure in this supposedly writer-led movement was Mark Ravenhill, who also provoked considerable media prurience with his Royal Court debut *Shopping and Fucking* (1996).

Although *Blasted* is said to have been the play that marked a resurgence in the Royal Court's reputation, Aleks Sierz is right to maintain that 'historians may be tempted to date the start of theatre's Cool Britannic phase from the play's premiere … But they would be wrong to do so'.[16] In fact, the play that preceded it at the Theatre Upstairs in December 1994 (*Ashes and Sand* by Judy Upton) was perhaps the first play that provided signs of what was to come from this new group of writers. Upton's play, about a violent girl-gang in a southern British seaside town, led the theatre critic Claire Armitstead to observe that 'suddenly the Royal Court has found a current and is swimming with it'.[17]

---

13   James Macdonald, 'They Never Got Her', *Observer Review*, 28 February 1999.
14   James Christopher 'Rat with Hand Exits Stage Left', *Independent*, 4 May 1998, pp. 6–7.
15   Cited in Susannah Clapp, 'West End Girls (and Boys)', *Observer*, 24 May 1998, p. 5.
16   Aleks Sierz, 'Cool Britannia? "In-yer-face" Writing in the British Theatre Today', *New Theatre Quarterly*, 56 (1998) 325.
17   Claire Armitstead, 'Riotous Assembly', *Guardian*, 8 December 1994, p. 8.

Aleks Sierz identifies even earlier writers from the decade who could claim to be precursors of what he terms 'in-yer-face' writers, and includes Anthony Neilson's *Penetrator* (1993) and Philip Ridley's *Ghost from a Perfect Place* (1992). In an uncanny echo of the initial reactions *Blasted* was to provoke, Tom Morris expressed the disquiet he felt about being in such close proximity to graphic staged violence: 'Watching the cruellest of these plays in a small studio theatre is like watching a simulated rape in your own living room. In very small theatres, it is impossible to walk out, so the audience is trapped in close proximity to the action, giving the playwright free reign to have his or her own say in the bluntest possible terms'.[18]

Nevertheless, *Blasted* brought theatre, temporarily at least, out of hibernation to dominate the cultural arena, and perhaps more importantly, its fortuitous scheduling at the beginning of the year focused critics' attention keenly, not only on the rest of the Royal Court's season, but on new writing in general. Hence, by the following year, plays such as Joe Penhall's *Pale Horse* and Mark Ravenhill's *Shopping and Fucking* had convinced some critics that a new generation of young writers was emerging. Benedict Nightingale for instance detected a shared vision: 'Certainly we can say that dramatists under forty are approaching the new millennium in an uneasy, uncertain yet unsolemn frame of mind ... There's a bravado in their evocation of a Britain they regard as being in disarray'.[19] Michael Billington and Lyn Gardner, writing in 1996, concur, and in their assessment they attempt to explain what has spawned this new drama: 'It is partly a reaction against the drab uniformity of television ... and where the single play, if not the film, is a dead duck. New writing at the moment is also driven by a total disillusion, often jauntily expressed, with social decay: specifically with the breakdown of any binding moral code or common sense of decency'.[20]

This disaffected group of dramatists quickly came to be known under a series of different names by theatre and cultural critics in an effort to describe what were seen to be the preoccupations of their work: epithets included 'the Britpack', 'the New Brutalists' and 'the Theatre of Urban Ennui'.[21] In 1998 Benedict Nightingale attempted to summarise their concerns:

> If one were to derive a capsule play from already performed work, it might involve gangs of girls adrift in a London where criminals dump bits of their

18 Tom Morris, 'Foul Deeds Fair Play', *Guardian*, 25 January, 1995.
19 Nightingale, *Future of Theatre*, p. 21.
20 Michael Billington and Lyn Gardner, 'Fabulous Five', *Guardian*, 13 March 1996, p. 10.
21 Nightingale, *Future of Theatre*, p. 20.

rivals in plastic bags, rent boys are casually raped, there's a lively back-street trade in stolen burglar alarms, and voracious spivs gather beside ageing charabanc drivers dying of a surfeit of porn. These dramatists are stronger on character and situation than conflict, tension and structure, preferring to offer vivid snapshots rather than concoct plots, maybe because plot implies some coherence in people's lives. They relish the oddball, the misfit, the bizarre; but they are troubled by the helplessness and unhappiness they see all around. They are vastly entertaining yet they radiate moral concern. They are Mrs Thatcher's disorientated children.[22]

From the pessimism that started 1995, its close prompted Michael Billington to note with enthusiasm, 'the abundance of new plays that both found an audience and addressed big issues'.[23] By the following year talk about a resurgence of new writing in British theatre had become 'listed along with pop, fashion, fine art and food as the fifth leg of the new Swinging London'.[24] The media, quick to respond to what they perceived as a new culture emerging, christened this flurry of artistic activity 'cool Britannia'. While Vera Gottlieb saw the whole thing as an artificial construct – 'The media and the market "named" something, then "made" something – and subsequently "claimed" something'[25] – a number of self-congratulatory newspaper articles started to appear around 1995. Robert Hewison's assessment was a typical response:

> We have the makings of a cultural renaissance, based on a new generation of young talent that is being recognised nationally and internationally. From Brit-pop to Bryn Terfel, from Stephen Daldry to Damien Hirst, from Jenny Saville to Nicholas Hytner, from Rachel Whiteread to Mark Wigglesworth, there is a renewed sense of creative vigour and excitement … We are on the threshold of either a decadent *fin de siècle* or the breakthrough that characterizes Vienna in 1900, when artists, playwrights, poets and composers launched twentieth century modernism.[26]

The mood of the time even began to permeate and influence interpretations of classical drama, such as Shakespeare. For instance, Mark Rylance's 1996 production of *Macbeth* saw 'the action … punctuated by loud, trippy trance-techno music, and when the grungy witches offered up their prophecies they slipped Macbeth a tab of acid for good measure'.[27]

22 *Ibid.*
23 Michael Billington, 'Review of 1995: An Irishman Captures London', *Guardian*, 27 December 1995, p. 6.
24 David Edgar (ed.), *State of Play Issue 1: Playwrights on Playwriting* (London, 1999), p. 28.
25 Vera Gottlieb, 'Lukewarm Britain', in Colin Chambers and Vera Gottlieb (eds), *Theatre in a Cool Climate* (Oxford, 1999), p. 209.
26 Robert Hewison, 'Rebirth of a Nation', *The Times*, 19 May 1996.
27 Andrew Smith, 'How to Get Rave Reviews?', *The Times*, 11 February 1996.

However, the concept of contemporary culture influencing classical theatre seemed to Benedict Nightingale a one-way process. Despite being a defender of the 'New Brutalists', he nevertheless saw a conspicuous absence, both in their work and in post-war drama, of 'an ear for metaphysics ... where people feel "tragically" ... they're [British dramatists] writing in a medium best suited to the conflict of the individual and the individual with his society'.[28]

The playwright David Edgar also had misgivings, in that while he applauded the resurgence of new writing in terms of the important issues it addressed (which he identifies as the crisis in masculinity), he nevertheless saw that in terms of *dramatic form* the new generation of dramatists were conservatives, 'operating within the context of a British television drama ... imprisoned within the homogenising constraints of genre. And the return to plays set in real rooms has been matched by the equally dramatic re-emergence of plays set in real time'.[29]

This is where Sarah Kane's drama most clearly deviates from the preoccupations of her contemporaries, or what she called 'plays about disaffected groups of youths exploring their sexuality'.[30] Although Aleks Sierz calls her work 'Harold Pinter and Edward Bond for the chemical generation',[31] Kane's drama is informed and influenced far more closely by classical and modern European theatre than 'rave culture'.

Jez Butterworth – whose play *Mojo* also made a spectacular debut at the Royal Court in the same year as *Blasted* – described as the 'undisputed leader of the stage brat-packers',[32] was also quick to ridicule the analogy: 'This idea of a motorcycle gang of playwrights I was leading just doesn't exist'.[33] Kane herself was equally disparaging, not only about the movement in general, but about her own work being seen at the vanguard:

I do not believe in movements. Movements define retrospectively and always on grounds of imitation. If you have three or four writers who do something interesting there will be ten others who are just copying it. At that moment you've got a movement. The media look for movements, even invent them. The writers themselves are not interested in it. Some of the writers who are said to belong to the movement I haven't even met. So, as far as I am concerned, I hope that my play [*Crave*] is not typical of anything.[34]

28 Nightingale. *Future of Theatre*, p. 25
29 Edgar, *State of Play*, p. 28.
30 Rebellato, 'Brief Encounter'.
31 Aleks Sierz, *Tribune*, 15 May 1998.
32 Billington and Gardner, *Guardian*, 13 March 1996.
33 Jim Shelly, 'The Idler', *Guardian*, 4 July 1998, p. 25.
34 Johan Thielmans, *Rehearsing the Future*, 4th European Directors Forum. Strategies for the emerging Director in Europe (London: Directors Guild of Great Britain *et al*, 1999), p. 10.

She was also sceptical about the term 'New Brutalism' to describe the drama being written from 1995 onwards:

> *Blasted* was considered the beginning of a movement called 'New Brutalism'. Someone said to a Scottish playwright that you couldn't call his work 'New Writing', because the play wasn't brutal enough. That is exactly the problem with movements, because they are exclusive rather than inclusive ... It is just a media label to refer to some things that might happen in a particular play. Actually it's not very helpful. When people come to see *Crave*, they will be surprised; or they will find that the label does not apply. I do not consider myself a New Brutalist.[35]

The relative worth of one dramatist over another is in the end a question of taste, and indeed the impact of late 1990s' British drama on the theatrical canon may be too early to assess, but Aleks Sierz is probably right that when assessing its impact theatrical revival alone will be the ultimate test of any individual play's artistic merit:

> Revivals of modern classics prove their theatrical vitality, even when the circumstances that informed their writing have changed. Plays such as *Trainspotting*, *Blasted*, *Mojo* and *Shopping and Fucking* owe much to their original directors and casts. Future revivals will show whether the issues they addressed so urgently have outlived their sell-by date – or whether they've become an established part of the theatrical vocabulary of social criticism.[36]

Sarah Kane's dramatic art: features, themes and issues

Non-realism

The theatre director James Macdonald, speaking about Sarah Kane's third play *Cleansed* (1998), makes a comment that can perhaps be applied to all her work. He observed that the play 'removes the psychological signposts and social geography that you get in the Great British play'.[37] He addressed this issue again following her death:

> At a time when much new writing was content to inhabit received dramatic form, each new play she wrote found a new structure to contain its ideas and

35 *Ibid.*
36 Sierz, 'Cool Britannia?', p. 333.
37 Christopher, *Independent*, 4 May 1998.

feelings. And in doing so, she gave the lie to a laziness in thinking which insists on the superiority of a certain kind of play – broadly, the Royal Court play of the Seventies and Eighties, driven by a clear political agenda, kitted out with signposts: indicating meaning and generally featuring a hefty state-of-the-nation speech somewhere near the end. More than any one, she knew that this template is no use to us now.[38]

It is this rejection, or at least manipulation, of the conventions of realism that is perhaps the key distinguishing feature of the dramatic strategy employed in Sarah Kane's work. Her characters make no lengthy 'state-of-the nation' speeches nor are they usually representative in themselves of any political or social issue. In fact her characters constantly elude psychological verisimilitude and do not allow us with any certainty to pin down their moral standpoint.

Whereas Kenneth Tynan in his now famous review of John Osborne's debut declared 'I doubt if I could love anyone who did not wish to see *Look Back in Anger*',[39] the overwhelming wave of hostility that greeted *Blasted* caused Stephen Daldry to comment 'one of our disappointments is that the metaphorical landscape has not been understood, or has been obscured by the controversy'.[40]

It becomes evident when re-reading the hysterical reviews that greeted the play, that what outraged the critics was not the sexual and physical violence – in fact many of the reviews almost seemed to revel in listing the outrages being committed onstage. Kane herself was both irritated and exasperated by this mode of criticism: 'My first play at the Theatre Upstairs got extremely negative press reactions, because of the content of the play. I am not really happy to list that content because that is what the press did. Actually taking events out of their context does not do justice to the play'.[41]

Michael Billington's review was a case in point. It warned his readers that the play 'contains scenes of masturbation, fellatio, frottage, micturition, defecation – ah those old familiar faeces! – homosexual rape, eye gouging and cannibalism'.[42] In fairness to Billington, he has since retracted much of what he originally said about *Blasted*, and while still not personally finding the play to his taste concedes that in retrospect, 'I deplored the tone with which I reviewed it, which was one of lofty derision. I can now see that it was a serious play, driven by moral ferocity'.[43]

38 Macdonald, *Observer Review*, 28 February 1999.
39 Stiltoe, *Look Back in Anger: A Casebook*, p. 51.
40 Clare Bayley, 'A Very Angry Young Woman', *Independent*, 23 January 1995.
41 Thielmans, *Rehearsing the Future*, p. 10
42 Michael Billington, 'The Good Fairies Desert the Court's Theatre of the Absurd', *Guardian*, 20 January 1995.
43 *Nightwaves*, BBC Radio 3; broadcast 23 June 2000.

Looking back at those early reviews, what in fact *really* seemed to disturb the critics about *Blasted* was that they ultimately failed to consider or make sense of either its structure or its content. Here was a play making demands that critics chose to either ignore, scornfully dismiss, or react against with mock outrage.

Kane could at least take succour from the fact that in this respect she was in good company. The initial critical reception to plays like Samuel Beckett's *Waiting for Godot* (1952) and Harold Pinter's *The Birthday Party* (1958) was a similar mixture of bafflement, irritation and dismissal when first performed. David Greig cites these and other writers in a letter to the *Guardian* newspaper complaining of Michael Billington's criteria of realism being used as the only yardstick on which to judge the merits of *Blasted*: 'What about Beckett, Artaud, Sartre, Heiner Muller, Howard Barker, Genet, almost all Greek tragedy, come to think of it *A Winter's Tale* contains very little "sense of external reality." An entire, important strand of theatrical writing concerns itself with internal reality, psychological reality'.[44]

Claire Armitstead, also writing in the *Guardian*, believes this reaction to be endemic in drama criticism, and when it comes to assessment of new work, John Osborne's *Look Back in Anger*, despite nearing its half-century vintage, is taken 'as their benchmark … we're still in the grip of the social realists. That's how they see theatre'. Despite this, Armitstead readily admits that as a critic, when confronted with a play like *Blasted* for the first time, which 'fundamentally challenges the very precepts by which you write: linguistic, logical, linear narrative structures the instinct is to feel intimidated and react by saying "this is not theatre"'.[45]

The dramatist Rebecca Prichard echoes these sentiments, illustrating this with examples from Phyllis Nagy's play *The Strip* (1995), as well as *Blasted*:

> Neither of these women felt tied to writing about the female experience: they felt they could just write about the world. They were making connections between very intimate, personal perspectives and a wider political reality. They're challenging an audience to deconstruct the values of their society as represented on stage, rather than merely asking them to empathise.[46]

To illustrate Claire Armitstead's point about the prejudice British theatre critics seem to hold against non-realistic forms in theatre, the

44 David Greig, letter to the *Guardian*, 24 January 1995.
45 Natasha Langridge and Heidi Stephenson, *Rage and Reason: Women Playwrights on Playwriting* (London, 1997) pp. xvii–xviii.
46 David Benedict, 'Essex Girl Writes Play Shock Horror', *Independent*, 22 October 1997.

following two quotations are representative of the newspaper reviews of *Blasted*, and reveal something of this obsession with what the dramatist David Greig describes as 'the naturalistic theatre of statistics':[47]

> Another problem is that her play is half-realistic, half-symbolic. She [Kane] has a vision of life and she illustrates it with characters who are either over-written or incomplete, both more or less than real people, in order to be illustrations.[48]

> At first you worry about the implausibilities. Then the whole question of plausibility ceases to arise, as the play loses its grip on any kind of reality and careers off into a gratuitous welter of carnage, cannibalism, male rape, eye-gouging and other atrocities.[49]

Critics' preoccupation with niceties of plotting and the trappings of realism were demonstrated even more clearly in their reviews about another play which was playing in London at the same time as *Blasted*. *Killer Joe*, by the American dramatist Tracy Letts, premiered at the Bush Theatre and was a dark comedy, also notable for its depiction of graphic violence. Several reviewers drew parallels between the two plays on this subject, but unlike *Blasted*, which was unanimously castigated, *Killer Joe* won widespread praise. The reasons seemed simple – Letts had obeyed the rules of plot and character progression whereas Kane had foolishly rejected them:

> But one reason why Tracy Letts's *Killer Joe* is bearable – in a way that Sarah Kane's *Blasted* at the Theatre Upstairs is not – is that it recognises the imperatives of art. In other words, the violence of Letts's brilliant play is related to social context and human character.[50]

> His [Letts's] play grips you with its narrative every step of the way and its shocks and horrors spring legitimately from the characters, their back-ground and their motivation. Ms Kane on the other hand, offers her audience scarcely a clue as to why her characters should behave as they do … It is an act of great injustice that it [*Killer Joe*] should open in a week when all the headlines on the subject of sex and violence in art are being stolen by a play which is not fit to lick its boots.[51]

Kane felt that it is often writers themselves who make the best critics and liked the idea of contemporaries reviewing each other's work. By the critic 'having another line of interest in art' rather than it being the

47 David Greig, letter to the *Guardian*, 25 January 1995.
48 Richard Morrison, 'Theatre's Chance to Stage a Recovery', *The Times*, 29 January 1995, p. 10.
49 John Gross, *Sunday Telegraph*, 22 January 1995.
50 Michael Billington, *Guardian*, 23 January 1995.
51 Jack Tinker, *Daily Mail*, 27 January 1995.

reviewer's sole 'profession', Kane felt that there was far more likelihood of critical practice being constructive than destructive: 'By genuinely caring if the play is good and actually wanting it to be good are pre-requisites and not this kind of joy in how vitriolic you can be'.[52]

One of Kane's most profound disappointments was the ignorance and incomprehension she perceived in the British practice of theatre criticism: 'What you get is a brief synopsis, and you get a list of things that happen and a little note at the end saying whether or not this particular middle-aged male journalist liked this play and whether or not you should go and see it – and it tells you nothing'.[53]

Kane contrasts this with the situation in Germany:

> They'd all read my work. They had intelligent questions to ask. They weren't rude or abusive ... and they'd actually prepared in the way you hope people will prepare when they come to see a work. And that's completely different to this country. The number of times the journalist will turn up and say 'I don't actually know any of your work'. Having said that, although I think the critics are much better out there, the standard of productions generally is much poorer and you have to allow a certain amount of cultural difference.[54]

Yet, Kane seemed resigned to the situation: 'All good art is subversive in form or content. And the best art is subversive in form *and* content. And often, the element that most outrages those who seek to impose censorship is form ... I suspect that if *Blasted* had been a piece of social realism it wouldn't have been so harshly received'.[55]

By the time of *Cleansed* some critics had begun to engage with the demands of Kane's work. For instance, Michael Billington commented, 'her new play displays far greater aesthetic control while remaining mysteriously cryptic'.[56] However, not until *Crave* was there a general will-ingness to accept that elements of her drama worked outside the confines of realism and naturalism.

Theatre and football

It is fair to say that Sarah Kane was as much a theatre practitioner as a writer. She has commented, 'I am a writer in the first place. Then I am a director, and in some cases, when I am under pressure, I act'.[57] Despite being that creature known as a 'Royal Court writer', Kane continued

52 Rebellato', Brief Encounter'.
53 *Ibid.*
54 *Ibid.*
55 Langridge and Stephenson, *Rage and Reason*, p. 130.
56 Michael Billington, *Guardian*, 7 May 1998.
57 Thielmans, *Rehearsing the Future*, p. 11.

throughout her career to move between and write for different theatres. For instance, immediately after *Blasted* ended its run she was working at the Gate Theatre in Notting Hill, London, where she wrote and directed her second play *Phaedra's Love* in May 1996. She later returned to the same theatre in October of the following year to direct a new translation of Georg Büchner's *Woyzeck*.

As literary associate for the Bush Theatre in March 1994 and resident dramatist for the new writers' touring company Paines Plough in August 1996, Kane always associated herself with theatres that supported new writing: 'I think that companies such as Paines Plough, the Royal Court and the Bush are important because they do new work. These companies create theatre history'.[58]

Kane even dabbled in acting, albeit reluctantly 'when under pressure'.[59] For instance, she played the role of Grace in the last three performances of *Cleansed* in 1998, after the actress Suzan Sylvester was injured. And during December 1998 when the British production of *Crave* toured to Maastricht and Copenhagen she stepped in to play the part of the young girl 'C' for five performances. Recalling in a letter to Edward Bond the experience of appearing in *Cleansed*, Kane remarked, 'as a result I now know a) how hard acting is and b) how easy it is. I'm taking no more crap from directors and actors about what is and isn't possible in performance. It can be such a simple thing, in fact I think it's the simplicity that makes it difficult, difficult but not complicated'.[60]

Apart from writing *Skin*, a short ten minute film for television, Kane wrote exclusively for theatre. Part of the reason for this was the immediacy the medium gave both performers and audience:

> It's always been the form I loved most because it's live. There's always going to be a relationship between the material and the audience that you don't really get with a film. I mean with the film I wrote, *Skin*, people can walk out or change channels or whatever, it doesn't make any difference to the performance. But with *Blasted*, when people got up and walked out it was actually part of the whole experience of it. And I like that, it's a completely reciprocal relationship between the play and the audience.[61]

This may have been due to the greater latitude in artistic freedom theatre allowed. Speaking about *Cleansed*, Kane once said: 'I made a deliberate

58 *Ibid.*
59 *Ibid.*
60 Sarah Kane, letter to Edward Bond, 2 November 1998. Also see the conversations below with Daniel Evans (p. 177), Mel Kenyon (p. 152) and Stuart McQuarrie (p. 187) on Sarah Kane acting in her own work.
61 Sarah Kane, interview with Nils Tabert, Brixton, London, 8 February 1998. Contained in Nils Tabert (ed.), *Playspotting: Die Londoner Theaterszene der 90er* (Reinbeck) 1998.

decision to write something that couldn't be a film or television ... Theatre might not be hip and cool, but at least there isn't any direct censorship, and you're never going to have that with film or tv'.[62]

Speaking in December of that year in a public interview, Kane picked up on the same idea:

> I would never work in television, and they wouldn't let me. There is too much censorship. As you cannot say what you want to say, I will not do it. Before Dennis Potter died, I already decided not to write for television. I do not see the point in writing for television. It really does not interest me. Film is another matter. I've written one eleven minute film, which was made for television. But they would not show it till after midnight. That says it all.[63]

The ephemeral nature of theatre, whereby each performance differs from the last, was seen by Kane as another of its strengths: 'Theatre has no memory, which makes it the most existential of the arts. No doubt that is why I keep coming back, in the hope that someone in a dark room somewhere will show me an image that burns itself into my mind, leaving a mark more permanent than the moment itself'.[64]

Moreover, the need to find a theatrical language for her own writing, one that is able to provoke a strong emotional and intellectual reaction, seems crucial; even if those reactions are uncomfortable or painful:

> The first previews of *Blasted* at the Royal Court – before I had any idea of quite how extreme the reaction was going to be we had a couple of people walk out ... And now I think it's bound to happen. If it doesn't then it's probably because something is not working. I've seen productions of *Blasted* where there was no reason to walk out because somehow they never connected emotionally, you could completely distance yourself from what was going on.[65]

That Kane attempted to make the theatre a disquieting and uncomfortable experience swam against a trivialisation director Dominic Dromgoole called *fake pain*:

> We live in a world of rampant cruelty, waste and injustice; we see it in every place, at every level. It's a given ... Yet in theatre, this didn't stop wealthy, healthy, middle-class folk looking at some inane subject like pensions or architecture or spying or newspapers and finding more rottenness than in any Denmark, more pain than in any holocaust, more apocalypse than any Hiroshima.[66]

62 Claire Armitstead, 'No Pain, No Kane, *Guardian*, 29 April 1998, p. 12.
63 Thielmans, *Rehearsing the Future*, pp. 13–14. See Mel Kenyon's account of Kane's forays in film and television, pp. 150–1.
64 Sarah Kane, 'The Only Thing I Remember is ...', *Guardian*, 13 August 1998, p. 12.
65 Kane, interview with Nils Tabert.
66 Mike Bradwell (ed.), *The Bush Theatre Book: Frontline Drama 5* (London, 1997) p. 73.

Kane was equally critical of theatre. Speaking in an early interview she not only expressed contempt for the critics who 'have the power to kill a show dead with their cynicism',[67] but also for a theatre that trivialises itself:

> I hate the idea of theatre just being an evening pastime. It should be emotionally and intellectually demanding. I love football. The level of analysis that you listen to on the terraces is astonishing. If people did that in the theatre … but they don't. They expect to sit back and not participate. If there's a place for musicals, opera or whatever, then there should be a place for good new writing, irrespective of box office.[68]

Kane discusses the football analogy again in an article written three years afterwards when she confesses, 'I frequently walk out of the theatre early without fear of missing anything. But however bad I've felt, I've never left a football match early, because you never know when a miracle might occur'.[69]

Kane's desire to see theatre more like a football match draws upon a famous comment made by the influential German theatre practitioner Bertolt Brecht. In an early essay he called for the same aesthetic to function in theatre, whereby 'we pin our hopes to the sporting public'.[70] For Kane also, 'performance is visceral. It puts you in direct physical contact with thought and feeling'.[71]

Her vision of theatre, in its use of both language and imagery has been described in similar terms: for instance, attention has been drawn to its qualities which range in intensity 'having your face rammed into an overflowing ashtray … and then having your whole head held down in a bucket of offal',[72] to a drama of 'almost unparalleled distilled intensity which is often unbearable to watch'.[73]

James Hansford in his assessment of Sarah Kane's work draws on parallels between Antonin Artaud's Theatre of Cruelty and Howard Barker's Theatre of Catastrophe. These analogies are useful, although we should be wary of applying them too rigidly. Hansford, while recognising that all three are concerned with pushing theatrical form to its limits, points out that while they appear to advocate excess, 'there is a declama-

---

67 Langridge and Stephenson, *Rage and Reason*, p. 132.
68 David Benedict, 'Disgusting Violence? Actually it's Quite a Peaceful Play', *Independent on Sunday*, 23 January 1995.
69 Sarah Kane, 'Drama with Balls', *Guardian*, 20 August 1998, p. 12.
70 Bertolt Brecht, 'Emphasis on Sport', in John Willett (ed. and trans). *Brecht on Theatre: The Development of an Aesthetic*, 2nd edn (London, 1992), p. 6.
71 Kane, *Guardian*, 20 August 1998.
72 Paul Taylor, 'Courting Disaster', *Independent*, 20 January 1995.
73 David Benedict, 'Real Live Horror Show', *Independent*, 9 May 1998.

tory economy and austerity in Kane's work that is not found in these other theoreticians and practitioners'.[74]

Moreover, in an interview conducted in February 1998 Kane confesses that it was only relatively late in her writing career that she had even begun to read and appreciate Artaud:

> It's pretty weird – because a lot of people said to me for a long time 'You must really like Artaud', and I hadn't read any of that. Artaud was recommended to me by a lecturer at university who I hated so much that I thought, 'Well I'm not going to read it if he thinks Artaud is good. He simply can't be'. So I only started reading him very recently. And the more I read it I thought, 'Now this is a definition of sanity; this man is completely and utterly sane and I understand everything he's saying'. And I was amazed on how it connects completely with my work. Also his writings about theatre are stunningly good. And it's amazing to me that I'd never read it.[75]

Artaud's call for a rejection of 'psychological theatre'[76] and Barker's assertion 'of no official interpretation' to a play are shared concerns; so too are other aspects of Kane's work, which at times seem to come close to Artaud's vision of 'total theatre': Kane's use of imagery that is often violent and extreme, or what Howard Barker calls 'beauty and terror'.[77] Here we encounter a theatre whereby the stage can become a makeshift grave for a man to huddle inside for comfort with the corpse of a dead baby; conversely it can also be the place where giant sunflowers miraculously sprout up through the ground. It can become a place where characters simultaneously undergo savage punishment and cruel suffering, yet it is also a place where we can witness moments of magic and bliss. In *Cleansed* for instance we see Carl ritually mutilated – his tongue cut out and hands amputated, yet we also see Grace and her dead brother Graham brought together in a dance of love for each other.

It could also be argued that Kane's startling theatrical imagery and her equally powerful use of sparse but vivid language at times get close to the elements of ritual and magic Artaud called his vision of theatre to 'double'. Scenes, such as in *Blasted*, where the blinded Ian is brought to despair in a series of silent tableaux (5:59-60), certainly have the potential to offer glimpses of what Artaud envisaged for his Theatre of Cruelty.

In interview, Kane confessed that such moments sometimes come about purely by accident, such as the fortuitous circumstances in

---

74 James Hansford, 'Sarah Kane' in Thomas Riggs (ed.) *Contemporary Dramatists*, 6th edn (Detroit, New York, 1999), p. 349.
75 Kane, interview with Nils Tabert.
76 Antonin Artaud *The Theatre and its Double*, trans. Victor Corti (London, 1999), p. 64.
77 Howard Barker, *Arguments for a Theatre*, 3rd edn (Manchester, 1999), p. 57.

rehearsals of *Blasted*, where the blinded Ian is sitting under the floor-boards with rain dripping onto his head:

> In *Blasted* Ian's almost kind of deified I think in a way that I didn't realise until I saw it performed. I went in for the technical run and when I watched at the end and he had all this blood and it started raining, and the blood was washed away, I thought it was kind of Christ-like.[78]

The serendipity of theatre, both in rehearsal and actual performance, underpins Kane's loyalty to its unpredictability:

> I decided on theatre because it's a live art. The direct communication with an audience I really like. When I go to a film, it doesn't matter what I do. It makes no difference. But when you go to the theatre, and you just cough, it may alter a performance. As a member of an audience I like the fact that I can change a performance. As a writer I like the fact that no performance will ever be the same.[79]

Nevertheless, Kane's relationship with theatre has also been a problematical one. Indeed, at times she almost seems to echo Hippolytus from her own play *Phaedra's Love* and his plea, 'if there could have been more moments like this' (8:103). On several occasions she spoke of the frustrations imposed by the constraints of theatre as a dramatic form, against what she identified as the sometimes more liberating aspects of other live performance mediums:

> I saw the *Jesus and Mary Chain* [a rock group] at the foot of Edinburgh Castle a few nights back, and found myself longing for a theatre that could speak so directly to an audience's experience. It rarely happens. But it happened at *The Ladyboys of Bangkok*, with the sheer joy of seeing a Thai trans-sexual lip-synching to 'I Am What I Am'. And it happened when I stumbled upon the Zimbabwean Nasa Theatre dancing and drumming to an exuberant crowd on the Lothian Road.[80]

In the same article Kane draws a further distinction between *performance* in the theatre and *text for performance*: 'Increasingly, I'm finding performance much more interesting than acting; theatre more compelling than plays. Unusually for me, I'm encouraging my friends to see my play *Crave* before reading it, because I think of it more as text for performance than as a play'.

Kane's choice of favouring performance over the text itself (despite the apparent contradiction of being a dramatist whose work starts with a written text), is perhaps not so surprising when she recalled two other

78 Sarah Kane, interview with Graham Saunders, Brixton, London, 12 June 1995.
79 Thielemans, *Rehearsing the Future*, p. 14.
80 Kane, *Guardian*, 20 August 1998.

memorable 'theatrical' performances which were both (in their own very different ways) completely devised and improvised:

> Number one was Jeremy Weller's 1992 Edinburgh Grassmarket Project, *Mad*. (Second was a live sex show in Amsterdam about a witch sucking the Grim Reaper's cock.) *Mad*, a devised play with professional and non-professional actors who all had first-hand experience of mental illness, remains the only piece of theatre to have changed my life.[81]

Despite Kane's professed need for the necessity of a live audience she believed that as a dramatist no concessions should be made in its direction – the audience she wrote for was probably the most exclusive of all – herself:

> I do not feel a responsibility towards the audience or to other women. What I always do when I write is to think: how does the play affect myself? If you are very specific in what you try to achieve, and it affects yourself, then it may affect other people too. On the other hand, if you have a target group in mind, and you think, 'I want to affect the eleven million people watching ITV on Sunday', then everything becomes bland So for me I am quite happy to aim at the smallest audience possible, which is myself, because I am the only person who is definitely going to see this play anyway. That's why I try to please myself.[82]

Jacobean or Calvinist?

In his book outlining trends for a post-millennium theatre, Benedict Nightingale predicts that a keener awareness and interest in the classics will take place. The reason he gives for a return to past theatrical forms is the inwardness and triviality that informs the concerns and subject matter of much contemporary British drama, and which gives rise to a hunger in audiences that can only be assuaged by returning to the riches of classical theatre:

> The Elizabethans and Jacobeans in particular ask you to suspend disbelief in the existence of titanic feelings and absolute values. They ask you to look at fierce, elemental encounters in a universe where the deity, though sometimes worryingly absent, has significance for the characters. And isn't there something invigorating about plays that avoid psychological or social explanations for human conduct and refuse to reduce good and evil into mere virtue and vice?[83]

---

81 Kane, *Guardian*, 13 August 1998.
82 Thielemans, *Rehearsing the Future*, p. 14.
83 Nightingale, *Future of Theatre*, p. 29.

It is this aspect of Sarah Kane's work that Mark Ravenhill, in an obituary appreciation, thinks lay behind the often tempestuous relationship she had with the British theatre establishment, being 'a contemporary writer with a classical sensibility', which was 'often abrasive for a modern audience … used to the reassurances of sociology or psychology'.[84]

If one were to trace similarities in Kane's drama to a particular group of dramatists, it would not be found in the work of her immediate contemporaries, but rather a group of playwrights who emerged in the late 1960s and early 1970s. They were even given the epithet 'New Jacobeans', and included Edward Bond, Peter Barnes, Howard Brenton and Howard Barker. These dramatists shared an overt sense of theatricality and a number of themes – most notably the depiction of violence and a fascination with the grotesque – which were frequently laced with a mordant black humour. John Russell Taylor, assessing new British writing in 1971, observes the following patterns emerging:

> Again and again these dramatists are attracted to such subjects as child murder, sex murder, rape, homosexuality, transvestism, religious mania, power mania, sadism, masochism. And although the angle of approach to these subjects varies enormously from play to play and writer to writer, one thing at least we may be sure about in advance: that it will not be any easily predictable, accepted angle … 'social problem' subjects will rarely if ever be approached as social problems, for solemn, semi-sociological or psychological dissection.[85]

Taylor saw this group of dramatists engaging in a project that went beyond 'literal-minded realism … as an approach to the extremes and complexities of modern experience', and concludes, 'In the world we live today, dark fantasy and savage comedy may well be the most direct, may even be the only possible way, of telling the truth without compromise'.[86] In what one reviewer of *Cleansed* saw as a distillation of 'epic themes and imagery … [and] tragic, neo-Classical excesses',[87] Sarah Kane's writing shares many of the same concerns as this earlier generation of 'New Jacobeans'.

While several critics, even in the earliest reviews of *Blasted*, noted its similarities with Shakespearian and Jacobean drama, often the only link made was between the depiction of stage violence – even here the connection was meant to be disparaging:

84   Mark Ravenhill, 'Obituary', *Independent*, 23 February 1999.
85   John Russell Taylor, 'British Dramatists: The New Arrivals: The Dark Fantastic', *Plays and Players*, 18 (1971), p. 24.
86   *Ibid.*, p. 27.
87   Sam Marlowe, *What's On*, 13 May 1998.

The revenge tragedians would probably think us a lily-livered lot to object to a spot of baby-eating and eye-ball chewing (no kidding) on stage. And Shakespeare was no slouch when it came to depicting horror and violence. But he did offer plot, character, poetry and a coherent moral framework. *Blasted* just provides incident upon incident of violence and degradation.[88]

A more considered assessment of this aspect of Kane's work started to emerge by the time of *Cleansed*. Claire Armitstead observed, 'Kane deals with Shakespearian passions. [Her] building blocks are the great metaphysical eruptions of classical drama'.[89]

Certainly, in comparison with many of the domestic settings and adherence to realism in the work of her contemporaries, Kane's drama is in possession of an overreaching feel in its grand attempt to make sense of the world rather than a specific event (although *Blasted* was influenced by the siege of Srebrenica in the former Yugoslavia) or social agenda. Moreover, like the Jacobean drama of William Shakespeare, Thomas Middleton and John Webster, Kane manages to condense great themes such as war and human salvation down to a series of stark memorable theatrical images: water dripping onto the head of the blinded Ian in *Blasted*, the mechanical toy car being operated aimlessly by Hippolytus around his palace in *Phaedra's Love* or the use of ritual dismemberment in *Cleansed*. It is this stark theatrical imagery that contributes towards what one commentator calls the 'chaste, visceral power'[90] of her theatre. Kane's 'classical sensibility' also extends to her embrace of tragic form. In *Blasted*, for instance, the tabloid journalist is made to undergo the savage experience of being blinded and sodomised by the soldier before being left alone to die; it also recalls the belief of the eponymous heroine of John Webster's *The Duchess of Malfi* that 'the greatest torture souls feel in hell / In hell: that they must live, and cannot die'.[91] (IV.i. 70–1) Speaking about *Blasted*, Kane seems to endorse this last sentiment in that, 'he [Ian] finds that the thing he has ridiculed – life after death – really does exist. And that life is worse than where he was before. It really is hell'.[92]

Yet simultaneously, the redemptive process of classical tragedy, whereby a character is made to gain insight through suffering, also operates throughout her work. When, for instance, we see the manifestly unpleasant journalist Ian in *Blasted* reduced to such a wretched state after his experience at the hands of the soldier, we are at last ready to feel pity

---

88   Sarah Hemming, *Financial Times*, 23 January 1995.
89   Armitstead, *Guardian*, 29 April 1998.
90   Hansford, 'Sarah Kane', p. 349.
91   John Webster, *The Duchess of Malfi*, (ed.) Elizabeth Brennan (London, 1983). All subsequent quotations from the play will use this edition.
92   Sarah Kane, letter to Graham Saunders, 31 October 1997.

for him: moreover, when we hear Ian's simple 'thank you' to the woman he has systematically abused during the course of the play, we are reminded of the same process Jonathan Dollimore finds in a play like Shakespeare's *King Lear* whereby, 'Through kindness and shared vulnerability human kind redeems itself in a universe where the gods are at best callously just, at worst sadistically vindictive'.[93]

Kane's second play, *Phaedra's Love*, not only retains the tragic protagonist from Seneca's classical Roman drama, but in its bloody climax also transposes elements from Elizabethan and Jacobean revenge tragedy. Kane's next play, *Cleansed*, perhaps most closely resembles – through shared exploration of the limits of madness and self-hood, as well as its treatment of imprisonment and 'life is a torture chamber',[94] – Webster's Jacobean tragedy *The Duchess of Malfi*. Together both plays attempt to 'represent a very great quantum of human pain'.[95] David Benedict observes that, 'the real shock is how powerfully the vivid images resound in your imagination afterwards'.[96] However, in the shifting identity and role as Grace's saviour/tormentor, Tinker also owes much to the figure of Bosola, the intelligencer and spy in John Webster's *The Duchess of Malfi*, who during the torture of the Duchess, adopts several disguises. These borrowings and echoes from Renaissance drama will be looked at more closely in the later chapters dealing with each individual play.

Kane's vision, like her Renaissance predecessors, is also an uncompromising one. For her, tragedy is a case of the writer, actor and audience 'descend[ing] into hell imaginatively in order to avoid going there in reality'.[97] Such a reaction is uncannily close to the philosophy that lurks behind Jacobean dramatists like John Webster, a writer also described as 'an extremist. [Who] embodied certain tendencies of his time to a greater extent than any of his contemporaries ... in a strange and highly individual way',[98] and whose plays, like Kane's, show 'Man's World ... [to be] a "deep pit of darkness," [where] mankind is "womanish and fearful" in the shadow of the pit'.[99]

Robert Watson believes such moments operate as 'accessible expressions of precious if painful insights',[100] and Kane's theatre also seems to

93 Jonathan Dollimore *Radical Tragedy: Religion, Ideology and Power in the Drama of Shakespeare and his Contemporaries* (London, 1984), p. 189.
94 Ralph Berry, *The Art of John Webster* (Oxford, 1972), p. 24.
95 *Ibid.*, p. 19.
96 Benedict, *Independent*, 9 May 1998.
97 Langridge and Stephenson, *Rage and Reason*, p. 133.
98 Berry, *The Art of John Webster*, p. 6.
99 Travis Bogard, *The Tragic Satire of John Webster* (California, 1955), p. 41.
100 Robert N.Watson, 'Tragedy', in A. Braunmuller and M. Hattaway, *The Cambridge Companion to English Renaissance Drama* (Cambridge, 1990), p. 301.

share a belief that extreme or brutal actions can become a stimulus for revelation or change in her audiences:

> If we can experience something through art, then we might be able to change our future, because experience engraves lessons on our hearts through suffering, whereas speculation leaves us untouched … It's crucial to chronicle and commit to memory events never experienced – in order to avoid them happening. I'd rather risk overdose in the theatre than in life.[101]

This embrace of the starker forms of Elizabethan and Jacobean drama, of souls either willingly embracing a tragic fate or cast into everlasting damnation, might seem at first to sit uneasily with Kane's reputation in the mid 1990s of being the chief representative of 'in-yer-face' theatre. However, the reasons for the choice of incorporating these models of classical tragedy into her drama also seem to have arisen from a personal schism Kane expressed between religious faith and loss of that faith:

> There is a debate I constantly have with myself because I was brought up as a Christian, and for the first sixteen years of my life I was absolutely convinced that there was a God, but more convinced … because it was a kind of Charismatic Christian church which was very much focused on the Second Coming … that I would never die. I seriously believed that Jesus was going to come again in my lifetime and that I wouldn't have to die. So, when I got to about eighteen and nineteen and it suddenly hit me that the thing I should have been dealing with from at the age of six – my own mortality – I hadn't dealt with at all. So, there is a constant debate in my head of really not wanting to die – being terrified of it – and also having this constant thing that you can't really shake if you've believed it that hard and that long as a child – that there is a God, and somehow I'm going to be saved. So, I suppose in a way that split is a split in my own kind of personality and intellect.[102]

Kane's estrangement from God – 'It was my first relationship break-up, I suppose'[103] – is a dominant theme in all her work. James Macdonald in his obituary appreciation recalls that one of Kane's favourite quotations was from Samuel Beckett's *Endgame* (1957), where the blind, wheelchair-bound Hamm after an attempt at supplication to God shouts out – 'The bastard! He doesn't exist'.[104] Kane in fact rewrites and reinterprets the line in *Blasted*, where Ian, also blinded, responds with the bitter rejoinder, 'the cunt' (4:57), to Cate's attempted explanation that God has intervened

101 Langridge and Stephenson, *Rage and Reason*, p. 133.
102 Interview with author.
103 Armitstead, *Guardian*, 29 April 1998, p. 12.
104 Samuel Beckett, *The Complete Dramatic Works* (London, 1990), p. 119. All further references to Beckett's plays will use this source.

to prevent his attempt at suicide. Like Beckett, Kane saw the remark as a bitter joke – 'Now I think it's hilarious, but nobody else did'.[105]

Morality and violence

One of the defining characteristics, not only of *Blasted,* but also the work of the so-called 'New Brutalists', was an overriding obsession with crime and violence. The stage, it was said, had become a stalking ground for drama whose primary concerns were an exploration of the gruesome and outlandish. Often the violence and bloodshed were accompanied by an equal reliance on black humour and a flippant sense of irony. This gave the group a reputation for moral ambiguity. Paul Taylor, writing in the *Independent,* outlines these aspects of their writing:

> Features of the urban landscape which would have had earlier Royal Court writers frothing with outrage, they scrutinise with an unindignant wit and a sharp eye for the quirks and contradictions. Characters who would once have been presented as straightforward victims are shown as being complicit in their own oppression. The protagonists peer with a kind of existential puzzlement at their own affectless, morally disconnected behaviour.[106]

Vera Gottlieb, in her discussion of the new British 1990s' dramatists, sees 'the use of verbal violence as a stylistic feature … both a continuum of Howard Barker's verbal abuse – and also the theatrical equivalent of such films as *Pulp Fiction, Reservoir Dogs* or *Natural Born Killers'*. As regards *Blasted,* she feels that it came somewhere between 'the kind of violence we are more used to seeing in the cinema – or in Jacobean tragedies'.[107] Early reviews of the play were also divided on the subject: Nick Curtis thought that 'ambivalence and Kane's enigmatic purpose lead one to conclude that this is no more than an artful chamber of horrors designed to shock and nothing more'.[108] John Peter felt the complete opposite, and believed that 'Kane's vision is born of unleavened, almost puritanical moral outrage', – but he warned – 'outrage, like violence, needs careful handling in the theatre … how much horror can you show, before an audience is overdosed?'[109] A few reviews did go beyond merely registering shock or outrage, and attempted to explain the morality they sensed underpinned the play. Louise Doughty commented: 'To dismiss *Blasted* as the work of a kiddie playing mud pies would be deeply naive.

105 Interview with author.
106 Paul Taylor, 'Ten Years in the Arts: *Angels in America*: The Play that Gave the Stage a New Direction', *Independent,* 11 October 1996.
107 Gottlieb, *Theatre in a Cool Climate,* p. 211.
108 Curtis, *Evening Standard,* 19 January 1995.
109 John Peter, *Sunday Times,* 29 January1995.

The soldier on the run from a terrible civil war and the horrors he describes may seem over the top to us, though a Bosnian refugee might beg to differ.[110]

Perhaps the most considered early assessment of *Blasted* during the storm of protest that greeted its short run came from Edward Bond, the dramatist, whose play *Saved* (1965), also performed at the Royal Court, had divided audiences and critics in its day over the depiction of violence in the theatre. *Saved* included the now infamous scene where a gang of youths are shown stoning a baby to death, and critics frequently made comparisons between the two dramatists until the time of *Cleansed*. Kane's admiration for Bond's work in general was profound: for instance she said: 'you can learn everything you need to know about the craft of play-writing from *Saved*',[111] and in one interview voiced her own strong initial reactions to Bond's play, and the influence it produced on her own writing: 'When I read *Saved*, I was shocked by the baby being stoned. But then I thought, there isn't anything you can't represent on stage. If you are saying you can't represent something, you are saying you can't talk about it, you are denying its existence, and that's an extraordinarily ignorant thing to do'.[112]

Looking back to the critical reaction to *Saved*, it shares many uncanny similarities with *Blasted*. For instance both plays were widely reviled, not only for the choice of subject matter but the way in which it was presented. For instance, Herbert Kretzmer wrote: 'From first to last Edward Bond's play is concerned with sexual and physical violence ... Nobody ... will deny that it is the function of the theatre to reflect the horrific undercurrents of contemporary life. But it cannot be allowed, even in the name of freedom of speech, to do so without aim, purpose or meaning'.[113] In contrast, Penelope Gilliat, writing in the *Observer* pointed out that *Saved* was not 'a brutish play ... It is a play about brutishness which is something quite different',[114] and that an underlying humanity informed the violence.

In what must have been a strange article to write, thirty years after *Saved* premiered at the Royal Court, Bond came to the defence of a play and its young writer also being accused of moral abnegation and trading in cheap sensationalism. In the article Bond drew attention to the

---

110 Louise Doughty, *Mail on Sunday*, 19 January 1995.
111 Ravenhill, *Independent*, 23 February 1999. For a detailed comparison of the two plays see Tom Sellar, '"Truth and Dare": Sarah Kane's *Blasted*, *Theater*', 1996 pp. 29–34.
112 Bayley, *Independent*, 23 January 1995.
113 Herbert Kretzmer, *Daily Express*, 4 November 1965.
114 Penelope Gilliat, *Observer*, 7 November 1965.

importance of the ancient theatrical forms in *Blasted* and also recognised the moral integrity that informed the play:

> The images in *Blasted* are ancient. They are seen in all great ages of art – in Greek and Jacobean theatre, Noh and Kabuki. The play changes some of the images – but all artists do that to bring the ancient imagery, changed and unchanged, into the focus of their age. The humanity of *Blasted* moved me. I worry for those too busy or so lost that they cannot see its humanity … But I do know this is the most important play on in London.[115]

Other playwrights also came to the defence of *Blasted* in the letter pages of the national newspapers. Caryl Churchill found it to be 'rather a tender play … able to move between into the surreal to show connections between local, domestic violence and the atrocities of war';[116] Martin Crimp, Paul Godfrey, Meredith Oakes and Gregory Motton writing as a collective voice believed 'the power of Ms Kane's play lies precisely in the fact that she dares to range beyond personal experience and bring the wars that rage at such convenient distance from this island right into its heart'[117] – while Harold Pinter made the distinction between *Blasted* and violence in the films of Quentin Tarantino. Whereas these were 'simply superficial', *Blasted* 'was facing something actual and true and ugly and painful – and therefore received the headlines saying this play should be banned'.[118]

Bond also makes a comparison between the morality operating in the films of Quentin Tarantino and *Blasted*:

> She [Sarah Kane] was able to penetrate very deeply what happens inside everybody, and that's not just a subjective thing it's how you relate to our external reality. If you let the outside world into yourself that is a chaotic and dramatic process and she was able to touch that process and people don't like it. There's a huge difference between Tarantino and *Blasted*. Both deal with chaos. One says chaos is dangerous for us but we have to go into chaos to find ourselves. The other says chaos is a gimmick, a new device – it's a trick. Tarantino will make his fortune. Sarah Kane kills herself.[119]

Kane herself was sceptical about the validity or moral purpose of Tarantino's films: 'he doesn't write about violence and he certainly doesn't write or make films about love … His films are about film convention and they're completely self referential, they refer to other historical films – that's all they do'.[120]

115 Bond, *Guardian*, 28 January 1995.
116 Caryl Churchill, 'A Bold Imagination for Action', *Guardian*, 25 January 1995, p. 19.
117 Martin Crimp et al., letter to the *Guardian*, 23 January 1995.
118 Harold Pinter, 'Life in the Old Dog Yet', *Daily Telegraph*, 16 March 1995.
119 *Nightwaves*.
120 Rebellato, 'Brief Encounter'.

She also expressed her displeasure at the way Tarantino's influence found its way into certain aspects of a 1996 production of *Blasted* in Hamburg, Germany:

> This man walked on-stage ... in a really trendy leather jacket, greased back hair, sun-glasses wrapped around – this 30 year old. And I thought 'Oh my God that's supposed to be Ian' – that's supposed to be a 45-year-old dying man. And I thought, 'where have I seen this character?' And it's Tarantino, and my heart just broke – I could hear this cracking in my chest! And in some ways that becomes quite insulting – the work is seen as part of a school which I abhor.[121]

The amorality Kane perceived in Tarantino's work also pervaded other aspects of the Hamburg production:

> My plays certainly exist within a theatrical tradition, though not many people would agree with that. I'm at the extreme end of the theatrical tradition. But they are not about other plays; they are not about methods of representation. On the whole they are about love and about survival and about hope, and to me that is an extremely different thing. So when I go to see a production of *Blasted*, in which all of the characters are complete shits and I don't care about them I get upset. In the Hamburg production, where Cate's been raped during the night, the lights came up and she's lying there on the bed, completely naked, legs apart, covered in blood and mouthing off at Ian; and I just wanted to die. I said to the director, 'you know she's been raped in the night, do you think its either believable, interesting, feasible or theatrically valid that she's lying there completely naked in front of the man who's raped her? Do you not think she might cover herself up for example?' And that's not to do with my feelings about nudity on stage. I've been naked myself on stage and I have no problem with it. Its simply about what is the truth at any given moment.[122]

It was therefore surprising that after the hostile reception to *Blasted*, Sarah Kane at first seemed reluctant to defend herself against accusations that the play glamorised violence. Although in two newspaper interviews[123] she spoke about the moral questions that the play raised following the outbreak of war in Bosnia, her Afterword in the collection of plays in which *Blasted* first appeared, seemed to be both weary of the argument, and at the same time wary in attempting to explain or justify the reasons behind the depiction of brutality and sexual violence in the play: '*Blasted* now exists independently of me – as it should do – and to attempt to sum up its genesis and meaning in a few paragraphs would be futile and of

121 *Ibid.*
122 *Ibid.*
123 Benedict, *Independent on Sunday*, 23 January, 1995; Bayley, *Independent*, 23 January 1995.

only passing interest. If a play is good, it breathes its own air and has a voice of its own. What you take that voice to be saying is no concern of mine. It is what it is. Take it or leave it'.[124]

In a later interview Kane expanded on her attitude to the role of the writer in justifying or attempting to explain their work:

> One of the major criticisms of *Blasted* was 'Sarah Kane doesn't know what she thinks'. And for me the job of an artist is someone who asks questions and a politician is someone who pretends to know the answers. And a bad artist is someone who's actually a politician. And I think what can I do other than say 'well there's this problem' and look at some of the aspects of the problem and let people make up their own minds ... which was actually what my afterword was about. It's not a case of not wanting to take more responsibility for what I've created, because for me the responsibility is taken in the act of writing it, and you make the decisions as you go along, that's when you take responsibility ... The one thing I don't think is the responsibility of playwrights is telling people what to think about the play afterwords. I adore Edward Bond's writing and I think that the forewords and afterwords he writes are brilliant, but there's no point in me trying to do that because I can't do it – it's not what I am. And I don't know what the play is about necessarily. I think it's up to other people to tell me.[125]

This reluctance to be the moral voice for her own work comes from Kane's belief that it is ultimately the audience alone who must take responsibility for what the play offers them. In a radio interview shortly after *Blasted* had finished its British run she stated:

> A lot of the people who have defended me over *Blasted* have said that it's a deeply moral play ... I don't think *Blasted* is a moral play – I think it's amoral, and I think that is one of the reasons people got terribly upset because there isn't a very defined moral framework within which to place yourself and assess your morality and therefore distance yourself from the material.[126]

While Kane seemed wary of asking others to look for a morality within the play itself, she was often prepared to state where the brutal imagery that characterises *Blasted* had come from:

> While the corpse of Yugoslavia was rotting on our doorstep, the press chose to get angry, not about the corpse, but about the cultural event that drew attention to it. That doesn't surprise me. Of course the press wish to deny that what happened in Central Europe has anything to do with us, of course they don't want us to be aware of the extent of the social sickness we're

124 Sarah Kane, Afterword to *Blasted*, in *Frontline Intelligence: New Plays for the Nineties*, selected and introduced by Pamela Edwardes (London, 1994), p. 51.
125 Interview with author.
126 *Start the Week*, BBC Radio 4; date unknown.

suffering from – the moment they acknowledge it, the ground opens up to swallow them. They celebrate the end of the Cold War then rapidly return to sex scandals (which sell more papers) and all that has been done to secure our future as a species is the reduction of the overkill factor.[127]

Kane also dismissed accusations that her plays glorify violence or revel in controversial issues for their own sake:

> Art isn't about the shock of something new. It's about arranging the old in such a way that you see it afresh. The press kept asking why it was necessary to show such acts of violence on stage. I think it was necessary because we normally see war atrocities as documentary or news footage. And *Blasted* is no documentary. So suddenly all those familiar images were presented in an odd theatrical form which provided no framework within which to locate oneself in relationship to the material. For me, that's an amoral representa-tion of violence – no commentary.[128]

At the same time she seemed aware that her work was also treated as symptomatic of the 'Britpack phenomenon', where at times the brutal was made to appear chic. Asked for instance whether she had been to see the controversial 1997 Saatchi art exhibition *Sensation,* and in particular the painting by Marcus Harvey, showing the face of Moors Murderer Myra Hindley constructed out of children's hand-prints, Kane gave the follow-ing reply:

> I didn't see it, I had very mixed feelings about it. Because on the one hand I suppose I would defend anyone's right to create a piece of art out of anything they want, and yet somehow with the Myra Hindley picture – without having seen it – I suspected that the artist's intentions were not entirely honest ... What I wouldn't want to do is upset someone by reference to someone like Myra Hindley or a specific situation ... Because then you are being cynical, you are using people's pain in order to justify your own work which I don't think is acceptable. As I've said I haven't seen it so I don't know whether the Myra Hindley picture has any resonance outside of the specifics of those children that were killed. And if it doesn't then it isn't justifiable because then you are tapping in on a group of people who have lost their kids.[129]

In retrospect, *Blasted* has been Sarah Kane's only work in which questions on the morality of a specific world event – namely the civil war in the former Yugoslavia – have informed one of the main themes of the play. Despite stating that *Blasted* was to be the first of a Trilogy about the nature of war – 'For me there isn't anything else to write about. It's the

127 Langridge and Stephenson, *Rage and Reason,* p. 131.
128 Kane, letter to Graham Saunders, 13 February 1998.
129 Kane, interview with Nils Tabert.

most pressing thing to confront'[130] – Kane's subsequent work was dominated by a move away from issues of mass conflict to the torments and
ecstasies of the individual. Kane's later plays concentrate on the search for
love, meaning and salvation in the lives of her characters, rather than on
specific world events affecting a collective humanity. Langridge and
Stephenson perhaps sum up this aspect of her work: 'Her plays ... offer
us a powerful warning, by showing the tragic but logical conclusion of
humanity's escalating, destructive behaviour. Simultaneously they force
us to confront our shared responsibility for the brutal reality which
already exists'.[131]

Issues of gender

The playwright David Edgar, commenting on the resurgence of British
theatre in the 1990s puts its success down to the rediscovery of a shared
subject matter – its exploration of masculinity:

> Whatever the distinctions between them, these plays address masculinity
> and its discontents as demonstrably as the plays of the early 1960s addressed
> class and those of the 1970s the failures of democracy. There are once again
> plays about the unintended consequences of huge social changes, plays
> which appear about twenty years after great tectonic shifts in the political,
> cultural and economic geology of the times. The decline of the dominant
> role of men – in the workplace and in the family – is probably the biggest
> single story of the last thirty years in the western countries.[132]

While these plays 'may have given a whole generation of young male playwrights – and some women playwrights too – a subject to embrace',[133] and
despite Michael Billington's belief in 'an equally powerful corps of women
playwrights capable of tackling everything under the sun'[134] many female
dramatists and theatre practitioners viewed the trend with either cynicism or abject horror. A few of the dissenting voices were male – most
notably Mark Ravenhill, who was sceptical about a trend which seemed
to be a reductive process, whereby an 'injection of testosterone and we'll
be ok again'.[135]

The dramatist Rebecca Prichard saw the vogue for such plays as
symptomatic of an admiration many young male British dramatists
seemed to share for American writers like David Mamet and Quentin

130 Bayley, *Independent*, 23 January 1995.
131 Langridge and Stephenson, *Rage and Reason*, p. 129
132 Edgar, *State of Play*, pp. 27–8.
133 *Ibid*. p. 28.
134 Michael Billington, *Guardian*, 27 January 1995.
135 Edgar, *State of Play*, p. 48.

Tarantino. Speaking about the former, she felt that in most cases a clumsy attempt was being made to emulate the violence and aggression in Mamet's language, while completely missing its moral imperative: 'We end up with plays which are a strange celebration of masculine culture but which at the same time totally emasculate theatre. They are supposed to look at power but they trivialise it'.[136]

Whereas a previous generation of female dramatists were perhaps more willing to see their work as an expression of their gender, Sarah Kane always saw the issue as irrelevant when assessing her role as a writer:

> My only responsibility as a writer is to the truth, however unpleasant that may be. I have no responsibility as a woman writer because I don't believe there's such a thing. When people talk about me as a writer, that's what I am, and that's how I want my work to be judged – on its quality, not on the basis of my age, gender, class, sexuality or race.[137]

This is not to say that Kane ignores issues of gender in her work – in fact the so-called 'crisis of masculinity' and the interplay of power between men and women dominate all her work. Ian and Cate in *Blasted*, Phaedra and Hippolytus in *Phaedra's Love*, Tinker and Grace/Woman in *Cleansed* and the unidentified voices in *Crave* and *4:48 Psychosis* vie for power and love. Despite commenting that 'an over-emphasis on sexual politics (or racial or class politics) is a diversion from our main problem',[138] almost all of Kane's work explores a diseased male identity and the effects these have on heterosexual (and in the case of *Cleansed* male homosexual as well) relationships. Yet the men who suffer in her plays often willingly embrace literal nihilism or suffer on a truly epic scale. Both Ian and Hippolytus for instance undergo extreme existential and physical torments, aimlessly counting out time, bitterly waiting for a glimpse of something that might make sense of their lives: both are ultimately waiting for death to claim them. Ian, for example, while still alive climbs gratefully into the grave of the baby, while Hippolytus thinks of each day as a weary struggle to 'Fill it up with tat Bric-a-brac, bits and bobs' (4:80). Finally, he welcomes disembowelment and mutilation at the hands of the mob. For Kane, these manipulative, abusive or violent male and female relationships seem to function as a metaphor and are 'symptomatic of societies based on violence or the threat of violence, not the cause'.[139]

Kane's work also seems to inhabit a world based on Julia's observation in Orwell's *Nineteen Eighty-Four* that hers is a society of repression,

---

136 *Ibid.*, p. 61.
137 Langridge and Stephenson, *Rage and Reason*, p. 134
138 *Ibid.*
139 *Ibid.*

of 'sex gone sour'.[140] Many of Kane's male protagonists such as Ian and Hippolytus use sex either as a form of punishment against women, or as an expression of their own deep sense of self-disgust. It is significant that even when there is an expression of a sexuality that is free from abuse or violence, such as the lovemaking between Grace/Graham and Carl/Rod in *Cleansed*, the interlude is short-lived or found to be lacking. For instance, Grace's relationship is delusional, based on her brother still being alive, and after Rod's declaration of love to Carl he is executed by Tinker.

Perhaps more disturbingly this debasement of women by male protagonists seems to offer them, paradoxically, a chance of salvation or partial redemption. Phaedra's declaration of love to Hippolytus contains elements that could be applied to the attitude many of the women in Kane's plays seem to hold: 'You're difficult. Moody, cynical, bitter, fat, decadent, spoilt. You stay in bed all day then watch TV all night, you crash around this house with sleep in your eyes and not a thought for anyone. You're in pain. I adore you' (4:79). Cate in *Blasted* returns like a latter-day Jane Eyre to feed and care for the blinded, traumatised Ian, while Phaedra's suicide is considered by Hippolytus as 'her present to me' (5:90), and constitutes part of his dying regret, 'If there could have been more moments like this' (8:103). Similarly, Tinker in *Cleansed* seems to undergo a process of moral redemption through the mutilation of Grace, and through it comes to accept love from the Woman in the booth, who he had previously also abused and kept captive. In *Crave*, while all the characters seem to be in some form of locked, private hell, the relationship between the young girl 'C' and the older man 'A' is also defined by his 'all-encompassing heart-enriching ... never ending love' (170), whereas the relationship for 'C' seems to culminate only in self-recrimination and self-loathing: 'I'm evil, I'm damaged, and no one can save me' (173).

Kane, speaking about *Phaedra's Love*, yet relevant to all the relationships that develop in her plays, likens the process in writing to a split in her own personality:

> I'm simultaneously Hippolytus and Phaedra, and both those things are completely possible, that lethal cynicism coupled with obsessional love for someone who is completely unlovable. And which is completely blind. So everytime I wrote a scene I was writing myself into rather opposite states and what it's like when these two people come together.[141]

However, Kane herself does not seem to see the gender relations in her drama being reduced to a dichotomy between aggressive self-torturing

140   George Orwell, *Nineteen Eighty-Four* (London, 1968), p. 109.
141   Kane, interview with Nils Tabert.

men and passive masochistic women: 'I write about human beings, and since I am one, the ways in which all human beings operate is feasibly within my understanding. I don't think of the world as being divided up into men and women, victims and perpetrators. I don't think those are constructive divisions to make, and they make for very poor writing'.[142]

Moreover, the male protagonists in her plays, despite showing the ability to inflict mental (and in the case of Tinker physical) torture on other people, have an underlying fragility, a desire to be loved and an almost pathetic tenderness that often lurks beneath their cruelty. James Hansford detects in the writing of *Blasted*, for instance, 'a perverse kind of tact that makes suppressed and inverted feelings of affection between her characters and yearnings for the ineffable within them subjects for serious attention'.[143] Kane saw her own work in much the same light, commenting, 'it never seemed to me they were really plays about violence or cruelty. Both things were incidental when it's about how you continue to love and hope when those things still exist'.[144]

Kane's male protagonists constantly veer from one extreme of contradictory behaviour to another. Ian for instance moves from calling Cate's brother a 'spazz … a retard … a Joey' to declaiming in almost the next exchange, 'You know I love you … Don't want you ever to leave' (1:5); Tinker, despite controlling the fates of the other inmates within the institution, attempts to pursue a hesitant, almost touching relationship with the woman who dances in the peep-show booth – 'Can we be friends? … I'll be anything you need' (6:122) he pleads. The self-confessed paedophile, named only 'A', in *Crave* inflicts untold emotional damage on the young girl 'C', yet simultaneously makes a long and ardent speech where he talks of all the ways in which he attempts to express his love – 'sit on the steps while you take a bath and massage your neck and kiss your feet …' (169). This trait of buried goodness lurking below monstrous acts of behaviour in the male protagonists is often combined with their honesty which is almost as cruel and ruthless as the abuse they inflict upon those trapped with them. Ian for instance is unmerciless to himself at the thought of dying from a terminal disease:

> IAN. I'm fucked.
> CATE. Can't you get a transplant?
> IAN. Don't be stupid. They give them to people with a life. Kids.
> CATE. People die in accidents all the time. They must have some spare.
> IAN. Why? What for? Keep me alive to die of cirrhosis in three months time.

---

142 Langridge and Stephenson, *Rage and Reason*, p. 133.
143 Hansford, 'Sarah Kane', p. 348.
144 Kane, interview with Nils Tabert.

CATE. You're making it worse, speeding it up.
IAN. Enjoy myself while I'm here.

(*Blasted* 1:11–12)

Hippolytus also pursues the same brutal truth, and despite his manifest unpleasantness to Phaedra and Strophe, he still manages to engage our sympathy. Kane remarked in an interview, 'Hippolytus is for me an ideal. If I was like him I'd be quite pleased with myself … he's always completely and utterly direct with everyone no matter what the outcome is going to be for him or for others … So I love Hippolytus. But then I love Ian as well'.[145]

This absolute ideal of honesty is also shared by the female protagonists. For instance, in a letter outlining casting and technical requirements during the student production of *Blasted* in 1993 at Birmingham University, Kane stated 'My stage direction[146] that she [Cate] is "beautiful" means she has an open and honest face, *not* that she has a good figure and long hair'. Kane's insistence on Cate's absolute integrity was another reason for her disappointment with the 1996 Hamburg production of *Blasted*:

> Again, Cate is just as honest. That's why it was such an annoying moment for me with the production in Hamburg of *Blasted* when Ian asks Cate, 'Have you ever had a fuck with a woman', and they cut her saying 'No'. It's a tiny detail, but for me it's important because again she is completely and utterly honest – up until the point when she finds the gun and he [Ian] asks, 'Have you got it?' And again she says 'No'. Up until then she does not tell a lie. And it's similar with *Phaedra*: she completely pursues what she wants. She's actually very in touch with herself about what she wants but she does pursue it completely honestly – to the point where she's prepared to die for it.[147]

Absolute honesty also manifests itself in the relationship between Carl and Rod in *Cleansed*, even when that integrity is painful to hear. Carl wants a pledge of undying love, but all Rod is willing to concede, in a speech which Dan Rebellato calls 'the most genuinely romantic speech in contemporary British playwriting',[148] the limits to which genuine honesty will allow:

> I love you *now*.
> I'm with you *now*.
> I'll do my best, moment to moment, not to betray you.

---

145 Kane, interview with Nils Tabert.
146 Subsequently cut in the final version.
147 Kane, interview with Nils Tabert.
148 Dan Rebellato, 'Sarah Kane: An Appreciation', *New Theatre Quarterly*, 59 (1999), p. 281.

Now.
That's it. No more. Don't make me lie to you.

(*Cleansed* 2:11)

This combination of cruelty underscored with tenderness and an almost ruthless belief and adherence to the truth seems to be at complete odds with the work of Kane's contemporaries from the so-called 'Theatre of Ennui', whose characters seem to believe in 'treating disaster with a breezy glee'.[149] Similarly, while Aleks Sierz believes that Kane's work along with Butterworth's and Ravenhill's 'explore the theme of masculinity in crisis, [yet] none offers an alternative vision',[150] it could be argued that the fate of her cruel male tormentors, grasping for fragments of goodness half-glimpsed within themselves after experiencing or inflicting terrible punishments, provides an alternative – even if that alternative is bleak and uncomfortable.

149   Nightingale, *Future of Theatre*, p. 21.
150   Sierz, 'Cool Britannia?', p. 331.

PART I The plays

2

'This disgusting feast of filth': *Blasted*

Finally I have been driven into the arms of Disgusted of Tunbridge Wells. For utterly and entirely disgusted I was by a play which appears to know no bounds of decency, yet has no message to convey by way of excuse. (Jack Tinker, *Daily Mail*, 19 January 1995)

Blasted will last. It's a very good play indeed and after the hysteria dies down it remains to be read and performed for years to come. (David Greig, letter to the *Guardian*, 24 January 1995)

The only contemporary play I wish I'd written, it is revolutionary. (Edward Bond, *Guardian*, 16 December 2000)

On certain rare occasions a play launches itself from a springboard of notoriety. Henrik Ibsen's *Ghosts* (1881) was famously described as 'an open drain; a loathsome sore unbandaged; a dirty act done publicly'[1] in the British press. More recently Edward Bond's *Saved* (1965) and Howard Brenton's *The Romans in Britain* (1980), described in one review as 'a nauseating load of rubbish from beginning to end',[2] were also castigated in some quarters for being works that peddled in obscenity.

Sitting in the audience during many of those early performances of her play, Sarah Kane must have felt that after the media had pounced

---

1 *Daily Telegraph*, 14 March 1891.
2 James Fenton, *Sunday Times*, 19 October 1980.

on *Blasted* it could no longer be judged on its own merits as a piece of drama:

> One of the disappointing things about *Blasted* was that no one could come and see it fresh anymore because everyone had read about it, but it did mean that when I was watching it and people got up and walked out, there was part of me that thought, 'why'd you come? If you're really going to get offended by a man raping another man, you knew it was going to happen.' We had one man who walked out twenty seconds before the end, just as the rain started falling on Ian's face, and I thought 'well, you've obviously found nothing to walk out about, but you want to walk out – you realise it's about to end, so you're going'.[3]

When *Blasted* made its debut at the Royal Court Theatre Upstairs in January 1995 Sarah Kane was 23 years of age, and her relative youthfulness was used against her by several critics. John Peter, for instance, chose to see *Blasted* as an early experiment from which better things would emerge with the onset of maturity – 'Kane has a lot to learn (she is 23), but I look forward to her next play to see what she has learned'.[4] Such responses seemed to imply that *Blasted* had been a hastily put-together affair, and that the Royal Court had cynically promoted Kane as an *enfant terrible* through which to regain the glory days of Edward Bond's *Saved* through staging controversial new work. *Blasted* had in fact undergone a protracted period of writing starting well over two years before, and involved a prior performance at the University of Birmingham in July 1993.

The fractured dramatic form of *Blasted*, in which the domestic first half of the play set in a Leeds hotel room, is suddenly transformed into an undisclosed war-zone, reflects the sudden change in subject matter during the process of writing. The impetus for this change in direction was brought about by the Bosnian civil war that ensued after 1990 when, with the collapse of Communism, the former state of Yugoslavia splintered into various republics all vying for independence:

> I think with *Blasted* that it was a direct response to material as it began to happen … I knew that I wanted to write a play about a man and a woman in a hotel room, and that there was a complete power imbalance which resulted in a rape. I'd been doing it for a few days and I switched on the news one night while I was having a break from writing, and there was a very old woman's face in Srebrenica just weeping and looking into the camera and saying – 'please, please, somebody help us, because we need the UN to come here and help us'. I thought this is absolutely terrible and I'm writing this

---

3 Interview with author.
4 Peter, *Sunday Times*, 29 January 1995.

ridiculous play about two people in a room. What's the point of carrying on? So this is what I wanted to write about, yet somehow this story about the man and the woman is still attracting me. So I thought what could possibly be the connection between a common rape in a Leeds hotel room and what's happening in Bosnia? And suddenly the penny dropped and I thought of course it's obvious, one is the seed and the other is the tree. I do think that the seeds of full-scale war can always be found in peace-time civilisation.[5]

At the time, Kane was at Bristol University, about to complete a degree in drama. Upon completion in the summer of 1992 she enrolled almost immediately to start on the MA Playwriting course at the University of Birmingham. This was run at the time by its founder, the dramatist David Edgar. Kane's year in Birmingham proved problematic:

> I do not remember why I did it, but I decided to apply for an MA in playwriting in Birmingham. I got funding, and that was the only reason I went really, because I needed the money. I didn't actually finish the course. When I was there I wrote the first half of *Blasted* and then I moved to London. The course itself was very academic. I did not think that was very useful. I did not go to most of the lectures because I felt they were inhibiting my writing. Living in Birmingham for a year helped more as an artist by just making me feel miserable. I was living in a city that I simply hated. The only thing it really gave me was that I wanted to write plays set in a very large industrial city, which was extremely unpleasant. That is what I did, and it became *Blasted*. In some respects it helped me, but at the same time you could say that is simply where I was in my life.[6]

Despite being reported to have said that her time at Birmingham 'nearly destroyed her as a writer',[7] the course culminated in a powerful and memorable performance of the first two scenes of *Blasted* before an audience. From evidence of early drafts of the play, Kane took advantage of this performance to rewrite and restructure the final play. The literary manager Mel Kenyon was in the audience, saw Kane's potential and eventually suggested *Blasted* to the Royal Court as a potential project. Kane recollects: 'In London I read a fairly finished version to the Royal Court and they said they'd pay me to finish it, or they would commission a new work. I took the commission but finished *Blasted* anyway. It was part of my Machiavellian scheme!'[8]

5 Rebellato, 'Brief Encounter'.
6 Thielemans, *Rehearsing the Future*, p. 13.
7 Langridge and Stephenson, *Rage and Reason*, p. 129.
8 Thielemans *Rehearsing the Future*, p. 13.

Structure

It is perhaps unproductive to talk overly of plot and narrative either in *Blasted* or in Kane's drama generally. Rather it is the *effect* that language and image produce rather than the 'narrating psychology'[9] Artaud so despised in western theatrical tradition. However, despite critical perplexity about a play that 'begins as a piece of gritty realism and ends (perhaps) as a cautionary fantasy',[10] *Blasted* has a carefully crafted, yet radical structure which is crucial to recognise in coming to an understanding of its concerns. Edward Bond believes that Kane's writing for theatre 'had an instinctive grasp of form which is the most important thing in playwriting' and that 'the form of *Blasted* is genuinely innovative'.[11] Kane was also aware at the time of its writing that *Blasted* was breaking received rules: 'What I attempted to do and I think I probably succeeded, was to create a form for which I couldn't think of an obvious direct precedent, so it wasn't possible to say this form is like a play written twenty years ago'.[12]

Kane's agent Mel Kenyon elaborates further to discuss specifics:

> I don't think it's accidental that in *Blasted* she took a three act structure and literally blew it apart. There is a bomb – it blows apart and we move from socio-realism to surrealism, to expressionism. So I think that was indicative of what she was trying to do. She found existing forms quite constraining or restraining because those big structures offer a kind of security and comfort which I think she felt was dishonest.[13]

Not everyone was in agreement that the dramatic form of *Blasted* deserved such praise for its innovation. Michael Billington, who in retrospect had come to admire its 'passionate moral vision or integrity', speaking in June 2000 continued to feel the structural division of the play was unsound – 'I think the connection between the Leeds hotel room to the war outside is never properly made, and I don't think you can simply have a bomb then translate the action from one place to another.' Billington saw this as evidence after her death for his assessment of Kane as 'a developing writer'.[14] Sarah Kane in turn saw such reactions by critics as indica-

---

9 Artaud, *The Theatre and its Double*, p. 57.
10 Curtis, *Evening Standard*, 19 January 1995.
11 Edward Bond, letter to Graham Saunders, 4 May 2000.
12 Rebellato, 'Brief Encounter'.
13 *Nightwaves*.
14 *Ibid.*

tive of a refusal to look beyond received dramatic form:' If they don't have a clear framework in which to locate the play then they can't talk about it ... Michael Billington couldn't say "ah this is a nice bit of social realism – I can talk about this"'.[15]

While the main reason for the structure of the play was an attempt to express the chaotic structure of war, another more mischievous purpose was also at work:

> I think that what happens in war is that suddenly, violently, without any warning whatsoever, people's lives are completely ripped to pieces. So I literally just picked a moment in the play, I thought I'll plant a bomb and blow the whole fucking thing up. I loved the idea of it as well, that you have a nice little box set in the studio theatre somewhere and you blow it up. You know you go to the Bush Theatre and you go in and you see the set ... and there's always a longing for it to blow up, so it was such a joy for me to be able to do that![16]

The opening scene of *Blasted* is firmly grounded in the theatrical traditions of Naturalism and psychological realism. Kane said in interview that 'the first section was influenced by Ibsen,'[17] and even the stage set showing the hotel interior is the very model of the 'fourth wall' inherited from Ibsen and Chekhov. Kane observed that this caused in reverse exactly the same sort of problems the second half of the play ran into when staged in Britain. Whereas critics here failed to understand how the first half of the play related to the second, with the entrance of the soldier, Kane observed that European critics and directors failed to engage with the first half because 'in Europe they've abandoned Naturalism, so they don't understand the play'.[18]

Although Kane said that, 'In terms of Aristotle's Unities, the time and action are disrupted while unity of place is retained',[19] unity of action is kept rigidly on course for most of the play. This is achieved not only through the characters, but also the use of props, which in many instances hold symbolic significance which is revealed as the action progresses. The items: *a large double bed; a mini-bar; champagne on ice; a large bouquet of flowers* (1:3), become tangible ciphers that help to demonstrate seduction, sexual abuse, misplaced love and rejection. Often unity of action is achieved by these objects changing their appearance and function as the play progresses. For instance, the bouquet of flowers by scene two are

15 Rebellato, 'Brief Encounter'.
16 *Ibid.*
17 Kane, interview with Nils Tabert.
18 Armitstead, *Guardian*, 29 April 1998.
19 Langridge and Stephenson, *Rage and Reason*, p. 130.

'*ripped apart and scattered around the room*' (2:24), exposing the hollow gesture of Ian's love token to Cate.

The importance of these specific props assumed crucial importance from the play's earliest beginnings. Prior to rehearsals for the Birmingham performance, in a letter outlining to the director casting and technical requirements, Kane lists the following props as 'vital, even in a workshop production'. These include, 'the bed, mini-bar and champagne, replica revolver and sniper rifle, under-arm holster, telephone, bouquet of flowers, bottles of Gordon's gin and cigarettes'. And in the play Ian's first action on entering the room is to throw '*a small pile of newspapers on the bed*'; from here he '*goes straight to the mini-bar and pours himself a large gin*' (1:3).

At other times Kane found the significance of the props and their contribution to unity of action purely by accident. For example, when Ian during the opening scene '*throws a small pile of newspapers on the bed*', we later see him '*shitting and then trying to clean it up with newspaper*' (5:59). The connection between the two actions only dawned on Kane through the process of rehearsal and subsequent performance: 'It's completely clear to me now, he should clean it up with newspaper. From the moment he comes in and throws them on the bed we have to follow those newspapers right the way through – they have their own story in there, because that's what they're full of. That's the logical conclusion'.[20]

In keeping with its naturalistic beginnings, the opening stage directions include brief but specific outlines about age, class, birthplace, accent and speech patterns of its two characters: IAN *is 45, Welsh born but lived in Leeds much of his life and picked up the accent.* CATE *is 21, a lower-middle class Southerner with a south London accent and a stutter when under pressure*' (1:3). The two early drafts of *Blasted* from the Birmingham production go even further and reveal ever more precise indicators to physical appearance and costume for the actor playing Ian. Kane specifies that he should be 'fat, with cropped hair and a trimmed ginger beard. He wears tinted glasses and a tan leather jacket'.

Ian's other life, away from journalism, is also introduced in the opening minutes when he produces a revolver, '*checks it is loaded and puts it under his pillow*'. Ian's role as a hit-man is made ambiguous in the play, and despite Cate's attempts at seduction to find out more, we learn only the most oblique references to the secret organisation Ian belongs to: 'Stood at stations, listened to conversations and given the nod ... Driving jobs. Picking people up, disposing of bodies, the lot' (2:30).

---

20 Interview with author.

In the 1993 drafts of the play,[21] Cate's tactic of seduction to get Ian to reveal more about his illegal activities is absent. Instead she confronts Ian directly, who is far more forthcoming:

CATE. Have you shot someone? Ian? You have you have.
IAN. I think someone's trying to kill me, Cate.
CATE. Why did you shoot them?
IAN. Someone's trying to kill me.
CATE. Have you done a murder?
IAN. Fucking hell. Cate, don't you listen? I'm a gunman. I work for MI5. Didn't you ever wonder why I had a gun?

We also learn something about Ian's respective targets: 'Irishmen. Terrorists', and the fact that the organisation now have Ian under surveillance – 'They've tapped my phone, my flat's bugged', and now plan to liquidate their one-time employee: 'I was poisoned last week. They think I can't keep a secret. What fucking use is that in the secret services?' This quite lengthy section was jettisoned early on, and even by the time of the student production the scene we are now familiar with had replaced it.

Kane's acknowledged debt to Ibsen also becomes apparent through her use of disease imagery. Like the syphilis that afflicts Dr Rank in *A Doll's House* (1879) and Oswald in *Ghosts* (1881), Kane uses the disclosure that Ian is dying from terminal lung cancer as a deliberate metaphor. The disease that eats away at his remaining lung, together with an acute awareness of the outward corruption of his body – 'Sweating again. Stink' (1:6) – function as manifestations for the moral corruption which Kane feels to be 'this thing rotting him from the inside which he feeds'.[22] This culminates later in his disclosure to Cate: 'when I came round, a surgeon brought in this lump of rotting pork, stank. My lung' (1:11). Again, in the pre-performance draft, both the motif of the physical source and moral effect of Ian's corruption is made more explicit. Here, Ian reveals, 'When the surgeon opened me up he was sick. The smell. Afterwards he showed it to me. It was white with cancer'.

Ian's corrupting influence upon Cate is also made in these same physical terms. At one point he ejaculates in her mouth. Immediately Cate '*spits frantically, trying to get every trace of him out of her mouth. She goes to the bathroom and we hear her cleaning her teeth*' (2:31). However, she still realises that 'I stink of you' (2:33), and almost immediately afterwards: '*Cate begins to cough and retch. She puts her fingers down her throat*

---

21 Two draft versions of the first two scenes exist from this production at Birmingham University. One was the final performance script used for the first two scenes of the play. The other version (corrected and amended in Sarah Kane's handwriting) was not used in rehearsals.
22 Interview with author.

and produces a hair.[23] *She holds it up and looks at Ian in disgust. She spits.*
It is only subsequently through the act of bathing and escape through the
bathroom window that Cate manages to temporarily escape from Ian's
malign influence.

Kane also talked about how Ibsen's influence decreased over the writing period, although at first psychological characterisation dominated:

> The first draft was about three times as long as what's there now and I don't
> think there's a single word in the first draft that is now in the final draft,
> because I suppose what I was writing was sub-text – great reams of it.
> Everyone having these huge monologues. It started off literally with what
> everyone feels and thinks. The whole thing about Stella – there was fucking
> reams of it, absolutely reams of it, but I thought it was more interesting
> because it's not everybody's wife who leaves them for another woman! And
> I thought, 'now that I know what they think … and then it was no we don't
> want any of that'.[24]

Kane said, 'I don't like writing things you really don't need, and my
favourite exercise is cutting – cut, cut, cut!'[25] It was through this process
of ruthlessly sloughing off superfluous dialogue that we reach in the final
text a characterisation that expresses itself through an almost minimalist,
telegraphic language in which only the barest outward form of meaning
is expressed: yet underneath lurks a multitude of partly realised and
unexpressed desires.

> I was doing this workshop in Birmingham the other day and someone said
> to me: 'I just want to know what you think about sub-text', I said, ' If I say the
> woman was Polish, I can say to you, where are you from? And what would
> you answer?' And she said 'Poland'. I said, 'Right, if I was writing this as a
> scene, what I'd have is me saying, where are you from, and then you saying,
> are you racist?' That is what sub-text is. It's nobody answers the question.
> Everyone goes around it in some way. Everyone puts up some kind of bar-
> rier. And I don't think it's deliberate. I think it's something you do all the
> time. And I suppose that is what happened with *Blasted*.[26]

The structure of the opening scenes between Ian and Cate show the
emotional and physical abuse that Ian inflicts upon Cate. He is more a
torturer than an ex-lover, and employs a complex armoury of cruel games

23 In the two drafts, written for the Birmingham production, the hair Cate plucks
     from her throat comes from Ian's beard. In the pre-performance draft the episode
     where Cate performs oral sex on Ian is absent, but it is included in the actual
     performance script. However, between the Birmingham production in 1993 and the
     Royal Court production in 1995 Kane must have seen the obvious logic in changing
     the source and typology of the hair!
24 Interview with author.
25 Rebellato, 'Brief Encounter'.
26 Interview with author.

and coercive tactics to both undermine and get what he wants. By scene two we learn that overnight Ian has forced himself violently upon Cate and that she is still bleeding from a bite administered during cunnilingus. In the Birmingham drafts of the play Ian calls the wound 'a love bite', and when Cate accuses him of rape Ian scoffs 'That wasn't rape. Don't know the meaning of the word'. Ian then carries out a further sexual assault when Cate lapses into an episode of *petit-mal.* As she succinctly concludes on waking, 'You're a nightmare' (2:33). Patricia Holland in her discussion of the play observes, 'Rape is shown not as a single brutal act, but as structured into a deeply unequal relationship, and performed with a whingeing self-pity'.[27]

It is this systematic abuse that acts as a lever for the structural collapse of the first section of *Blasted* in on itself, taking literally part of the hotel room with it. The collapse of this seemingly up to now archetypal 'well-made play' is achieved mainly through the device of the soldier, who turns the tables on Ian and subjects him to a terrible physical and mental ordeal. In several interviews Kane stressed the importance in at least discerning the deliberate link she made within the abusive domestic first half of the play and the 'odd theatrical form part war-zone, part dreamscape'[28] of the second part:

> The form and content attempt to be one – the form is the meaning. The tension of the first half of the play, this appalling social, psychological and sexual tension, is almost a premonition of the disaster to come. And when it does come, the structure fractures to allow it entry … The form is a direct parallel to the truth of the war it portrays – a traditional form is suddenly and violently disrupted by the entrance of an unexpected element that drags the characters and the play into a chaotic pit without logical explanation … The unity of place suggests a paper-thin wall between the safety and civilization of peacetime Britain and the chaotic violence of civil war. A wall that can be torn down at any time, without warning.[29]

In a later interview Kane said more about the culpability of Ian's actions in the first section of the play bringing about the cataclysmic effects of the second half:

> With *Blasted* you do know what this situation is even though it's not specifically defined, and it's a two way thing, because the soldier is the way he is

27 Patricia Holland, 'Monstrous Regiment', *Independent*, 27 January 1995.
28 Langridge and Stephenson, *Rage and Reason*, p. 131.
29 *Ibid.*, pp. 130–1. Greg Hobbs who first played the role of Ian at the Birmingham production of *Blasted* remembers that during rehearsals Kane spoke about Claire McIntyre's play *My Heart's a Suitcase* (1990) as a precedent for structure: 'if she [McIntyre] could make people walk through walls, then I can transport the hotel room to Bosnia'. Interview with Aleks Sierz and Greg Hobbs, 23 October 2000.

because of the situation, but that situation exists because of what Ian has created in that room, of what he has done to Cate – and he does it with this self deprecating self pity which seems to me completely accurate; I mean when people are intensely violent they manage to make the victim feel guilty. So basically, it's a completely self perpetuating circle of emotional and physical violence. If you skip the connection between all this, if you skip the emotional reason, the play does appear to be completely broken backed, just split into two halves which means it fails totally.[30]

The soldier's function can be interpreted on many levels. He is certainly the integral link to the physical and mental abuse Ian perpetrates on Cate in the first part of the play, and this Kane attempts to communicate through the repetition of rape. However, the critical reaction to the scene left her feeling both frustrated and disappointed:

I mean it's interesting the way the scene was perceived. I was reading all these reviews and thinking, 'but that's not what I wrote at all!' What was being described was a soldier comes in and randomly rapes Ian. And what they kept ignoring was the fact that he does it with a gun to his head which Ian has done to Cate earlier – and he's crying his eyes out as he does it. Well, I think both these things have changed that theatrical image completely. But then I think critics have problems discussing theatrical imagery anyway. And we've been reduced to this fear of the word so much. What's the point of writing a play that doesn't have an image structure, but that image structure seemed to be completely ignored and it takes away the meaning. And then they just take the meaning from the words, which is why I end up accused of being racist, and the characters as racist. You have to look at the context of the image.[31]

Kane also sees the soldier in some ways as an expression of Ian himself; a metaphorical creation, summoned up from the darkest recesses of his subconscious:

The soldier is a kind of personification of Ian's psyche in some sense, and it was a very deliberate thing. I thought the person who comes crashing through that door actually has to make Ian look like a baby in terms of violence – and I think that's successful. It's difficult because when you look at what Ian does to Cate it's utterly appalling, and you think 'I can't imagine anything worse' and then something worse happens.[32]

Ian at least partly recognises the similarities he shares with his tormentor. When the soldier takes the last drops of gin from the bottle, Ian even chuckles in recognition – 'worse than me' (3:40). In one of the early drafts of the play written at Birmingham, the parallels are made more

30 Kane, interview with Nils Tabert.
31 Interview with author.
32 *Ibid.*

obvious as the soldier is also intent on raping Cate. The episode begins the same way, with the soldier finding a pair of Cate's knickers while searching the room:

> (*He stuffs them down the front of his trousers and rubs them over his genitals with pleasure. He stops suddenly and looks at Ian with hate.*)
> VLADEK. English shit.
> (*He spits in Ian's face. Vladek looks towards the bathroom.*)
> Is your girl in there?
> Is she good?
> Does she fuck?
> I will see.

The atrocities the soldier relates to Ian in the final version of *Blasted* seem to make the latter's acts of cruelty to Cate seem petty in comparison. The two men even vie with each other in a twisted competition to establish the depth to which their amorality has reached:

> SOLDIER. I broke a woman's neck. Stabbed up between her legs, on the fifth stab snapped her spine.
> IAN. (*Looks sick.*)
> SOLDIER. You couldn't do that.
> IAN. No.
> SOLDIER. You never killed.
> IAN. Not like that.
> SOLDIER. Not
> Like
> That
> IAN. I'm not a torturer.
> SOLDIER. You're close to them, gun to head. Tie them up, tell them what you're going to do to them, make them wait for it, then … what?
> IAN. Shoot them.
> SOLDIER. You haven't got a clue.
> (*Blasted* 3:47)

The most obvious link with the first part of the play is the re-enactment of the rape Ian originally perpetrated on Cate. It is also carried out with a gun held to Ian's head, yet we realise that throughout this vicious and dehumanising act '*the soldier is crying his heart out*' (3:49), and is a form of re-enactment, as he physically copies what other soldiers have done to his girlfriend – 'He ate her eyes. Poor bastard. Poor love. Poor fucking bastard' (3:50). Kane points out about his subsequent suicide, that 'the only way he can ever learn what his girlfriend had to go through is when he's pulling the trigger … the next moment is the moment of his death'.[33]

---

33 Kane, interview with Nils Tabert.

Kane also wanted to draw comparisons between acts of rape in the play against the part mass rape played in the Serbian policy of 'ethnic cleansing':

> I was working on this with some actors and someone said 'there's nothing kind of unusual about the fact that there's rape camps in Bosnia, or people are raped during war. That's what war is'. Certainly the Vietcong it seems didn't rape. They just didn't. And when Western women were captured by the Vietcong and they were finally rescued, and people said, 'Oh God, what happened. Were you raped?' – gleefully, for stories, and there just weren't any. And similarly the Chinese army ... Isolated incidents, but it really isn't kind of used as a war weapon. Certainly, it's happening in Yugoslavia. It's being used systematically to degrade Muslim women. And so I tend to think there's got to be something cultural about that.[34]

That 'the play collapses into one of Cate's fits'[35] is significant, for these form the other principal doorway into the second part of the play, and contribute not only to the 'strange, almost hallucinatory authority'[36] Edward Bond believes to be operating in *Blasted*, but are also the device that triggers the nightmarish suffering to which Ian and Cate are subjected to following the soldier's invasion of the hotel room.

Cate's fits are a mysterious and disturbing phenomenon. She reveals that once under their influence she 'can be away for minutes or months sometimes, then I come back just where I was' (1:10); and that when they strike, 'The world don't exist, not like this' (1:22). These episodes seem benign, and Cate compares them at one point to a masturbatory fantasy:[37] 'Just before I'm wondering what it'll be like, and just after I'm thinking about the next one, but just as it happens it's lovely, I don't think of nothing else' (1:23).

However, Kane clearly seems to intend these episodes to became a gateway and a metaphor in which to articulate theatrically the extreme behaviour we witness later. She commented in interview, 'War is confused and illogical, therefore it is wrong to use a form that is predictable. Acts of violence simply happen in life, they don't have a dramatic build-up, and they are horrible'.[38]

---

34 Interview with author.
35 Langridge and Stephenson, *Rage and Reason*, p. 130.
36 Bond, *Guardian*, 28 January 1995.
37 In both the Birmingham drafts of *Blasted*, the line 'It's like that when I have an orgasm' is substituted for 'It's like that when I have a fit' (1:22). There is also an analogy made to time standing still and the game of football. This material was cut by the time of the Royal Court production – 'Straight after someone equalises, or even if they don't I feel sick and certain that it won't be safe till we've got another [goal] ... But for one moment I'm not thinking of anything else'.
38 Bayley, *Independent*, 23 January 1995.

Kane also provides several clear intimations of the gathering cataclysm in the first part of the play. For instance, the opening stage direction: '*A very expensive hotel room in Leeds – the kind that is so expensive it could be anywhere in the world*' (1:3), blurs right from the start boundaries concerning locale and prepares us for when the hotel room becomes 'at best merely a bombed out shelter'.[39]

Similarly, Cate's question to Ian as to whether he has slept with a man (1:19) presages the rape Ian will later undergo, while Cate's first words, 'You're a nightmare' (4:51), when she finds the blinded Ian huddled inside the baby's grave are a direct repetition of the phrase used in the earlier section of the play to express disgust towards her ex-lover (2:33).

These boundaries between dream and reality are questioned by Ian himself when trapped with the soldier – 'Don't know what the sides are here. Don't know where … Think I might be drunk', but the soldier is quick to dispel such thoughts – 'No. It's real' (3:40).

The ending of the play is problematic. Nick Curtis believes that 'the final scenes are a systematic trawl through the deepest pits of human degradation',[40] yet they could be interpreted as an indication of hope, in that Ian's last words to Cate of 'thank you' (5:61) indicate partial redemption for Ian, and reconciliation and forgiveness between the pair. A more pessimistic interpretation is that both simply eke out an existence in the bombed-out shelter of the hotel room, and that Cate's return to Ian is an act of passive acceptance and capitulation.

Edward Bond sees the final scene as a desperate form of optimism, based around a true scenario:

> You open a door. Inside in the gloom three children sit and play the ancient game of straws … Instead we see that the children are sitting on a naked body. The body is putrescent … Perhaps the children draw straws for the last breadcrumb or drop of water? They do not fight for it. And perhaps the dead woman is their mother and isn't it natural for children to cling to their mother? But surely this is a terrible perversion of the world? No it is their normality. How did it come to that? Oh – bit by bit. And all is not lost – the children are not yet eating their straws.[41]

Bond concludes, '*Blasted*, I think, comes from the game of straws, from the centre of our humanity and our ancient need for theatre'.[42] Kane herself was far more ambiguous regarding the ending of the play. This is borne out by a significant cut that she made to the first published edition. Here, Cate has a speech which makes explicit the sacrifice she had to make

---

39 Hansford, 'Sarah Kane', p. 348.
40 Curtis, *Evening Standard*, 19 January 1995.
41 Bond, *Guardian*, 28 January 1995.
42 *Ibid.*

in order to obtain the food and drink that will sustain herself and Ian as the war wages outside. Also underscored is the Beckettian motif of attempting but failing to leave:

> CATE. Did it in the back of a van.
> He smelt of cigarettes and sweat.
> What he did -
> What he did with his wife he said.
> Did it quickly. Made me bleed.
> Gave me a sausage, some bread and this.
> (*She pours gin in* Ian's *mouth*)
> Want to go home now.[43]

Removal of this speech *possibly* makes the outcome of Cate's long-term future bound to Ian more problematic; perhaps the real reason for its removal was the beginning of a practice Kane would develop in later work, whereby the dramatic image would function over that of language. Asked whether she would change any aspects of *Blasted* as it currently stood in 1995, she replied, 'If I was going to rewrite it I'd try the purifying images even more, and I'd cut even more words out if such a thing is possible, because for me the language of theatre is image'.[44] This is why in the second edition of the play she dispenses with Cate's explanatory speech because the stage direction, '*There is blood seeping from between her legs*' (5:57; *Frontline Intelligence*, p. 49), common to both versions, is enough to indicate what has happened to Cate without her telling the audience.

Other small but immensely important changes Kane made to the second edition were to do with a specific time scale. In the original edition the sense of time in which the action was operating remained unclear, but in rehearsals for the Royal Court production 'there was also the use of rain, which was James Macdonald's idea, about having rain between scenes which gradually gets harder to the point where it comes through the roof'.[45] Kane took this imagery and inserted stage directions in the second edition that relate the rain to different seasons. So, '*The sound of spring rain*' (1:24) marks the point where Ian sexually assaults Cate, to the meeting and ordeal with the soldier. Spring passes until we hear '*the sound of autumn rain*' (3:50), and Cate's first meeting with Ian lasts another season until the '*sound of heavy winter rain*' (3:57) completes the play. This use of seasons to mark the passing of time contributes to the feeling that from the entrance of the soldier the play indeed slips into one of Cate's fits whereby, 'Time slows down. A dream I get stuck in'

(1:22). This manipulation of time also contributes to the sense of night-mare, whereby Ian's rape and blinding by the soldier is made to stretch out interminably over summer and autumn.

'Our town now': issues of nationalism

'State of Britain' plays have been a popular theme in post-war drama ever since *Look Back in Anger*, or indeed Osborne's *The Entertainer* (1957), and it is against this benchmark that Peter Ansorge criticises Sarah Kane's generation of dramatists for being too narrow in their outlook: 'perhaps because they had experience of a world war ... [that] young writers like Osborne and Wesker could produce work on a much broader canvas'.[46]

Blasted I would argue is a notable exception. The play works on many levels, and while much of its dominant themes concern themselves with the relationship between Ian and Cate, and later Ian's personal agonies and partial redemption, its other dominant ideas focus around the question of nationhood. It is a play that asks uncomfortable questions about British identity, and in bringing a foreign war straight into a Leeds hotel room also asks questions about British engagement with a broader Europe.

These aspects of nationhood are shown principally through the character of Ian, his profession as a tabloid journalist and his embroilment in the mysterious right-wing organisation who now want him dead. Ian is Welsh by birth but we are told in the opening stage directions that he has lived in Leeds for most of his life. To Ian, 'English and Welsh is the same. British' (3:41). But his sense of national identity is based almost entirely on a sense of a racism – 'Hate this city. Stinks. Wogs and Pakis taking over' (1:4) – and racial purity: 'Come over from God knows where have their kids and call them English they're not English born' (3:41). Ian's involvement in the sinister organisation seems to be motivated out of this misplaced sense of Britishness – 'Done the jobs they asked. Because I love this land' (2:30).

Ian's sense of nationhood is narrow and parochial; nowhere is this revealed more than in the newspaper stories he writes – 'I'm a home journalist for Yorkshire. I don't cover foreign affairs' (3:48) – but we do hear Ian working on one story which is set abroad:

---

46   Ansorge, *From Liverpool to Los Angeles*, p. 60.

A serial killer slaughtered British tourist Samantha Scarce, S - C - R - A - C - E, in a sick murder ritual comma, police revealed yesterday point new par. The bubbly nineteen-year old from Leeds was among seven victims found buried in identical triangular tombs in an isolated New Zealand forest point new par. Each had been stabbed more than twenty times and placed face down comma, hands bound behind their backs new par. Caps up, ashes at the site showed the maniac had stayed to cook a meal, caps down point new par. Samantha comma, a beautiful redhead with dreams of becoming a model comma, was on the trip of a lifetime after finishing her A levels last year point. (*Blasted* 1:12–13).

Ian's dictation of the article is a notable omission from the two Birmingham drafts of *Blasted,* and it is possible that the inclusion was made in order to make a stronger dramatic point about Ian being made later to confront literally some of the events he reports from a comfortable distance at home. As Patricia Holland observes, 'Ian operates with a set of values borrowed from the tabloid paper on which he works',[47] and the article reflects many of these beliefs. The story concentrates on just the single murdered girl whose connection to Leeds is the sole justification for the story in Ian's newspaper. The other victims, who we assume to be from other nationalities, are ignored almost completely. The article is also a mixture of the prurient and self-righteous. The way Samantha met her death is described in some detail and we are also told of the plans she had to become a model. This is mixed together with the image of 'Samantha's heartbroken Mum', yet Ian's technical instructions for punctuation produce a distancing effect to any real sense of shock or revulsion to the event. The implicit sexual titillation Ian has deliberately added to a story of genuine human suffering is immediately reinforced after finishing his dictation by telephone: Ian and his colleague talk about a 'Scouse tart, spread her legs. No forget it. Tears and lies, not worth the space' (1:13).

Kane's belief in the connection between Ian's character and profession is also made explicit in the origin of the newspaper stories used in the play: 'Both the stories that Ian dictates and the one he reads are actually straight from the *Sun*. They're not fictional at all. I just changed the names and the places and I think added a couple of details and took a couple of things out – just because I wanted to make them slightly different, but I did want them to be the real thing'.[48]

The narrow boundaries of national self-interest that Ian and his paper operate within is explored in greater detail with the appearance of the soldier. In the two Birmingham drafts of *Blasted* the soldier is very

47 Holland, *Independent,* 27 January 1995.
48 Interview with author. The other story Ian narrates is the one to the soldier: 'Kinky car dealer' (3:48).

much a product of events taking place in the former Yugoslavia. Here, the soldier is even given a Serbian name, Vladek. To him, Leeds and indeed all of Britain is just another piece of territory:

> VLADEK. English shit. Why did you fuckers recognise Croatia?
> (*Ian is confused.*)
> Why are you English spineless dogs sniffing Germany's arse?
> IAN. That was the government. I'm not the government.
> VLADEK. This is a Serbian town now. And you are English shit.
> (*He spits in Ian's face.*)

Despite erasing such specific references to the Yugoslavian conflict, early critical defence of *Blasted* identified this as the main idea behind the play, and its attempt to 'range beyond personal experience and bring the wars that rage at such a convenient distance from this island'.[49]

Others saw the confrontation between Ian and the soldier to be a continuation of the issues from the first part of the play where 'the imagery of racism and obscenity so enthusiastically peddled by the media' comes to a brutal conclusion; and 'through a series of stark theatrical images, eschewing the realism of the preceding action attempts to reveal the country's own dark imagination and fearful subconscious'.[50]

The cataclysm that engulfs Ian comes partly from his profession as a tabloid journalist. The soldier wants him to write about the scarring experiences that the war have created – 'that's your job … Proving it happened' (3:47). However, Ian abnegates any moral responsibility for the journalism he practises – to him they are just 'stories': 'I do other stuff. Shootings and rapes and kids getting fiddled by queer priests and schoolteachers' (3:48). Ian believes that his particular form of Anglocentric reporting, despite the fact that a civil war has suddenly erupted around him, and even invaded the space of the Leeds hotel room he occupies, 'isn't a story anyone wants to hear' (3:48). In his self-appointed role as arbiter and filter for 'truth', Ian helps to shape public perceptions on who are to be perceived as heroes and villains in the minds of the British public. Despite the Soldier's insistence for Ian to 'tell them … you saw me', Ian believes there is no interest in 'soldiers screwing each other for a patch of land. It has to be … personal. Your girlfriend, she's a story. Soft and clean. Not like you. Filthy, like the wogs. No joy in a story about blacks who gives a shit? Why bring you to light' (3:48).

The irony is that the soldier will be the last person Ian will see before his eyes are put out. The metaphor of blinding had an obvious appeal to Kane: 'Given also that Ian was a tabloid journalist I thought in a way it was

49 Crimp *et al.*, letter to the *Guardian*, 23 January 1995.
50 Nick Drake, letter to the *Guardian*, 24 January 1995.

a kind of castration, because obviously if you're a reporter your eyes are actually your main organ. So I thought rather than have him castrated, which I thought felt melodramatic, I could go for a more kind of metaphorical castration'.[51]

The media furore that greeted *Blasted* soon became a case in point of life imitating art, and as Kane observed: 'The week the play opened there was an earthquake in Japan in which thousands of people died, and in this country a fifteen-year-old girl had been raped and murdered in a wood, but *Blasted* got more coverage in some newspapers than either of these events. And I'm not only talking about tabloids'.[52]

Influences

In Sarah Kane's last play, *4:48 Psychosis*, one of the speakers announces themselves to be 'Last in a long line of literary kleptomaniacs' (a time honoured tradition, p. 213). A significant feature of Sarah Kane's drama is the degree to which it is informed and influenced by an eclectic collection of theatrical, literary and musical sources: these range from the King James version of the Bible, to poetry, novels and pop music lyrics. Some of these influences are directly acknowledged; others are unconscious, and while Vera Gottlieb writing at the time of *Crave* commented – 'the virulence of the attacks on Kane seemed to have driven her into a withdrawal, imitating the "language"-based drama of Pinter and Beckett, but without their often profound content'[53] – it is hard to see Kane as simply a derivative writer.

Kane displayed a refreshing candour in revealing and discussing these influences and the effects they produced on her own writing. In an interview she revealed the principle texts that inform *Blasted*: 'I think with everything I write there are usually a couple of books that I read again and again when writing. With *Blasted* it was *King Lear* and *Waiting for Godot* – well it was strange with *Blasted* because for me there are kind of three sections: the first one was very influenced by Ibsen, the second one by Brecht, and the third one by Beckett'.[54]

51 Interview with author.
52 Langridge and Stephenson, *Rage and Reason*, p. 130.
53 Gottlieb, *Theatre in a Cool Climate*, p. 211.
54 Kane, interview with Nils Tabert.

Samuel Beckett's influence looms large in all of Sarah Kane's work. This is not only through the stylistic approach of stripping language down to its bare meaning, but more particularly in *Blasted* an attempt to reinterpret certain images and themes from *Waiting for Godot* (1952). For instance, despite Kane being specific about the last section of *Blasted* being influenced by Beckett, thematically it also informs the whole play through the motif of entrapment. While fellow dramatist Mark Ravenhill felt that in *Blasted* 'with its great passions locked in a small room … constantly reminded me of Racine',[55] Ian and Cate's relationship of mutual co-dependency has far more in common with the characters from *Waiting for Godot*. In Beckett's play the characters Vladimir/Estragon and Pozzo/Lucky seem consigned to spend their lives bound to each other. Despite having the opportunity to leave his master after being struck blind, Lucky continues to choose servitude, and while both the tramps frequently believe they 'weren't made for the same road' (1:52), they both recognise that 'they need each other to in order to exist – to *prove* their own identities – and so their attempts to leave one another during the course of the play either fail or they end up returning to each other eventually'.[56]

Despite reminding her ex-lover that she is only 'here for the night' (1:5), Ian is determined to prevent Cate from leaving the confines of the hotel room and his own stifling influence. Cate in turn seems predisposed to continuing this smothering attachment. At one point Ian asks Cate to marry him, but her excuse is 'I couldn't leave Mum'. When Ian reminds her, 'have to one day', Cate's immediate rejoinder is 'why?' to which Ian *'opens his mouth to answer but can't think of one'* (1:6).

Ian sees Cate and himself as inextricably linked. To him 'we're one' (2:26), and on learning Cate is about to embark on another relationship, Ian asserts, 'You're more mine than his' (1:16). At times Ian's tactics to keep Cate with him become desperate, even farcical:

CATE. Want to go home now.
IAN. It's not even seven. There won't be a train.
CATE. I'll wait at the station.
IAN. It's raining.
CATE. It's not.
IAN. Want you to stay here. Till after breakfast at least.
CATE. No.
IAN. Cate. After breakfast.
CATE. No.
     (Ian locks the door and pockets the key.)

55 Ravenhill, *Independent*, 23 February 1999.
56 Richard Coe, *Beckett* (Edinburgh and London, 1964), p. 81.

IAN. I love you.
CATE. I don't want to stay.
IAN. Please.
CATE. Don't want to.
IAN. You make me feel safe.
CATE. Nothing to be scared of.

(*Blasted* 2:27–8).

This relationship, based on a cleaving to one another, is a reciprocal one. Despite leaving on two occasions, Cate ultimately returns to Ian and the play ends, as it does in *Waiting for Godot*, with the characters still inhabiting the stage together. The precarious sanctuary that the hotel room provides, also echoes the importance Vladimir places on the tree as both a landmark and proof of existence and memory in *Waiting for Godot*, or the room that Hamm and Clov stay bounded by in *Endgame*.

The metaphor of the room as both refuge and conduit for the elements of menace and chaos that lurk immediately outside is also reminiscent of early work by Harold Pinter. *Blasted* is most similar in this respect to *The Dumb Waiter* (1960). There are also other similarities which include Gus, Ben and Ian all working as hired killers for sinister organisations, the continual checking and rechecking of their guns as well as the device of a mysterious outside agency that supplies Ben and Gus with items such as matches to light the kettle. In *Blasted* this manifests itself as the hotel's ghostly but efficient room service that supplies gin, sandwiches and cooked English breakfasts outside the door with an almost supernatural speed. Although Ian puts a face to the person delivering these items – 'Probably the wog with the sarnies' (1:6), and Cate a name – 'Andrew' (1:17), his presence (if indeed it is the same person) is only announced by the sound of a knock. In both plays knocks at the door signify danger. In *The Dumb Waiter* this sense of threat is laced with humour:

BEN. If there's a knock on the door you don't answer it.
GUS. If there's a knock on the door I don't answer it.
BEN. But there won't be a knock on the door.
GUS. So I won't answer it.[57]

In *Blasted* a knock on the door is ominous both to Ian, who believes that the organisation he worked for now want to kill him, and later to Cate, who perhaps with a prescience that comes from her fits pleads with Ian: 'DON'T ANSWER IT DON'T ANSWER IT DON'T ANSWER IT' (2:34).

---

57 Harold Pinter, *The Dumb Waiter*, in *Plays 1* (London, 1989), pp. 142–3.

James Hollis in a comment regarding Harold Pinter's *The Room* (1960) speaks about how an innocuous everyday object like a door can be imbued with menace within the context of the play:

> A door which does not explain itself or from which we expect some kind of explanation becomes mysterious, even ominous – it seems absurd to think of a door as ominous, but we find ourselves wondering if someone will knock on the door, come in, and make demands on us ... the door becomes an extension of one's identity as well.[58]

In *Blasted* the door is also made into a disquieting object. This comes about through Ian and Cate's anxiety whenever they hear a knock, to the lack of human agency that delivers their food to the final disclosure that the soldier waits outside to claim Ian. With the arrival of Ian's nemesis tension is maintained as both protagonists on either side of the door play an elaborate game of cat and mouse with each other:

> *There are two loud knocks at the outer door.*
> IAN *draws his gun, goes to the door and listens.*
> *The door is tried from outside. It is locked.*
> *There are two more loud knocks.*
> IAN. Who's there?
> *Silence.*
> *Then two more loud knocks.*
> IAN. Who's there?
> *Silence.*
> *Then two more loud knocks.*
> IAN *looks at the door.*
> *Then he knocks twice.*
> *Silence.*
> *Then two more knocks from outside.*
> IAN *thinks.*
> *Then he knocks three times.*
> *Silence.*
> *Three knocks from outside.*
> IAN *knocks once.*
> *One knock from outside.*
> IAN *knocks twice.*
> *Two knocks.*
> IAN *puts his gun back in the holster and unlocks the door.*
> (*Blasted* 2:35–6).

The idea for the intricate system of knocks and counter knocks was a later addition to the play. In both versions of the Birmingham scripts the

---

58   James Hollis, *Harold Pinter: The Poetics of Silence* (Illinois, 1970), p. 20.

stage directions are far more simple: '*There is a loud knock at the outer door ... The door is tried from the outside. It is still locked. A foreign voice speaks its own language*'. Kane's alteration of the episode seems to show that she was perhaps keen to instil a greater sense of mystery (by removing the sound of the soldier's voice) and a build-up of dramatic tension (including an intricate set of directions relating to the number of knocks upon the door) prior to their encounter. Structurally, this small scene is crucial to the dynamics of the play as the door literally functions as the device through which the soldier's entry triggers the radical switch in mood and tone that occupies the second half of the play.

The influence *Waiting for Godot* produces on *Blasted* is in turn dependent on its other principal source, that of Shakespeare's *King Lear* (c.1604–5). In some respects it is not surprising that Kane chooses to draw elements from what has generally been considered to be Shakespeare's starkest, most brutal play. The critic A.C. Bradley has commented that, 'In no other of his tragedies does humanity appear more pitiably infirm or more hopelessly bad,'[59] while Kenneth Muir described the play as 'a human body in anguished movement, tugged, wrenched, beaten, pierced, stung, scourged, dislocated, flayed, gashed, scalded, tortured and finally broken on the rack'.[60] The influence *King Lear* exerts over *Blasted* extends even down to its title:

> I was doing a workshop with this person who script edited it and he said, 'right I'm going to the toilet, and when I come back tell me what the title of the play is you're going to write', and I thought 'oh, for fuck's sake', and I knew it was about someone who got drunk a lot, so he came out and I said 'I'm going to call it *Blasted*. 'It was only when I was into about the fourth draft I suddenly thought, 'of course, it's the blasted heath!' And by that time I was already reading *Lear, and* it was beginning to influence it, but it was just sheer coincidence, but once that happened I thought that maybe this is – I hate to say destiny and things – but I thought maybe there's some subconscious drive to rewrite that play.[61]

However, Kane reveals that the idea to reinterpret the Shakespearian text was by no means an immediate process:

> The first two drafts of *Blasted* were written emotionally rather than technically. And although parts of it are very deliberate reworkings of *King Lear*, I didn't make that decision until some time into the process. Many of the thematic similarities were already there, but I didn't become consciously aware

59 A. C. Bradley, *Shakespearean Tragedy* (London, 1967), p. 273.
60 Kenneth Muir (ed.), *King Lear: The Arden Shakespeare* (London, 1977), p. 25.
61 Interview with author.

of them until the third draft, after someone suggested that I should re-read *King Lear*.[62]

As Jan Kott[63] has noted the similarity between *King Lear* and Beckett's *Waiting for Godot* and *Endgame*, Sarah Kane in turn distils an amalgamation of material common to all three works. One of the most striking and disturbing of these is the image of the blinded Ian willingly crawling into the baby's makeshift grave in order to wait for death to claim him. The image comes from two connected expressions that appear in both *King Lear* and *Waiting for Godot*. In the former, Lear's 'crawl toward death' (I.i.41) is halted by his youngest daughter Cordelia. However, Lear upbraids her, complaining, 'You do me wrong to take me o'th' grave' (V.i.38). Samuel Beckett builds upon this image of Lear's slow journey to the comfort of death in a speech by Pozzo in which he laments over the human condition, 'they give birth astride of a grave' (II. 82). Like Lear, Ian also finds solace by making literal Lear's journey by seeking the infant's makeshift resting place. However, Kane denies Ian the solace death is supposed to bring. She explains, 'He's dead, he's in hell – and it's exactly the same place he was in before, except that now it's raining.'[64]

The scene is also laced with a grim cruelty: after Ian 'dies with relief' (5:60), he quickly discovers that nothing has changed – he is back exactly where he was before and mocks Cate's Christian interpretation earlier in the play – 'you fall asleep and then you wake up' (1:10). It is Cate however who also mocks the blinded Ian when she returns:

CATE. You're sitting under a hole.
IAN. I know.
CATE. Get wet.
IAN. Aye.
CATE. Stupid bastard.
                    (*Blasted* 5:60)

The other revisited scenes from the other two plays are the farcical attempts made at suicide. In *Waiting for Godot*, the tramps attempt to take their own lives in the hope that 'it'd give us an erection!' (I.18) However, their efforts are hampered by indecision and a poor rope, while in *King Lear* the blinded Gloucester believes that his disguised son Edgar will assist his leap from Dover cliff. Edgar in fact, while appearing to help, is there to thwart the attempt. He somewhat cruelly allows his father to fall a small harmless distance from the summit:

62 Kane, letter to Graham Saunders, 31 October 1997.
63 Jan Kott, *Shakespeare our Contemporary*, trans. Boleslaw Taborski, rev. edn (London, 1967).
64 Kane, letter to Graham Saunders, 31 October 1997.

GLOUCESTER. But have I fall'n, or no?
EDGAR. From the dread summit of this chalky bourn.
  Look up a-height. The shrill gorged lark so far
  Cannot be seen or heard. Do but look up.

(King Lear IV.iv.55–63)

Sarah Kane moulded this scene into the framework of *Blasted*: 'I struggled with scene four for a long time. It was a void in the play – I knew *something* went in there, I just couldn't think what. And then it dropped into my head "It's Ian's Dover scene." As straightforward as that. A blatant rewrite of Shakespeare'.[65] In Kane's version the blinded Ian urges Cate to allow him to end his life, but she abets the suicide only in so far as handing Ian the soldier's gun, which she first renders useless by removing its ammunition:

IAN. End it. Got to Cate, I'm ill. Just speeding it up a bit.
CATE. (*thinks hard*)
IAN. Please.
CATE. (*gives him the gun*)
IAN. (*Takes the gun and puts it in his mouth. He takes it out again*)
  Don't stand behind me.
IAN. (*Puts the gun back in his mouth.*
  He pulls the trigger. The gun clicks, empty. He shoots again. And again and
  again. He takes the gun out of his mouth.)
  Fuck.
CATE. Fate, see. You're not meant to do it. God –
IAN. The cunt.

(Blasted (4:56–7)

Cate's attempts at dissuasion because 'God wouldn't like it' (4:55) echoes Edgar's somewhat pat exhortation, citing the hand of divine intervention in saving his father: 'Therefore, thou happy father / Think that the clearest gods, who make them honours / Of men's impossibilities, have preserved thee' (IV.v.72–4).

Like Ian's bitter remark about God being 'the cunt', Gloucester also curses the heavens for depriving him of a way of ending worldly sufferings:

Is wretchedness deprived that benefit
To end itself by death? 'Twas yet some comfort
When misery could beguile the tyrants rage
And frustrate his proud will.

(King Lear IV.v.61–4).

King Lear's other most famous, or perhaps notorious, scene is the one in which Gloucester is forced to 'smell his way to Dover' (III.vii. 91–2) –

---

65 Kane, letter to Graham Saunders, 3 March 1998.

namely the blinding scene. Samuel Johnson believed it to be 'an act too horrid to be endured in dramatick exhibition, and as such must always compel the mind to relieve its distress by incredulity',[66] while A. C. Bradley objected to the scene on the grounds that 'the physical horror of such a spectacle would in the theatre be a sensation so violent as to overpower the purely tragic emotions'.[67] Kane's decision for Ian to be blinded also came about through another literary source:

> I'd been reading Bill Bruford's *Among Thugs* which is about football violence. He joined up with a group of Manchester United supporters and went round beating people up, and there was one particular incident in it, where there was an undercover policeman, and he got into a row with someone from another firm, and someone just went up to him at a party, grabbed his head – sucked his eye out, bit it off and spat it on the floor. And this policeman, he was just unconscious as soon as the person did it. He was in such shock. And then I read *Lear* and I thought there's something about blinding that is really theatrically powerful.[68]

The other celebrated incident in *King Lear* is the storm scene. Here, Shakespeare uses the cataclysm of 'all-shaking thunder' (III.ii.6) which finally shreds the remnants of Lear's authority as 'the tragically authentic voice of nature crumbling into chaos'.[69]

However, this disintegration of self is followed by the beginnings of partial redemption, or what Lou Lappin refers to as 'a process of psychic dissolution, exposure and self recognition'.[70] G. K. Hunter thinks of Lear's exposure on the blasted heath as a form of trial by ordeal which simultaneously 'strips and reduces human dignity [yet] also shows with the greatest force and detail the process of restoration by which humanity can recover from degradation … [Lear's] retreat into the isolated darkness of his own mind is also a descent into the seed bed of a new life'.[71]

In *Blasted*, Kane takes this same process, whereby Ian is also stripped of power and made to feel extremes of physical and mental anguish before he can begin to rediscover his lost humanity. However, Kane chooses to forego the physical presence of the storm itself as a force of nature, and attempts instead to show Ian's dissolution in a series of

66 Samuel Johnson, *Johnson on Shakespeare*, vol. II (ed.) Bertrand H. Bronson (London, 1968), p. 703.
67 Bradley, *Shakespearean Tragedy*, p. 251.
68 Interview with author.
69 Northrop Frye, *Fools of Time: Studies in Shakespearean Tragedy* (Oxford, 1967), p. 116.
70 Lou Lappin, *The Art and Politics of Edward Bond* (New York, 1987), p. 122.
71 G. K. Hunter, *Dramatic Identities and Cultural Tradition: Studies in Shakespeare and his Contemporaries* (Liverpool, 1978), pp. 251–2.

episodic, wordless scenes – this is perhaps what she meant in interview as the Brechtian-inspired section of the play.

Kane's own particular interpretation of the 'storm scene' in *Blasted* recalls a comment Sir John Gielgud made about a technique he used for playing Lear's confrontation with the storm. Instead of attempting to simply react against the raging elements, Gielgud tried to make Lear *himself* portray the storm.[72] In the same way in *Blasted*, Ian dominates as the epicentre of a catastrophic *psychomachia*:

> *Darkness.*
> *Light.*
> IAN *masturbating.*
> IAN cunt cunt cunt cunt cunt cunt cunt cunt cunt cunt cunt
> *Darkness.*
> *Light.*
> IAN *strangling himself.*
> *Darkness.*
> *Light.*
> IAN *shitting.*
> *and then trying to clean it up with newspaper.*
> *Darkness.*
> *Light.*
> IAN *laughing hysterically.*
> *Darkness.*
> *Light.*
> IAN *having a nightmare.*
> *Darkness.*
> *Light.*
> IAN *crying huge bloody tears.*
> *He is hugging the* SOLDIER'S *body for comfort.*
> *Darkness.*
> *Light.*
> IAN *lying very still, weak with hunger.*
> *Darkness.*
> *Light.*
> IAN *tears the cross out of the ground, rips up the boards and lifts the baby's body out.*
> *He eats the baby.*
> *He puts the sheet the baby was wrapped in back in the hole. A beat, then he climbs in after it and lies down, head poking out of the floor.* (*Blasted* 5:59–60)

The processes Ian carries out onstage seem disturbing and bizarre, but they identify and serve to remind us – from the first image of frenzied

---

72 John Gielgud, *Early Stages* (London, 1953), pp. 157–8.

masturbation, to the occupancy inside the child's grave – of some of the events which we have witnessed in the first part of the play. The opening image for instance works almost like a condensation of Ian's old self, showing us the remnants of his abusive sexual nature. Although Aleks Sierz maintains that the primary aim of this is to shock, and points out, 'If "cunt" is still a taboo word … Kane makes Ian … say it eleven times while masturbating,'[73] Kane explains how the genesis of this scene came about:

> Well, I mean the wanking thing kind of started off as a joke. I was talking with a bloke who's a really close friend, and we were talking about the differences between men's and women's sexual fantasies and he said 'it seems to me women's sexual fantasies are like eighteenth-century novels. There's all this stuff around it, but there's never actually any sex. The fantasy is about the build up and the restraint, and the fact that it doesn't happen.' And then I said 'so what are men's sexual fantasies like? They're just basically cunt aren't they? An array of genitalia.' And then of course I thought, 'that's where Ian has to go.'[74]

When asked about the similarities between the series of short tableaux scenes and the storm in *King Lear*, Kane said she only recognised the connection during the writing of *Blasted*. However, despite the different image structure employed she believes the intention was the same:

> For Ian to experience a moment of utter terror, he has to get as low as humanly possible before he dies. I decided to take the most basic human activities – eating, sleeping, wanking, shitting – and see how awful they can be when you're really alone – which is pretty awful. But, as a storm scene in the same way as *King Lear* I suppose it does become one because Ian gets as low as he can get – he really does. But for me, it got to the point where I didn't know what words to use anymore, and it was a complete breakdown of language. I thought I'm going to have to do this purely through image, which I'm happier doing anyway.[75]

Ian's death and resurrection are a case in point. The stage directions make this clear, but how can this be made explicit onstage? Kane had mixed feelings about the first performances at the Royal Court: 'Well, I actually thought that in terms of the production it was one of the least successful parts, but in terms of the writing it's one of the most successful parts of the play. Whenever I read it I think I'm really proud of this bit of writing.'[76] During rehearsal and subsequent performance of this par-

73 Sierz, 'Cool Britannia?', p. 328.
74 Interview with author.
75 Kane, letter to Graham Saunders, 31 March 1997.
76 Interview with author.

ticular scene, Kane found that it was producing new reverberations on the existing play: 'once we went into rehearsal there were certain things where I thought I could take that image further'. These new images also developed previous thematic material within the play which Kane had not intended:

> There was one thing I really liked about it, because it brought out a thing that I hadn't thought when I articulated it to the director, and he hadn't thought of it either. Ian says earlier 'God – the cunt'. And then when he's masturbating cunt, cunt, cunt, cunt'. It was really interesting because Pip Donaghy [the actor playing Ian] was looking up and it looked like he was praying, and it sets off all kinds of resonances about that thing about God being a cunt; and it was completely spontaneous. None of us had planned it at all, but I thought that was where the production takes over, which is good because it should start setting up its own resonances.[77]

This unwitting contribution to the debate about the existence of God and the question of life after death, already set up in the play, comes to a partial resolution in performance with the final image from the tableaux scenes, where Ian is inside the infant's grave with water dripping onto his head:

> Ian is deified in a way that I didn't really realise until I saw the play performed for the first time. When I watched the blood being washed away by the rain I saw just how Christ-like the image is. Which isn't to say that Ian isn't punished. He is, of course, he dies, and he finds that the thing he has ridiculed – life after death – really does exist. And that life is worse than where he was before. It really is hell.[78]

Ian's prolonged punishment and sense of isolation during these scenes bring to mind echoes of Christ's Passion at the Crucifixion, as does his death and subsequent return to earth which parodies Christ's burial on the Friday evening, His descent to Hell on Saturday and resurrection on Sunday morning. However, Ian's fate seems to be one of a slow and painful education in which his simple acknowledgement of 'thank you' to Cate is only the beginning of what will be a long and painful journey towards self-awareness. It is perhaps worth placing Ian's treatment in this scene against a comment Kane made about both her own sensibility and the characters in her plays: 'Probably all my characters in some way are completely Romantic. I think nihilism is the most extreme form of Romanticism. And that I think is where the plays get misunderstood. I think I'm a complete and utter Romantic, in the tradition of Keats and Wilfred Owen'.[79]

77 Ibid.
78 Kane, letter to Graham Saunders, 31 October 1997.
79 Kane, interview with Nils Tabert.

If we interpret what happens to Ian in the light of this comment, then his nightmarish ordeal with its promise of hope through a process of prolonged atonement for past sins places him amongst figures from myth and literature such as Samuel Taylor Coleridge's *The Rime of the Ancient Mariner* (1798). Here, the eponymous Mariner commits a transgressive act against Nature through the senseless killing of an albatross – for this he is punished by supernatural forces and is made to endure thirst, despair and isolation as his shipmates die and he is left alone to witness a corrupted ('The very deep did rot') and pitiless nature ('the death – fires danced at night').This lasts until the Mariner is able to bless the water snakes ('O happy living things!') and attempt to heal the breach he has caused. Even then, like Ian's return from the dead, the Mariner is not fully absolved by the Polar Spirit's 'fellow daemons', one of whom decrees, 'The man hath penance done / And penance more will do'.

Both Coleridge's Mariner and Ian undergo 'a form of purgatorial fire',[80] while the unexplained act of cruelty against the albatross echoes Ian's cruel treatment of Cate – neither have done any of the protagonists harm, yet both feel compelled to destroy these representatives of simple goodness. Virginia Radley in her comment on the Mariner, which could equally well apply to Ian, recognises 'at the outset [he] is a being who is experienced, worldly, corrupted, and thereby set in opposition to the Albatross who is unworldly, natural, hence uncorrupted'.[81]

In answer to the question posed during an interview as to whether Ian is punished or redeemed at the end of the play, Kane answered 'both',[82] and figures such as Ian and the Mariner share a paradox in that they achieve heroic status through acts of transgression:

> The Mariner has done a guilty thing, and he is certainly punished. Yet had he not done it, his sense of the universe (and ours through him) would be more limited. If he is a guilty man, he is also something of a hero simply because he has gone further in experience than others. In an admittedly qualified way, he is akin to the romantic heroes that were to become so common in nineteenth-century writing – some of them Byronic, others patterned after Faust – who by violating laws acquire a depth of experience that others lack'.[83]

Their suffering is also a form of rebirth which 'involves the almost total destruction of the old self in order to make room for the new'.[84] Coleridge uses this model of suffering and rebirth through partial redemption to

---

80   Richard Holmes, *Coleridge* (Oxford, 1982), p. 87.
81   Virginia L. Radley, *Samuel Taylor Coleridge* (New York, 1966), p. 64.
82   Interview with author.
83   Walker Jackson Bate, *Coleridge*, (New York, 1968), p. 57.
84   *Ibid.*, pp. 62–3.

moralise – 'He prayeth well, who loveth well' – and discloses to the reader that the Wedding Guest leaves the encounter, 'A sadder and a wiser man'. *Blasted* avoids such an overt approach, and instead we witness the first tiny gesture of this process of spiritual rebirth through Ian's acknowledgement of 'thanks' to the woman he has systematically abused in the first half of the play.

The incident that provoked the most ridicule and offence in equal measures was the incident where Ian eats the baby. Again, Kane was frustrated by the literal interpretation most critics took, yet initially she also had doubts about the scene in regard to how it would translate from text to performance:

> A lot of people said to me when they read it before it was performed 'we're not sure about the baby eating', and I kept looking and thinking 'is it gratuitous? What does gratuitous mean anyway? And does it become unbelievable?' I can't remember who it was who said it, that when *King Lear* is read the blinding of Gloucester is somehow more acceptable. I find the opposite. Reading *Blasted* is much harder work than watching it, because when you read it, it's literally *he eats the baby*. When you see it he's clearly not eating the baby. It's absolutely fucking obvious. This is a theatrical image. He's not doing it at all. So in a way it's more demanding because it throws you back on your own imagination. But somehow, I don't know – it's more realistic when you read the scene because you get simply the act.[85]

Eating the baby is the last thing Ian does before he dies, and it provides a way of trying to encapsulate the utter nihilism and despair he feels after the blinding. The use of the baby also, by contrast, provides an element of hope. Cate has willingly taken responsibility for the infant after it has been handed to her by a stranger, and even though the baby eventually dies, Cate gives it the dignity of a Christian burial. Her prayer to the departed child again reveals a belief in the afterlife, and these simple acts of human faith and compassion assume greater importance when they are compared with Ian's bleakness of vision. To Ian the baby is worthless: 'they shit and cry. Hopeless' (4:52). He also ridicules the trouble Cate goes to in burying and praying for her dead charge:

CATE. I don't know her name.
IAN. Don't matter. No one's going to visit.
CATE. I was supposed to look after her.
IAN. Can bury me next to her soon. Dance on my grave.

(*Blasted* 5:57).

85 Interview with author.*

A production of *Blasted* in Brussels chose to reinterpret the play in order to make the incident with the baby of central importance. In most cases Sarah Kane was sensitive to textual reinterpretation of her work, but felt that in foreign productions the writer 'must allow a certain amount of cultural difference',[86] and here she felt the production was an interesting experiment:

> I do not think that the production in Brussels had very much to do with what I've written. It's not to say that I didn't like it, on the contrary. It is not one of those productions that I would not want as the first production of one of my plays. It could not help me as a writer to develop. But coming from another country, I found it interesting. The play was produced at the time of the Dutroux affair. When I was in Brussels at the time, bodies were uncovered; there was an enormous amount of guilt. Whenever I met someone, they were always saying: 'I am ashamed to be a Belgian', which I found quite extraordinary. I can't imagine that happening in England, someone saying I am ashamed to be British. *Blasted* became almost completely about a baby which dies. At the point when the baby was being buried, people in the audience were crying. I certainly felt that it was not because of the play, but because of what was going on outside the theatre. The production took the play and reinterpreted it in terms of what was happening in that city. That's fine. If that situation was happening in London with a first production of a play I would be extremely unhappy, and I would probably withdraw the play.[87]

Kane's response to *King Lear* extended to examine its domestic themes. She explained, 'for me [*King Lear*] it's really a play about father-hood',[88] and in *Blasted* the claustrophobic and pathological relationship between Ian and Cate parodies and echoes the 'darker purpose' (I.i.36) between Lear and Cordelia, accentuating through the disparities in age the incestuous overtones that exist between father and daughter in Shake-speare's play. A. C. Bradley contends that the famous speech of Lear to Cordelia – 'Come let's away to prison / We two alone will sing like birds i'th cage' (V.iii. 8–9) – is enough to suggest 'He [Lear] meant to live with Cordelia and her alone'.[89] Ian, as we have seen, also tries desperately, through a combination of cajoling, emotional blackmail and bullying, to keep Cate exclusively to himself.

Just as the issue of the missing queen in *King Lear* exerts a troubling, ghostly presence throughout the play, absent and even sinister manifesta-tions of fatherhood haunt the periphery of *Blasted*. Cate for instance talks of her fits returning 'since Dad came back' (1:10), while Ian believes his

86 Rebellato, 'Brief Encounter'.
87 Thielemans, *Rehearsing the Future*, p. 11.
88 Interview with author.
89 Bradley, *Shakespearean Tragedy*, p. 250.

estranged son Matthew hates him. Ian's bitter comment, 'I'll send him an invite for the funeral' (1:18), expresses the gulf of absence between father and son.

However, just as in Cordelia's return to Lear, Cate's return to Ian seems to promise reconciliation, although the scene in Kane's play is perhaps more significant in terms of marking a change in our perceptions of character. Previously, Cate has had to constantly battle against Ian's patronising view of her: 'You think I'm stupid. I'm not stupid ... Can look after myself'[90] (1:21). Her departure from Ian and experiences in the war-zone show she has the ability to survive, and is prepared to even sell herself for food, including meat. Her earlier moral objections, 'Dead meat. Blood. Can't eat an animal' (1:7), have given way to a pragmatism, brought about through the need to survive the chaos of the war. Kane also believes that Cate shows a degree of flexibility within the play that is outwardly surprising:

> Well, the thing is you see, I seem to have a completely different take to the rest of the world, which is I don't think Cate is simple. For me, Cate constantly surprises me, she has this very idealised image of what sex should be, but it's not from a position of naivety. I see her as possibly the most intelligent of all of them. I think the thing that stops Cate being a stereotype is those surprising things. She has sex with people which you don't expect, and I think everything is grounded specifically. I don't think there's any aspect of her supposed simpleness which isn't grounded – and again it may have been an unconscious thing because I was reading a lot of Shakespeare at the time, and also I read *Waiting for Godot*, which okay, they're not fools, but they're clowns, again who are capable of massive insight.[91]

James Hansford in his discussion of the play also sees Cate as mercurial, 'capable of sudden expressions of lust and affection',[92] yet she is also shown, as Kane mentioned, with intelligent insight and a fierce resilience. These traits, together with a refusal to be constantly passive against Ian's aggression, are demonstrated throughout the play. For example, when Ian asserts that Adolf Hitler 'should have gone for scum ... the wogs and fucking football fans' (1:19) Cate challenges this by revealing that she is a football fan and turns Ian's logic against itself – 'I go to Elland Road sometimes. Would you bomb me?' (1:20)

Cate is also far from being an epitome of simple goodness. She exacts revenge on Ian several times in retaliation against his abuse – biting his

---

90 In the pre-performance draft of the Birmingham University script, Ian comments, 'I'm in trouble because of you. It's not my fault you're ignorant. If you're ignorant, you're ignorant, you *are* fucking ignorant. I've never met anyone so fucking ignorant'.

91 Kane, interview with author.

92 Hansford, 'Sarah Kane', p. 348.

penis, ripping the arms off his jacket and launching a sustained physical attack. She also ignores Ian when he is in pain even though '*it looks very much as if he is dying*' (2:24), and despite her return in the second half of the play, she refuses to pray for him. Although Cate feeds the blinded Ian food, afterwards she '*sits apart from him, huddled for warmth*' (5:61).

This harsher side to Cate also comes across more strongly in the two Birmingham drafts of the play. In both versions Cate makes greater use of obscene language such as simple exclamations ('Ham. Fuck's sake'), and expresses rage more powerfully against Ian. For instance, in the final version of the play when Ian holds the gun to her head, Cate is defiant: 'Do it. Go on, shoot me. Can't be no worse than what you've done already. Shoot me if you want, then turn it on yourself and do the world a favour' (2:34). However, in the pre-performance draft this becomes – 'Go on, do it, shoot me, then turn it on yourself you shit and do the world a fucking favour'.

Kane also made another small but immensely significant change to Cate's character after the Birmingham performance had been completed. Shortly after Cate enters the hotel room she is '*sucking her thumb*' (1:4). The action is repeated again at the end of the play when she is alone with Ian. Not only does the action underpin the father/daughter dynamics and abuse within her relationship with Ian, but when this is combined with Cate's epileptic seizures somehow this also underscores her innocence and unworldliness.

This relative harshness of Cate in the early drafts also finds the opposite taking place in Ian. Here he uses far more polite registers to his speech ('Bring a bottle of Gordon's up please'), but by the time of the final Royal Court script these have all been expunged in order to make his final 'thank you' produce a far greater impact.

Kane's debut was nothing less than remarkable. It reached further than the vistas offered by John Osborne's now famous stage props of ironing board and sofa, or the hackneyed 'truism' that women dramatists like to keep their subject matter narrow. Kane's concerns in *Blasted* weren't merely domestic – they embraced questions existential and cosmic, questions such as the existence of God, suicide, damnation, life after death and the extent of human brutality. These thematic aspects of *Blasted* as well as the theatrical effects employed also placed it firmly in a European milieu of non-realism, away from the socio-realism that had come to dominate much post-war British drama.

What is perhaps even more important about *Blasted* was that it served an important and timely function in reminding critics and public alike that theatre was more than the sum of West End musicals, classical revivals and pleasant undemanding comedies, but an artistic force which still had the ability to shock and stimulate, as well as bring about new ways of thinking about ourselves. In short, *Blasted* restored back to the British theatre its missing venom and bile.

3

'If there could have been more moments like this': *Phaedra's Love*

Phaedra's Love, Sarah Kane's second full-length play, came out sixteen months after *Blasted* in May 1996 at London's Gate Theatre, a small fringe venue in Notting Hill.[1] On the surface, *Phaedra's Love* appears to be a very different play from *Blasted*, in both its thematic and structural approach. Kane also took the decision to direct the play herself:

> The thing that I felt strongly about was that in lots of productions of *Blasted*, sometimes I was looking at the stage and I wasn't seeing exactly the images I'd written. And so I thought if I direct *Phaedra's Love* myself there's no one to blame. If the image doesn't happen it's completely my own fault and I find out how difficult it is.[2]

The play came to be written out of a commission by the Gate Theatre for a new work influenced by a canonical play from the past. Kane chose the Roman playwright and philosopher Seneca's version of the Phaedra story as the basis for her own play. As the critic Ruby Cohn observes, 'American playwrights venture rarely into Greek myth, and English playwrights even more rarely',[3] and initially Kane had no natural inclination to reinterpret a play from the ancient classics:

---

1 See Mel Kenyon's account of how the commission from the Gate Theatre took place, pp. 149–50.
2 Kane, interview with Nils Tabert.
3 Ruby Cohn, *Currents in Contemporary Drama* (Bloomington, 1969), pp. 102–3.

They [the Gate Theatre] asked me to rewrite a classic and my original choice was *Woyzeck*. But they were already planning to do a season of all Büchner's plays, so *Woyzeck* was out. Then I said I'd do Brecht's *Baal*, because it's loosely based on *Woyzeck*. But the Gate thought of all the possible problems with the Brecht estate and we did not really want to get into that. So in the end it was the Gate which suggested something Greek or Roman, and I thought, 'Oh, I've always hated those plays. Everything happens off-stage, and what's the point?' But I decided to read one of them and see what I'd get. I chose Seneca because Caryl Churchill had done a version of one of his plays [*Thyestes*] which I had liked very much. I read *Phaedra* and surprisingly enough it interested me.[4]

Kane's discovery and interest in Seneca should perhaps not be unduly surprising as his work shares thematic similarities reminiscent of *Blasted*, and its view of humanity whereby 'the world of … Seneca's tragedies seems one in which to be human is to suffer, to be alive is to be entrapped in evil, to exist to be located in the midst of a universe conspicuous for its apparent perversity … for its dissection of the human spirit, even for its malice'.[5]

The Phaedra myth, in which tragedy arises out of the hopeless love of the Queen for her royal stepson, is one which has endured and pervaded the entire western dramatic tradition. Most celebrated is of course Jean Racine's *Phèdre* (1677), a reworking of the tale, based on material from both the Greek dramatist Euripides and Seneca's versions of the story.

Sarah Kane's exploration of the Phaedra myth, while using Seneca's version as a loose model, is very much a personal reinterpretation of the source material: 'I read Euripides after I'd written *Phaedra's Love*. And I've never read Racine so far. Also, I only read Seneca once. I didn't want to get too much into it – I certainly didn't want to write a play that you couldn't understand unless you knew the original. I wanted it to stand completely on its own.'[6]

Phaedra's Love, as in previous versions of the myth, retains the essential core of the tragedy – that of the queen's overwhelming passion for her stepson. However, Kane's play departs radically from the Senecan source in a number of its concerns: these include the nature of the queen's love for Hippolytus and the role of free will in embracing a tragic fate. The play is also a continuation and expansion of the issues and concerns that

---

4   Kane, interview with Nils Tabert. Kane eventually directed a production of *Woyzeck* in October 1997 as part of the Gate Theatre's season of plays devoted to Georg Büchner.

5   A. J. Boyle (trans), *Seneca's Phaedra* (Liverpool, 1987), p. 37.

6   Kane, interview with Nils Tabert.

preoccupied *Blasted* - concerns that involve the dissection of a male sensibility that is diseased and nihilistic, the existence of God, life after death and the effects of violence.

While the title of the play, and despite Kane's own early protestations on the subject,[7] the character of Phaedra is supplanted in her version by Hippolytus, who becomes the focus of the play in terms of his active participation in the tragedy that he unleashes upon himself. In a later interview Kane conceded that the play concentrates on Hippolytus:

> I suppose I set out to write a play about depression because of my state of being at that time. And so inevitably it did become more about Hippolytus. Except that it was also about that split in my own personality ... The act of writing the play was to try and connect two extremes in my own head. Which in the end wasn't only a depressing experience but also very liberating.[8]

Hippolytus' dominance in the play is perhaps not so surprising when one considers the similarities he shares with Ian from *Blasted*. Both men are embittered nihilists who play out their frustrations on the women trapped with them, and both are also subjected to savage experiences that paradoxically result in insight being gained from catastrophe.

Using the figure of Hippolytus, Kane goes against the traditional depiction of the young prince, recognising that like the Senecan model he is 'less the product of a noble vision than of a deranged psychology, as its connection with a ferocious misogynism reveals'.[9]

> The other interesting thing about [Seneca's] *Phaedra* was that I thought Hippolytus was so unattractive for someone supposed to be so pure and puritanical, and I thought actually the way to make him attractive is to make him unattractive but with the puritanism inverted – because I wanted to write about an attitude to life – not about a lifestyle. So I made him pursue honesty rather than sexual purity which I hadn't cared for anyway ... And besides, before I'd even asked the Gate about doing *Baal* I'd already done some work on my version of it, and then the Gate said no, so I had these scenes with Baal and various people. And when I looked at them again I thought actually Hippolytus and Baal are the same character, so I can just use this material in *Phaedra's Love*. The scene with Hippolytus and the priest was originally written for *Baal*.[10]

Kane's use of Albert Camus' novel *The Outsider* as another literary influence for the play[11] manifests itself partly in Hippolytus' pursuit of

---

7   See Langridge and Stephenson, *Rage and Reason*, p. 134
8   Kane, interview with Nils Tabert.
9   Boyle, *Seneca's Phaedra*, p. 64.
10 Kane, interview with Nils Tabert.
11 *Ibid.*

absolute honesty. This is also the defining characteristic of Camus' anti-hero Mersault, 'who is driven by a tenacious and therefore profound passion, the passion for an absolute and for truth'.[12]

Kane also presents her central protagonist as the archetypal anti-hero; and whereas Seneca portrays Hippolytus as a hunter of prowess and a fearless warrior, in *Phaedra's Love* he is a man subject to and imprisoned by gross appetites. His sexual voracity seems to be modelled on the debauched poet/protagonist from Kane's abandoned *Baal* play, a figure who is given over to 'a vision of life of self-indulgent amoralism'. Yet, whereas Baal's philosophy is one of 'extracting the maximum intensity of pleasure from each passing moment',[13] Kane seems to base her Hippolytus on the physical deterioration and slothful boredom drawn from accounts of the reclusive Elvis Presley of the 1970s. In *Phaedra's Love* the palace of Theseus has become a kitsch Graceland, a monument to the spiritual emptiness that gnaws at the royal family. Parallels between the royal prince and stories of music's self-proclaimed 'king' and his tormented last years abound throughout the play: both are bloated on a diet of junk-food staples, most notably hamburgers and peanut butter (1:65), and both give themselves over to a life of sloth, abetted by the television and intermittently interrupted by anonymous sexual encounters with women (and men in the case of Hippolytus) who willingly seek the allure of celebrity and power – 'Everyone wants a royal cock' (4:74). Whereas successive plays based on the Phaedra myth chose to depict the queen as suffering from a sickness of the soul that gives rise to her obsession for Hippolytus, following in the wake of *Blasted*, Kane returns to an exploration of a male identity in which the processes of life no longer hold any meaning or joy. Both Ian and Hippolytus are counting out time, bitterly waiting for a glimpse of something that might make sense of their lives: both are ultimately waiting for death to claim them. Hippolytus' daily existence is a weary struggle to 'Fill it up with tat Bric-a-brac, bits and bobs, getting by' (4:80).

Hippolytus' chief displacement activity, unlike the chaste prince of previous versions of the myth, is to fill the void with sex. However, Kane's Hippolytus like Ian in *Blasted* is 'a sexual disaster area' (3:73), and throws himself into a succession of joyless encounters with strangers. While previous retellings of the play, including Seneca's, point to Phaedra's obsession with Hippolytus being the source of sexual corruption that taints the

---

12 Afterword, Albert Camus, *The Stranger*, trans. Joseph Laredo (Harmondsworth, 1983), p. 119.
13 Ronald Spiers, 'Baal', in Siegfried Mews (ed.), *Critical Essays on Bertolt Brecht* (Boston, 1989), p. 20.

house of Theseus, *Phaedra's Love* locates the source of the contagion within Hippolytus himself. His debasement of sex and denial of love – as with Ian in *Blasted* – are revealed in motifs such as the sexually transmitted 'Inch of pleurococcus' (5:85) that coats the royal tongue 'like the top of a wall', or Hippolytus' elaborate masturbation rituals involving the contents of his sock drawer.

Similarly, the motif of incest that underscores Phaedra's desire for Hippolytus (despite there being no blood tie between the pair) and brings about the fall of the royal household is expanded by Kane. As Albert Gerard observes in successive dramatic versions of the myth, the motif of incest 'exemplifies the utter disruption of natural order and moral hierarchies'.[14] In Kane's version, Phaedra's daughter Strophe has not only slept previously with Hippolytus but has also shared her mother's new husband Theseus. Kane also uses the characters of Phaedra and Strophe to comment upon and draw parallels to the British royal family. Both mother and daughter are depicted as outsiders to the royal household, and in a cynical move are brought in by the old order in an attempt to refresh and restore its mystique. Hippolytus, during the crisis that threatens the future of his family, mocks Strophe's role in its hierarchy and her loyalty to its corrupt ideals as she attempts to save him from the anger of the mob – 'Strange. The one person in the family who has no claim to its history is the most sickeningly loyal. Poor relation who wants to be what she never will' (5:88).

The play, written before the death of Princess Diana, becomes eerily resonant as the death of Phaedra elevates the queen to iconic status as mob hysteria prevails in an outpouring of hostility against the old order. Kane, in an interview less than six months after Diana's death, felt that 'it would be a really good time for a production [*Phaedra's Love*] in Britain'.[15] For instance, the sentiments that figures in the crowd display towards the dead Phaedra – 'She was the only one had anything going for her' (8:98) echoed the sometimes hysterical reactions of some quarters in the media and the public during the height of mourning for Diana, 'when written tributes to the princess simultaneously evinced anger with the Royal Family, and took the line that Diana was the best of the lot or worth more than all the other royals put together'.[16]

It is against such a background that Phaedra's desire for Hippolytus operates. As in the versions of the myth by Seneca and Racine, Phaedra's

14   Albert Gerard, *The Phaedra Syndrome: of Shame and Grief in Drama*, (Amsterdam, 1993), p. 2.
15   Kane, interview with Nils Tabert.
16   Rosalind Blunt, 'Princess Diana: A Sign of the Times', in Jeffrey Richards, Scott Wilson and Linda Woodhead (eds), *Diana: The Making of a Media Saint* (London, 1999), p. 29.

passion for her doomed lover is expressed as a mysterious and over-whelming force; yet while Seneca shows Phaedra driven towards a love which repulses her, Kane portrays the emotion as one impossible to resist: 'Can't switch this off. Can't crush it. Can't. Wake up with it burning me. Think I'll crack open I want him so much' (3:71).

Yet Kane does provide something in the way of a possible explanation for the attraction that draws Phaedra irresistibly forward. This involves the queen succumbing to another equally old and cogent myth – that of her own ability to change Hippolytus through the strength of her love: 'You're difficult. Moody, cynical, bitter, fat, decadent, spoilt. You stay in bed all day then watch TV all night, you crash around this house with sleep in your eyes and not a thought for anyone. You're in pain. I adore you' (4:79).

Kane described her conception of Hippolytus as a puritan who desires brutal truth over flattery and empty rhetoric, even when that truth can be harmful to others:

> Hippolytus, as he is in the original story, is deeply unattractive. Though he's physically beautiful, he's chaste, a puritan, a hater of mankind. For me, puritanism isn't about lifestyle, but an attitude. Instead of pursuing what is traditionally seen as pure, my Hippolytus pursues honesty, both physically and morally – even when that means he has to destroy himself and everyone else. The purity of his self-hatred makes him much more attractive as a character than the virginal original.[17]

While the Hippolytus in Kane's play is not the chaste misogynist of Seneca who condemns all womankind as 'a damned race',[18] he recognises the hate Phaedra feels for herself to be just as strong as the feelings of self-loathing he harbours within himself (4:85). He is also aware of Phaedra's romantic fantasy of being a ministering angel to him, and also the frisson of excitement to be gained from conducting an illicit affair with her step-son. As a consequence he deliberately and savagely crushes the notions of romantic love with which Phaedra imbues the brief and tawdry sexual act between them.

Whereas previous plays based on the Phaedra myth rely on the conflict that arises out of this opposition between desire and repulsion, *Phaedra's Love* shows the consequences that consummation brings. Instead of being the culmination of Phaedra's longing, the sexual act is wantonly deconstructed and trivialised by Hippolytus, and so becomes redundant and passionless, punctuated by the rustle of the bored prince's sweetbag and his cruel comment after ejaculating into his stepmother's mouth –

---

17 Langridge and Stephenson, *Rage and Reason*, p. 132.
18 Boyle, *Seneca's Phaedra*, p. 37.

'There. Mystery over' (4:81). Hippolytus compounds the cruelty by disclosing that in the past he has slept with her daughter Strophe, and in the final humiliation informs Phaedra that in all probability she has caught gonorrhoea. 'Hate me now?' (4:85) he chides.

The use of sex as a form of punishment, and especially the use of rape explored in *Blasted*, continues in *Phaedra's Love*. As in Seneca's version of the play, Kane retains Phaedra's accusation of rape against Hippolytus, and here there is perhaps justification for the charge; indeed one could see how Hippolytus' brutal contempt and rejection of her obsessive love for him could be likened to a form of mental rape. Kane commented, 'what Hippolytus does to Phaedra is not rape – the English language doesn't contain the words to describe the emotional decimation he inflicts. "Rape" is the best word Phaedra can find for it, the most violent and potent'.[19]

Phaedra's act is immensely significant, and Kane believed, 'Phaedra is the first person to become active in the play – her accusation and later suicide liberate Hippolytus and set off the most extraordinary chain of events leading to the collapse of the monarchy'.[20] Like Hippolytus Kane recognised that 'Phaedra completely pursues what she wants. She's not actually very in touch with herself about what she wants but she does pursue it completely honestly. To the point where she's prepared to die for it.'[21] Ironically it is Phaedra's death that provides the incontrovertible proof needed for Hippolytus to be convinced of her love for him. Hippolytus sees Phaedra's sacrifice as 'her present to me' (5:90), an act that finally provides a release from his own torment. Phaedra's death is paradoxically Hippolytus' salvation: 'Not many people get a chance like this. This isn't tat. This isn't bric-a-brac.'

Phaedra's suicide also leads to Hippolytus accepting the tragic fate that arises as a direct consequence of his actions with a strange kind of joy. News that the people riot outside the palace following Phaedra's accusation causes Hippolyus to rejoice, 'Life at last.' It is a sentiment shared by Kane's source material of Brecht's *Baal* and Camus' Mersault. The former for instance 'is not concerned with mere survival [but] accelerates his own destruction by the pursuit of the utmost intensity of experience',[22] while the latter becomes 'a hero and martyr for truth'.[23]

The act also satisfies Hippolytus' simultaneous cravings for change and release through death, and despite being urged to defend himself by

19 Langridge and Stephenson, *Rage and Reason*, p. 132.
20 *Ibid.* p. 134.
21 Kane, interview with Nils Tabert.
22 Spiers, 'Baal', p. 23.
23 Conor Cruise O'Brien, *Camus* (London, 1970), p. 20.

Strophe and the priest against accusations of the rape, he willingly chooses public execution by the rioting mob. His final words, 'If there could have been more moments like this' (8:103), bring together concerns in a play that like its Senecan model is based upon the 'presentiment of life as sin, as obscenity ... the death-wish [being] integral to Phaedra's tragic world'.[24]

Sarah Kane described *Phaedra's Love* as 'my comedy',[25] and of all her work it is perhaps the most overtly and darkly humorous. Much of the humour resides in the cynical retorts and brutal honesty that Hippolytus uses to cut through the defences and pretensions of the other characters – this is where Kane believed the source of the comedy lies: 'Hippolytus is a complete shit, but he's also very funny, and for me that's always redeeming. I think there are people who can treat you really badly, but if they do it with a sense of humour then actually you can forgive them'.[26]

Michael Billington describes the humour in play as being 'laconically funny',[27] and when asked to define this aspect of the play Kane believed much of the laughter arises from its bleakness:

> It's probably a life-saving humour. When I was first thinking about writing that play I read an article in a newspaper written by a man who'd been suffering from clinical depression for three years. And he said the only thing that he'd had to hang onto was this really morbid sense of humour. It was the only thing that made him bearable to be with. And that kept him rooted. I suppose that was the thing with *Phaedra's Love*. I think when you are depressed oddly your sense of humour is the last thing to go; when that goes then you completely lose it. And actually Hippolytus never ever loses it.[28]

Imprisoned on the charge of raping his stepmother, Hippolytus is visited by a priest. This scene continues another debate, started in *Blasted*, involving the existence of God and the issue of personal redemption. Like Ian, Hippolytus follows a creed of atheism based on a logic that makes it impossible to seek Christian salvation: 'What do you suggest, a last-minute conversion just in case? Die as if there is a God, knowing that there isn't? No, if there is a God, I'd like to look him in the face knowing I'd died as I'd lived. In conscious sin' (6:94).

In *Phaedra's Love* the priest urges Hippolytus to deny the crime of raping his stepmother as he foresees revolution amongst the people if the prince confesses. The priest retains a moral pragmatism that wishes to sustain order and power in the earthly life through the system of church

---

24 Boyle, *Seneca's Phaedra*, p. 37.
25 Kane, interview with Nils Tabert.
26 *Ibid.*
27 Michael Billington, *Guardian*, 21 May 1996, p. 2.
28 Kane, interview with Nils Tabert.

and monarchy. The priest is quite happy to serve two masters simultaneously – God and Hippolytus. This ambiguous morality and shifting loyalty are reflected in the passive act of fellatio the priest performs on Hippolytus, prompted only by the silent cue of the prince undoing his trousers. The hypocrisy of the priest disgusts Hippolytus and makes him even more determined to gladly accept the tragic fate that awaits him: 'I know what I am. And always will be. But you. You sin knowing you'll confess. Then you're forgiven. And then you start all over again. How do you dare mock a God so powerful? Unless you don't really believe' (6:96).

Kane saw the scene as illustrating a particular point: 'If you're not sure God exists you can cover your arse, living your life carefully just in case, or you can live your life as you want to live it. If there is a God who can't accept the honesty of that then, well, tough.'[29] For Kane, this is the quality in Hippolytus that, while not placing him in the mould of a classical tragic hero, is one that she found deeply attractive, both in art and life:

> For me Hippolytus was always sympathetic because he's always completely and utterly direct with everyone no matter what the outcome is going to be for him and for others. You can never misunderstand anything that he's saying. And I suppose that's one of the things I personally strive for – to be completely and utterly understood. Hippolytus is for me an ideal. If I was like him I'd be quite pleased with myself … There is a politician here, Alan Clark, the most appallingly right wing unpleasant person, and he fucks everyone he can. He has written his diaries now, about his affairs. His behaviour is utterly revolting but then he's so funny that his diaries are utterly compelling. And somehow you forgive him. You think, well at least he's not pretending to be something that he's not. He's completely open about the fact that he's sexually corrupt.[30]

For Kane, the resolution to live by complete honesty, while leading to annihilation, was the only conception of a tragic hero that she could countenance:

> Someone said to me this thing which ended up in *Phaedra's Love* – because I was going on about how important it is to tell the truth and how depressing life is because nobody really does and you can't have honest relationships. And they said, 'but that's because you've got your values wrong. You take honesty as an absolute. And it isn't. Life is an absolute. And within that you accept that there is dishonesty. And if you can accept that you'd be fine'. And I thought 'that's true'. If I can accept that if not being completely honest

29 'Obituary' *Independent*, 23 February 1999.
30 Kane, interview with Nils Tabert. Kane is referring to the *Alan Clark Diaries* (London, 1994).

doesn't matter then I'd feel much better. But somehow I couldn't and so Hippolytus can't. And that's what kills him in the end.[31]

Phaedra's Love not only retains the tragic protagonist from Seneca's classical Roman drama, but its bloody climax also transposes elements from Elizabethan and Jacobean revenge tragedy, in which a form of staged violence is performed that is both outlandish and shocking to the sensibilities. This is potentially a dangerous venture to put before a modern audience. Stage directions that include genitals and bowels being thrown into a fire and vultures descending from the sky, not only risk estranging an audience, but possibly provoking its sense of ridicule. However, this was one of the original ideas that had intrigued Kane about reinterpreting a Roman tragedy: 'I thought you *can* subvert the convention of everything happening off-stage and have it on-stage and see how that works.'[32]

The other major challenge during the process of directing the production was its depiction of violence:

> We made a decision that I would try to do the violence as realistically as possible. If it didn't work then we'd try something else. But that was the starting point to see how it went. And the very first time when we did the final scene with all the blood and the false bowels by the end of it we were all severely traumatized. All the actors were standing there covered in blood having just raped and slit their throats; and then one of them said, 'this is the most disgusting play I've ever been in', and he walked out. But because of the work we'd done before, all of us knew that point was reached because of a series of emotional journeys that had been made. So none of us felt it was unjustified, it was just completely unpleasant … And it turned out to be a lot easier than you would think it is. I mean you write something like *his bowels are torn out,* and that seemed an incredibly difficult thing to do. But actually audiences are really willing to believe something is happening if you give them the slightest suggestion that it is.[33]

Kane's direction for the production also concentrated on attempting to break down the barriers between audience and the actors where seating was dispersed around the theatre, and no single playing space selected. Nowhere was this more apparent than the bloody climax of the play when members of the audience suddenly found that their up to then silent neighbour turned out to be from the cast. The barrier between stage and audience was then further broken down (and made extremely uncomfortable for the audience at times) when the slaughter of Hippoly-

---

31 Kane, interview with Nils Tabert.
32 *Ibid.*
33 *Ibid.*

tus was carried out 'with bleeding body parts chucked over the audience's heads'.[34]

Hippolytus' last line, 'If there could have been more moments like this', spoken as '*a vulture descends and starts to eat his body*', is both poignant and humorous. The ending finds its inspiration from the abandoned *Baal* play. Brecht's protagonist sings: 'Baal will watch the vultures in the star-shot sky hovering patiently to see when Baal will die. Sometimes Baal shams dead. The vultures swoop. Baal without a word will dine on vulture soup.'[35] Hippolytus' death is the culmination of a brief flowering of meaning since the death of his stepmother: 'The only way back to any kind of sanity is to connect physically with who you are, emotionally and spiritually and mentally. And the thing with Hippolytus is that in his moment of death everything suddenly connects. He has one moment of complete sanity and humanity. But in order to get there he has to die.'[36] Kane believed Hippolytus 'recognizes the inanity of his condition in finding meaning and contentment through embracing a violent and bloody death ... I don't think he's taking the piss in the last line, but I don't think he's unaware of the fact that it's funny. He's aware of the paradox.'[37] This connection between the spiritual and physical is represented in an even more extreme manner in Kane's next play, *Cleansed*, and would remain a dominant theme in her last two works, *Crave* and *4:48 Psychosis*.

34　Sarah Hemming, *Financial Times*, 23 May 1996.
35　Bertolt Brecht, *Baal*, in *Plays 1*, trans. Peter Tegel, Ralph Manheim, John Willett and Steve Gooch (London, 1987), p. 56.
36　Kane, interview with Nils Tabert.
37　*Ibid.*

1 Sarah Kane and Michael Shannon (playing the title role) in rehearsal for
   Woyzeck, The Gate Theatre, 16 October 1997

2 Sarah Kane (in baseball cap) at rehearsals for *Woyzeck*

3 Sarah Kane and cast members in rehearsal for *Woyzeck*

4 'Getting dark thank Christ day's nearly over.' Cas Harkins as Hippolytus in *Phaedra's Love*, The Gate Theatre, May 1996

5 'You enjoyed that?' Cas Harkins and Phillipa Williams in *Phaedra's Love*

6 *Blasted* becomes a news item. In this Heath cartoon, 'This time they've gone
too far!' (31 January 1995), John Major's problems with the 'Euro-sceptic'
faction in the Conservative administration find their way into Kane's debut
(Reprinted courtesy of the artist and the *Independent*)

7 Paines Plough's production of *Crave*, November, 1998. Left to right: Ingrid
Craigie, Alan Williams, Sharon Duncan-Brewster and Paul Thomas Hickey

4

'This sensible hell': *Cleansed*

> I my brother know
> Yet living in my glass. Even such and so
> In favour was my brother, and he went
> Still in this fashion, colour, ornament,
> For him I imitate.
>
> (Shakespeare, *Twelfth Night* III.iv. 371–5)

The performances of *Cleansed* in April 1998 marked Sarah Kane's return not only to the Royal Court but also for the first time onto the main stage in one of its major productions of that season. The play was both highly experimental and ambitious in its scope: as Dominic Cavendish observed, 'Kane is boldly lowering the theatre's drawbridge and letting the barbarous world in.'[1] This was due in no small part to the bold use of stage set and theatrical effects which included 'some of the most extraordinary hydraulic designs on the London stage'.[2] Jeremy Herbert's scenography, described as a 'series of vividly lit, cunningly designed tableaux',[3] where characters 'lie on violently tilted hospital beds' or 'sprawl on steeply raked platforms as if stuck in a fly-trap',[4] seemed to come close at times to an Artaudian conception of theatre whereby 'the

1 Dominic Cavendish, *Independent*, 18 May 1998.
2 Michael Coveney, *Daily Mail*, 7 May 1998.
3 Susannah Clapp, *Observer*, 10 May 1998, p. 13.
4 *Ibid.*

archetypal theatre language will be formed around staging not simply viewed as one degree of refraction of the script on stage, but as a starting point for theatrical creation'.[5]

The play, set in a former university now transformed into a sinister institution, also marked a further retreat from realism in Kane's work:

> I was having a fit about all this naturalistic rubbish that was being written and I decided that I wanted to write a play that could never ever be turned into a film – it could never ever be shot for television; it could never be turned into a novel. The only thing that could ever be done with it was it could be staged, and believe it or not that play is *Cleansed*. You may say it can't be staged, but it can't be anything else either'.[6]

The choice of acknowledged sources[7] that inform *Cleansed* was also the widest and most disparate in all of Kane's work, and again provided a strong indication of a further move away from realism. These secondary influences included Franz Kafka's *The Trial* (1925), Georg Büchner's *Woyzeck* (1837), George Orwell's *Nineteen Eighty-Four* (1949), Shakespeare's *Twelfth Night* (c.1601) and August Strindberg's *The Ghost Sonata* (1907). The episodic structure of the play, which Susannah Clapp commented 'does not so much unfold as accumulate'[8] – is based on Büchner's play *Woyzeck*, in which the relationship between story and plot (i.e. the order in which events occur to produce narrative) has disappeared:

> Now Büchner's *Woyzeck* is an absolutely perfect gem of a play ... in that anything remotely extraneous or explanatory is completely cut and all you get is those moments of extremely high drama. And what I was trying to do with *Cleansed* was a similar thing but in a different way, and when I finished *Cleansed* I was directing *Woyzeck* and I was playing around with all the different versions as he [Büchner] died before completing the play so nobody really knows the order he meant the scenes to go in. And I sat there with all the scenes with all these different bits of card, moving them around and I thought 'where have I done this before? It was in *Cleansed*!' And I wrote all the story-lines – if you like the Rod and Carl story / the Grace / Graham story / the Robin / Grace story and the Tinker / Stripper story separately, and I thought 'where do they connect?' And so I was doing all this moving things around and going completely insane thinking – 'there's a scene missing – where's the scene?' Until eventually I had the thing that I wanted ... And I think that in a lot of other plays there are things like 'so he runs off and tells his father' or if you look at Greek drama a messenger comes on – all of which

5 Artaud, *The Theatre and its Double*, p. 72.
6 Rebellato, 'Brief Encounter'.
7 Kane, interview with Nils Tabert.
8 Clapp, *Observer*, 10 May 1998.

is a lot easier to take and gives you a chance to calm down. But I didn't want to give people a chance to calm down.[9]

Kane's eschewal of realism in language, which had begun in *Blasted* and *Phaedra's Love*, became even starker in *Cleansed*, together with the depiction and function of character. Susannah Clapp described them as not 'so much characters as states of being',[10] and *Cleansed* began a process, which would continue in *Crave* (1998) and *4:48 Psychosis* (written 1999, performed 2000), in which character became more an expression of emotion than the outward manifestations of psychology and social inter-action. Kane had the chance to directly engage in these experiments with characterisation when she stepped in to play the part of Grace for the last three performances of the British premiere when the actress Suzan Sylvester was injured. She paradoxically felt the task to be, in the case of *Cleansed*, both simultaneously easy and difficult: 'I can't talk about all acting but what *Cleansed* asked for was extreme simplicity and that's a very difficult thing to do when you're standing in front of four hundred people with no clothes on ... Your instinct is to run away, but actually it's a very simple thing. What do I want? What do I feel? And how do I enable myself to feel that?'[11]

Cleansed also moved further in the process of Kane's project to pare language down to a stark minimalism. She commented in interview, 'I wanted to strip everything down. I wanted it to be as small – when I say small I mean minimal and poetic, and I didn't want to waste any words.'[12] Instead *Cleansed* frequently relies on theatrical imagery to add a further dimension to linguistic meaning: James Macdonald commented, 'Words are literally only a third of the play ... The bulk of the meaning is carried through the imagery. That's incredibly rare for a British playwright.'[13]

Despite *Phaedra's Love*, the release of her short film *Skin* in 1997, and directing *Woyzeck* at the Gate Theatre in October of the same year, *Cleansed* was regarded by many critics as the follow-up to *Blasted*. Not surprisingly, several of the reviews concentrated on the depiction of vio-lence in the play, but the hysteria and mock outrage that had constituted criticism then now gave way to a more considered assessment. While some in the British press still considered Kane to be 'a naughty schoolgirl trying to shock',[14] and the play itself 'portentous drivel, exquisitely dressed

9   Rebellato, 'Brief Encounter'. See Daniel Evans' comments on the influence *Woyzeck* made on the structure of *Cleansed*, p. 170.
10   Clapp, *Observer*, 10 May 1998.
11   Rebellato, 'Brief Encounter'.
12   *Ibid.*
13   Christopher, *Independent*, 4 May 1998.
14   Sheridan Morley, *Spectator*, 16 May 1998.

in designer chic',[15] there was now more of a general readiness to treat the play on its own terms. Even more conservative tabloid papers such as the *Daily Express* conceded that 'this feverish work has a bizarre integrity to it and a feeling that it has been ripped fresh from a hellish personal vision and nightmare landscape'.[16]

Although in truth the so-called acts of atrocity in *Blasted* were themselves all highly stylised pieces of theatre, *Cleansed* goes even further to redefine the representation of staged violence, and to provoke a response in the audience through the effect that lies behind the action. The director James Macdonald commented, 'Though it is equally shocking in what is being transacted between one person and another, what we've done in *Cleansed* is focus the audience on why these things are being done rather than the mechanics.'[17]

In interview, Kane looked in some detail at the stage direction: '*He* [Tinker] *takes Carl by the arms and cuts off his hands*' (8:129):

> It's not about the actual chop. It's about that person who can no longer express love with his hands, and what does that mean? And I think the less naturalistically you show those things the more likely people are to be thinking what is the meaning of this act rather than 'fucking hell, how do they do that'! That's a far more interesting response to elicit from an audience because David Copperfield can do that.[18]

Violence in the play is also ritualised, where for a stage direction such as '*Tinker produces a large pair of scissors and cuts off Carl's tongue*' (4:118), the mutilation is shown through a piece of red cloth being extruded from the mouth and cut. A similar effect, using red streamers, is also used for when Tinker amputates Carl's hands and feet. The effect was reminiscent of Peter Brook's celebrated 1955 Stratford production of Shakespeare's *Titus Andronicus* (c.1590), where such atrocities were depicted in a highly stylised way whereby 'the violence was muted by an intense, mythic, even abstract quality. Thus Lavinia appears after her rape and mutilation with red streamers, symbolising blood flowing from her mouth and hands'.[19] The idea that seemed to operate in both plays was to 'formalise the horrors, to confine them within a ritualistic framework so that the agonies were distanced'.[20]

15 Georgina Brown, *Mail on Sunday*, 24 May 1998.
16 *Daily Express*, 20 May 1998.
17 Christopher, *Independent*, 4 May 1998.
18 Rebellato, 'Brief Encounter'. David Copperfield is an American stage magician and illusionist.
19 Maurice Charney, *Titus Andronicus* (Hemel Hempstead, 1990), p. xv.
20 Beauman, Sally, *The Royal Shakespeare Company: A History of Ten Decades* (Oxford, 1982), p. 225.

However, this is not to say that the violence in *Cleansed* failed to be disturbing by not being realistic. Such imagery left one critic 'feeling bruised to the bone, tight in the stomach and hopeless',[21] and again one must go back to Brook's comment about *Titus Andronicus*, whereby 'if one wants to create a fresh emotional response to the violence, blood and multiple mutilations of *Titus Andronicus*, one must shock the imagination and subconscious with visual images that recall the richness and depth of primitive rituals'.[22]

Some of the violent imagery employed is a combination of intertextuality and the stylised set against the modern and the real. For instance the torture of Carl involving a pole being inserted through the anus immediately brings to mind the torture of the eponymous *Edward II* (1592) in Christopher Marlowe's play, yet Kane explained that the torture, where a pole is inserted until it comes out through the shoulder, is 'a form of crucifixion which Serbian soldiers used against Muslims in Bosnia, and they would do it to hundreds and hundreds of Muslims and hang them all up and leave them there; and it would take them about five days to die'.[23]

Cleansed is also the most *neo-Jacobean* of Kane's plays, whereby every word, action and gesture are uncompromising and *in extremis*. This is perhaps best expressed by Grace's stark sentiment to her brother – 'love me or kill me' (5:120).[24] Several critics' reactions registered this pain. Susannah Clapp described the play as a 'howl of horror';[25] while John Peter, writing in the *Sunday Times*, commented:

> *Cleansed* is a nightmare of a play, it unreels somewhere between the back of your eyes and the centre of your brain with an unpredictable but remorseless logic. As with a nightmare, you cannot shut it out because nightmares are experienced with your whole body. As with a nightmare you feel that

---

21 John Peter, *Sunday Times*, 10 May 1998.
22 Gerald Freedman, *Titus Andronicus* (London, 1970), pp. 3–5.
23 Rebellato, 'Brief Encounter'.
24 The line is an almost direct borrowing from John Ford's early Caroline tragedy *'Tis Pity She's a Whore* (1633), which also follows the passionate but incestuous love between a brother (Giovanni) and sister (Annabella):
ANNABELLA. On my knees,
   Brother, even by our mother's dust I charge you,
   Do not betray me to your mirth or hate;
   Love me or kill me, brother.
GIOVANNI. On my knees,
   Sister, even by my mother's dust I charge you,
   Do not betray me to your mirth or hate;
   Love me or kill me, sister.
                                    (I.11.242–8)
25 Clapp, *Observer*, 10 May 1998.

somebody else is dreaming it for you, spinning the images out of some need that you don't want to think of as your own.[26]

Many features of *Cleansed* – the diminution of language, the extraordinary set and theatrical imagery, the ritualised cruelty, its extremes of love and pain and its Jacobean sensibility – bring to mind Artaud's writings about his envisaged Theatre of Cruelty. What is perhaps more extraordinary is that at the time Kane, while aware of Artaud's name, had not read any of his work. Speaking about this aspect of *Cleansed*, Janette Smith, the assistant director on the Royal Court production, commented that while the play eschews Artaud's idea about breaking down the barrier between actor and audience, she believed, 'there is a kind of "total theatre" approach through the imagery written in the script. The lighting and sound are used in conjunction with the acting to create effect. The rat sounds in particular are used in a metaphoric way rather than a literal one.'[27] Smith went on to include another specific Artaudian image – that of Carl's silent scream at the end of the play (18:146) – as it developed through rehearsals:

> Artaud was interested in the power of the scream for the actor. At the end of *Cleansed* Carl screams silently. This used to be vocal, but was changed in rehearsal after discussion with people from Amnesty International. They told us about the way in which a victim watched another being tortured. They felt they were screaming, but in fact they became paralysed with fear, and though they wanted to, they could not scream. So, in the penultimate scene we have Carl physically screaming, but without the sound.[28]

While *Cleansed* is undoubtedly a dark play, Kane also believed it is essentially hopeful in its central theme: on how love for all the characters can survive even the most extreme and savage of situations: 'They're all just in love. I actually thought it's all very sixties and hippy. They are all emanating this great love and need and going after what they need, and the obstacles in their way are all extremely unpleasant but that's not what the play is about. What drives people is need, not the obstacle.'[29]

Speaking in February 1998 prior to its performance, Kane explained the apparent contradiction of the two conditions:

> When I was working on *Cleansed* I was in a very extreme state. I was going through the most appalling depression, but on the other hand I was so com-

26   Peter, *Sunday Times*, 10 May 1998. Other reviews expressed much the same reaction. See Benedict, *Independent*, 9 May 1998; Nicholas de Jongh, *Evening Standard*, 7 May 1998.

27   Mal Smith, *Antonin Artaud and his Legacy* (Theatre Museum Education Pack, London, 1999).

28   *Ibid.*

29   Rebellato, 'Brief Encounter'.

pletely and utterly and madly in love that those two things didn't seem to be any contradiction at all. These days it does. So sometimes when I read *Cleansed* it's like it's by another writer. I now could not write it. But it was never about the violence, it was about how much these people love. I think *Cleansed* more than any of my other plays uses violence as a metaphor.[30]

Kane's use of Orwell's *Nineteen Eighty-Four* as a direct influence is also significant here, as one of its principal themes is also about the exploration of love, both as an act of defiance – a counteraction against repressive forces – and also how those very forces police and crush through torture any attempt at expression of love. Both Kane and Orwell seem to be aware of the paradox of durability and fragility, whereby 'As an emotion love is stronger than anything else in the world but as a social force it suffers from a great disadvantage. It is purely individual in its action. The condition of love is isolation from the rest of the world.'[31] In an interview Kane explains that the play is based around the idea of love when placed in extremity, and how love develops or survives under these conditions: 'If you want to write about extreme love, you can only write about it in an extreme way, otherwise it doesn't mean anything. So I suppose both *Blasted* and *Cleansed* are about distressing things which we'd like to think we would survive. If people can still love after that, then love is the most powerful thing.'[32]

The connection between these extreme images of violence placed against motifs of tenderness was noticed by several critics after the British production. For instance, Paul Taylor commented, 'For the first time in my estimation, the yearning for some loving, purifying alternative to the horror; symbolised in the incestuous devotion between a brother and a sister; made a deeper impact in a Kane play than the atrocities.'[33] While the relationship between Grace and Graham is dominant, its director James Macdonald went further in explaining, 'In fact there are four love stories. Everybody's in love. It is a play about the nature of love and its relationship to brutalisation. Love is a kind of madness and ecstasy.'[34]

These four relationships involve Graham/Grace, Carl/Rod, Robin/Grace and Tinker/Woman. Love as a purifying force is demonstrated through various manifestations of theatrical image such as the single sunflower bursting through the stage after Grace and Graham make love (5:120), followed by a whole profusion of Wordsworthian daffodils ('*their yellow covering the entire stage*') after Grace is beaten and raped by the

---

30 Kane, interview with Nils Tabert.
31 John Atkins, *George Orwell* (London, 1954), p. 248.
32 Armitstead, *Guardian*, 29 April 1998.
33 Taylor, 'Tuesday Review', *Independent*, 23 February 1999.
34 Christopher, *Independent*, 4 May 1998.

voices (11:133); the use of song (5:119;13:136); and physical actions such as the dance of love Graham/Grace, Carl/Rod (5:119; 13:136) perform for each other.

Central to the idea of love surviving repression was Kane's reading of the French literary critic Roland Barthes' *A Lover's Discourse*:

> There's a point in *A Lover's Discourse* when he says the situation of a rejected lover is not unlike the situation of a prisoner in Dachau. And when I read it I was just appalled and thought how can he possibly suggest the pain of love is as bad as that. But then the more I thought about it I thought actually I do know what he is saying. It's about the loss of self. And when you lose yourself where do you go? There's nowhere to go, it's actually a kind of madness. And thinking about that I made the connection with *Cleansed*. If you put people in a situation in which they lose themselves and what you're writing about is an emotion which people lose themselves then you can make that connection between the two. As long as you don't start writing things like 'Auschwitz 1944' which would be reductive anyway.[35]

This duality within the play between tenderness and affirmation in love placed against annihilation and loss of self-hood is found within the title of the play itself, where *Cleansed* might either allude to the redemptive love Tinker seems to find at the end of the play, or to the destruction of self-hood, or even the physical slaughter of the inmates within the institution.[36] The similarities to Tinker's conversion of the former university into a death camp also give the play, despite its introspective feel, a wider political resonance, closer in fact to the response *Blasted* made about the new Europe that had emerged since the fall of the Berlin Wall in 1989.

Kane's approach, to combine a deluded and obsessive form of love set inside a repressive institution that attempts to crush this particular emotion, brings together these two strands of the personal and political in a very distinct way:

> When you love obsessively, you do lose yourself. And when you then lose the object of your love, you have none of the normal resources to fall back on. It can completely destroy you. And very obviously concentration camps are about dehumanizing people before they are killed. I wanted to raise some questions about these two extreme and apparently different situations.[37]

Kane herself was aware that political readings were bound to be made about the play, and while believing these to be valid, was wary

---

35 Kane, interview with Nils Tabert.
36 See conversation with Nils Tabert on the problems of translating the title into German, pp. 139–40.
37 Kate Stadllon, 'Extreme measures', *Time Out*, 25 March 1998.

that *Cleansed* would become categorised by any particular geographical location or historical situation:

> With *Cleansed* I didn't want to get into the situation of: this is about Germany and the Jews. It definitely had a strong impact on me but the play is not about that, so why use that as to give something a context? Because then you are being cynical, you are using people's pain in order to justify your own work which I don't think is acceptable. Also I think there's the problem that when you get so specific something actually stops having resonance beyond that specific ... Whereas I hope that *Cleansed* and *Blasted* have resonance beyond what happened in Bosnia or Germany specifically.[38]

This refusal to set the play in a specific location or time does much to give it the feeling of occupying a dreamscape, a similarity *Cleansed* shares with one of its direct sources, Strindberg's *The Ghost Sonata*. The unreal locales of Tinker's institution and Hummel's house are juxtaposed against the empiricism of the real world. Strindberg achieves this at the beginning of the play by placing Hummel and the student outside the house where we can see everyday objects like a water fountain and poster-hoardings advertising a performance of Wagner's *The Valkyrie,* to take place that evening. Likewise in *Cleansed*, at one point we hear evidence of the 'real' world through '*the sound of a cricket match in progress on the other side of the perimeter fence*' (2:109). The figures of Grace and the student initially see these places as fulfilling some need within themselves. For the student the house at first stands as the pinnacle of his worldly aspirations, 'imagining all the beauty and luxury inside' (1:255),[39] while for Grace, Tinker's institution promises to provide the means to reunite her with her brother. However, both house and institution are snares rather than sanctuaries, as the student later realises: 'There's something very rotten here. And yet ... I thought it was a paradise' (3:285).

Both plays also make use of rooms that are assigned names, each having a specific function. In *The Ghost Sonata* we find the Hyacinth Room, and both plays contain a Round Room – the one in *Cleansed* at one time being the university library. There are also the following in Kane's play: the White Room – which was formerly the university sanatorium; the Black Room – with '*the showers in the university sports hall converted into peep-show booths*' (6:121); and the Red Room – once the university sports hall but now given over to a torture chamber. The use of rooms as places of discovery and revelation for characters constitutes a form of ongoing journey or pilgrimage, and is a distinctive feature of

---

38 Kane, interview with Nils Tabert.
39 August Strindberg, *The Ghost Sonata*, in *Miss Julie and Other Plays*, trans. Michael Robinson (Oxford, 1998). All subsequent quotations from the play will use this edition.

Strindberg's later dramatic work. This technique, called *Stationen* drama, became an important motif in later expressionistic theatre. The path the Student takes through the house shares similarities with Grace's sojourn in the institution, where 'his moving inwards – from the street through the Round Room to the Hyacinth Room – is an inverted pilgrimage from paradise via purgatorio to inferno'.[40] In the case of *Cleansed*, Grace's journey within the institution moves in a similarly apocalyptic path: tender moments such as teaching Robin to read and write give way to being beaten, raped and surgically experimented upon.

The central relationship in *Cleansed* between Grace and her brother is taken from Shakespeare's *Twelfth Night*.[41] Here, in his last festive comedy, two women grieve for their lost brothers: Viola, separated from her brother Sebastian in a shipwreck, thinks him dead, whereas Olivia's brother has died. However, whereas Olivia's obsessive grief for her dead brother is used as a source of comedy, Kane shows that Grace is unable to accept her brother's death and drifts into a delusional state by resurrecting him in her imagination. And whereas by the end of *Twelfth Night*, in keeping with the genre of Elizabethan comedy, gender identities are restored to their natural order; in *Cleansed* Grace is crudely operated on by Tinker to more fully resemble her brother.

Kane also takes the motif of disguise in *Twelfth Night*, where Viola becomes the male page Cesario to pass as a man. However, in Shakespeare's play Viola's donning of male apparel is not done in a bid to *become* her brother. As Stephen Greenblatt observes, the practice of women disguising themselves as men in Shakespearian comedy is a device whereby 'characters like Rosalind and Viola [can] pass through a state of being men in order to become women'.[42] In *Cleansed* this use of disguise is not done for theatrical or comic effect. Grace adopts the clothing and mannerisms of her brother in an attempt to actually *become* her brother, with the objective of being seen in the same way as Duke Orsino remarks on seeing Viola and Sebastian together for the first time as brother and sister: 'One face, one voice, one habit, and two persons' (V.i.213). Grace craves the same recognition and demands to be seen as such by others: 'I look like him. Say you thought I was a man' (3:114).

40 Egil Tonnquist, *Strindbergian Drama: Themes and Structure* (Stockholm, 1982), p. 197.

41 In the other significant play of that year – Patrick Marber's *Closer* – a man takes on a woman's persona during internet correspondence. Marber saw this as 'updating Shakespeare's *Twelfth Night*, where a woman pretends to be a man'. Cited in Sierz, *In-yer-face Theatre*, p. 193.

42 Stephen Greenblatt, 'Fiction and Friction', in R. S. White (ed.), *New Casebooks: Twelfth Night* (Basingstoke, 1996), p. 117.

Integral to the theme of love in *Cleansed* are the ways in which love is tested. Often this is brought about in the most violent and brutal ways by the figure of Tinker. It is a name that on the one hand suggests a theatrical joke – alluding perhaps to the theatre critic Jack Tinker who provided *Blasted* with its most infamous review – while also suggesting a character reminiscent of Jacobean City comedies, such as Ben Jonson's *Volpone* (1605) or *The Alchemist* (1610), where a name is used to describe both a character's nature and function. Tinker is certainly a meddler in the fates of his charges, testing their desires, their delusions and professions of love; often to savagely logical conclusions.

Tinker is a chameleon-like presence throughout the play, and this mercurial identity is established right from the start when he tells Graham, 'I'm a dealer not a doctor' (1:107). Later he tells the Woman, 'I'll be anything you need' (7:122), and after carrying out the phalloplasty on Grace he leaves with the admission, 'I'm sorry. I'm not really a doctor' (18:146).

This fluidity of identity, ranging from torturer to redeemer, make Tinker one of the most problematic characters in all of Kane's plays. His puzzling and contradictory identity seems in part to come from the amalgamation of several of the literary sources that influenced *Cleansed*.

Partly he is a Mephistophelian figure granting foolish wishes. For instance, on overhearing Grace's desire to change her body, 'so it looked like it feels. Graham outside like Graham inside' (7:126), Tinker eventually grants the wish in a savage mockery of Viola's comic aside in *Twelfth Night*, 'a little thing would make me tell them how much I lack of a man' (III.iv.293–4), through the transplant of Carl's phallus onto Grace's genitalia along with the removal of her breasts.

In his brutal repression of love, Tinker, like Hippolytus, is another of Kane's puritan figures; he is also reminiscent of the puritan steward Malvolio in *Twelfth Night*, who despite being a figure of satire and a comic dupe still 'stalks the stage as anti-mirth'.[43] Tinker is a far darker version of Malvolio but his function is the same: policing the stage and snuffing out the smallest expressions of human affection and love in others, and whereas Malvolio is made to undergo temporary imprisonment and accused of being out of his wits, in *Cleansed* Tinker is the jailer and active in reinforcing Grace's psychotic delusions.

He is also the soothing torturer, reminiscent of Orwell's O'Brien in *Nineteen Eighty-Four*, and described as the 'tormentor … the protector … the inquisition … the friend'.[44] In *Cleansed*, during the beating of Carl by a group of men, Tinker intervenes to '*kiss Carl's face gently*' (4:116).

43 J. M. Gregson, *Twelfth Night* (London, 1980), p. 51.
44 Orwell, *Nineteen Eighty-Four*, p. 196.

Tinker is also something of a voyeur and creature of the shadows who tests the pledge of love Carl and Rod swear to each other. Whereas in Orwell's dystopian future O'Brien tortures Winston into betraying and denying his lover Julia, in Kane's rewriting of the episode Tinker tortures Carl, who despite earlier asserting, 'I'll never turn away from you' (2:111), eventually betrays Rod in a direct echo of Winston's act against Julia (4:117). This is compared to the behaviour of Rod, who despite his initial reluctance in taking any form of vow, asserting 'I wouldn't die for you', and his promise to 'do my best not to betray you' (2:111), ultimately demonstrates his love for Carl which endures right up until the point where he dies when forced to choose by Tinker (16:142).

Kane also uses the motif of a ring to show the endurance of the pair's love. This perhaps reflects her interest in Elizabethan and Jacobean drama, where the exchange of rings, as in Shakespeare's *Merchant of Venice* for instance, becomes the vehicle for the humorous test of fidelity between the romantic Belmont lovers. In a play like *The Duchess of Malfi* (*c*.1612)[45] ring imagery is used for both romantic love and darker, sinister themes. When for instance the Duchess claims her wedding ring has healing properties and presses it against the bloodshot eye of her lover Antonio (I.ii.323–36), it acts as a prelude to being placed on Antonio's finger by the Duchess and pronouncing him to be her second husband. The same ring is later used during the Duchess's imprisonment and torture when her brother Ferdinand presents her with a severed hand and its wedding ring still attached, which he says is taken from Antonio (IV.i.40–55).

In *Cleansed*, Kane uses this dual ring imagery not only as a romantic and affirming symbol of love, but also as a demonstration of how love is savagely tested in Tinker's institution. For instance, its role as pledge and token between Carl and Rod places it within the conventions of Elizabethan comedy, where the playful banter centring around exchange, and Rod's refusal to part with his ring or vow his eternal love (2:109–12), recalls similar moments out of Shakespeare's Elizabethan comedies such as *Much Ado About Nothing* (*c*.1598) and *As You Like It* (*c*.1599).

The darker Jacobean elements to the ring imagery are later revealed in Tinker's attempt to destroy Rod and Carl's love thorough the symbolism of the ring. This is why Tinker reminds Carl while he is being tortured, 'I love you Rod I'd die for you' (4:117), and with Carl's eventual betrayal of his lover ('Not me please not me … Rod not me') Tinker

---

45 Sheridan Morley noticed the connection but commented, 'What we have here is a bad attempt to combine *Waiting for Godot* with *The Duchess of Malfi* and it misses both by more than a mile', *Evening Standard*, 16 May 1998.

carries out a symbolic act of violence to signify the death of love: with a pair of scissors he removes Carl's tongue – the organ of betrayal – and makes him swallow Rod's ring. Tinker's act, while attempting to annihilate love, ultimately fails as Rod forgives Carl his act of treachery and also renews the bond of love with Carl when he '*picks up the severed left hand and takes off the ring he put there*' (8:129).

Their love is later tested by Tinker when, after hearing the song of a child, Carl '*begins … a dance of love for Rod*' (13:136). This follows on from the dance of love Graham performs for Grace (5:119), but again Tinker intervenes to crush this new expression of love by the choice of punishment – namely the removal of Carl's feet, which the rats later carry away.

Rod's final pledge of love comes just before Tinker tests their loyalty for the final time. After making love, Rod affirms to Carl, 'I will always love you / I will never lie to you / I will never betray you / On my life.' This final declaration is made through a reversal of Tinker's previous act involving the ring: now, in a gesture more resembling the Sacrament, Rod '*takes off the ring and makes Carl swallow it*' (16:142). In his discussion of *Cleansed*, Dan Rebellato sees such imagery operating under conditions where 'the play strips romantic love of all its unknowable promises, its claims of eternity, and asks what is left … this irreducible core is the extraordinary and hard-won affirmation of the play'.[46]

Tinker's attempts to crush all expressions of love extend to others in the play. When another inmate, Robin, draws a picture of a sunflower – the motif signifying the love between Graham and Grace – Tinker '*sets light to the paper and burns the whole thing*' (7:129). Also, when Robin, who is in love with Grace, buys her a box of chocolates, Tinker's punishment is to make him eat its entire contents. The distress this causes makes Robin involuntarily urinate, and in his panic and embarrassment at Tinker's commands to 'Clean it up, woman' (15:141),[47] he inadvertently carries out an act of betrayal by tearing out the pages from the books Grace had been teaching him to read. Grace however, in a heavily tranquillised state, is unable to realize the consequences of Robin's actions, and in fact warms her hands by the blaze created from the books.

The supreme irony regarding Tinker, is that someone who so systematically attempts to destroy love in others is in fact yearning to express and reciprocate love himself. This is conducted principally through the figure of the Woman, who seems to be imprisoned as an erotic dancer in a peep-show booth. Their relationship is a puzzling one

46 Rebellato, 'Sarah Kane', p. 280.
47 See Daniel Evans discussion of this incident, p. 170.

and the ultimate answer is perhaps kept deliberately ambiguous by Kane, who commented that, 'almost every line in *Cleansed* has more than one meaning'.[48] However, it is perhaps worth looking at Strindberg's *The Ghost Sonata*, and the figure of the Mummy in order to understand something of these particular scenes from *Cleansed*. In Strindberg's expressionistic, dream-like play the Mummy also 'lives in the closet mostly, both to avoid seeing and being seen' (2:268): she is like 'a pitiful monster of some kind, waiting to be released from the terrible spell placed on her by some wicked magician'.[49] Both the Mummy and the Woman appear to be prisoners, where 'crimes and secrets and guilt bind us together' (2:270). We learn that the old man Hummel, who in his mephisophelean powers closely resembles Tinker, has been a past lover of the Mummy but had abandoned her. Harry Carlson makes an interesting point that could be applied to both Hummel and Tinker in that the relationships with these female characters 'psychologically … represent elements that Hummel has fled or rejected all his life: love and compassion. They are aspects of himself that were never released or assimilated.'[50]

The Mummy reverts back to her former self as Amelia after Hummel replaces her in the closet; similarly, once Grace's identity has been obliterated both Tinker and the Woman seem free to become lovers. This process is similar to that which takes place in *Phaedra's Love* through which the liberation of Hippolytus is achieved through the death of his stepmother.

Even while *Cleansed* was in production, Kane spoke in one newspaper interview about her next play *Crave*, which she had completed while living in America. Hints as to the departure it took from previous work were already evident: 'I wanted to find out how good a poet I could be while still writing something dramatic … As soon as you've written and used a theatrical form, it becomes redundant.'[51]

---

48 Armitstead, *Guardian*, 29 April 1998.
49 Harry G. Carlson, *Strindberg and the Poetry of Myth* (Berkeley and Los Angeles, 1982), p. 197.
50 *Ibid.*
51 Armitstead, *Guardian*, 29 April 1998.

5

'Only love can save me and love has destroyed me': *Crave*

These fragments I have shored against my ruins. (T.S. Eliot, *The Waste Land*)

Less than 3 months after *Cleansed*, came another play by Sarah Kane. *Crave* premiered at the Traverse Theatre in Edinburgh during August and September 1998 as part of its yearly festival programme, and subsequently transferred to the Royal Court during September and early October, as well as touring during the same period to Dublin and Berlin. It later went on to a short tour during November, consisting of three performances in Copenhagen, and one in Maastricht on the 2nd December 1998.

For Kane, *Crave's* opening in Edinburgh, its tour and the production itself stood as the most fully realised of her plays, and in a letter to Edward Bond she commented, 'For once I liked this performance very much, so much so that I saw about forty performances.'[1]

The relatively short interval between having two plays produced so quickly together would have been unusual for any dramatist, but considering the gap of nearly two years between *Phaedra's Love* and *Cleansed*, the production of a new play, albeit only 45 minutes in length was surprising. Vicky Featherstone, Artistic Director of the new writing company Paines Plough (and subsequently director of *Crave*), kindled the

---

1 Kane, Letter to Edward Bond, 2 November 1998.

initial idea of the play by giving Kane a snap 'commission' for a new work during the same period in which *Cleansed* was being written.[2]

Kane spoke of the event that inspired *Crave* coming from a fortuitous accident: 'I walked into Vicky's office one day and found she was not there. But I saw a copy of [Rainer Werner] Fassbinder's *Pre-Paradise Sorry Now* which I started to read. While reading it I suddenly had the idea of *Crave*.'[3] A 20 minute first draft then underwent a rehearsed reading to see how it would stand up in performance. This was a new departure for Kane as far as the writing process was concerned, but a valuable one:

> We did a reading at lunch-time with four different actors. Vicky had orches-trated the rhythm and by listening to it I realised how much further I could go in terms of musicality. The 'yes, no, yes, no' sections suddenly came to my mind by listening to the rhythm, and I thought, 'how extreme can I be with this?' I wouldn't have known that just by writing it at my desk.[4]

Kane then departed to America to do workshops with The New Dramatists, a theatre group based in New York, and subsequently worked on *Crave* during this period. The experience of living and working in America had a profound effect. Despite believing it to be, 'a cultural waste land ... it did change my writing because I was losing my cultural articu-lacy. The number of words I was using was getting smaller and smaller, and my writing became stranger and stranger.'[5]

Nevertheless, despite the radical shift in dramatic form that did much to distinguish *Crave* from her previous work, Kane's intentions and expectations while writing the play seem to have remained clear: 'I wanted to find out how good a poet I could be while still writing some-thing dramatic.'[6] Kane has also said that she intended the play to be, 'deliberately an experiment with form, and language and rhythm and music'.[7]

This preoccupation with form and structure dominated the early stages of writing *Crave*, and sometimes overshadowed its content:

> Personally I do not do an awful lot of rewriting during rehearsals, but I always do some. Sometimes it is only when you hear voices saying the words that you know whether they are right or not. Particularly with *Crave* I could hear where the music could be better. Normally when I am writing, I know what the intention and the meaning of the line is. With *Crave* I knew what the rhythm was, but I did not know what I was going to say. There are a

---

2 For an account of this story see the interview with Vicky Featherstone, pp. 128–9.

3 Thielemans, *Rehearsing the Future*, p. 13.

4 *Ibid.*, p. 14.

5 Armitstead, *Guardian*, 29 May 1998, p. 12.

6 *Ibid.*

7 Thielemans, *Rehearsing the Future*, p. 10.

couple of times I used musical notation, only the rhythm without actual words.[8]

Given the often stormy relationship with British critics, *Crave* also marked a significant breakthrough in an appreciation and understanding of Kane's work that had tentatively begun with *Cleansed*. For instance, retrospectively Michael Billington believes *Crave* to be, 'by far her most achieved work'[9] while previously hostile reviewers saw her as 'born again'[10] and 'a commanding talent'.[11]

Such a benevolent response was also surprising considering *Crave's* further retreat from realism and formal characterisation, and its experimentation with rhythm and poetic language. Those critics who disliked the depiction of physical and sexual violence in Kane's work, praised *Crave* as a breakthrough. While a significant feature of each preceding play had witnessed a gradual evolutionary progress in finding a new form to fit content, *Crave* was significant in that it made new demands on its audience by breaking lose from what one perhaps expected a Sarah Kane play to contain.

No one was more aware of this than Kane herself, and when it was originally read out at the Paines Plough script meeting, a pseudonym of Marie Kelvedon was used. This startling figure, whose potted biography included, 'being sent down from St Hilda's college, Oxford ... for an act of unspeakable Dadaism in the college dinning hall',[12] was a device primarily used to break preconceptions of what people had come to expect from her work. Vicky Featherstone explained the reasoning behind this initial decision:

> In one way, she [Sarah] thought it was funny. Marie was her middle name, Kelvedon was a town near where she was born. But in another way, it was deadly serious. She had spent a lot of time shaking off the negative effects of *Blasted*. She really wanted to write something that could be judged for what it was, rather than for the fact that it had been written by Sarah Kane.[13]

The principle influence that guides *Crave* in both form and content is T.S. Eliot's landmark poem *The Waste Land*[14] (1922), which, in its use of speaking voices, acted as a prelude to Eliot's later move into writing verse drama. Eliot's outline for the poem is similar to many of Kane's intentions

8   *Ibid.*, p. 12.
9   *Nightwaves*.
10 Nicholas de Jongh, *Evening Standard*, 24 August 1998.
11 Irving Wardle, *Sunday Telegraph*, 13 September 1998.
12 Sarah Kane, *Crave* (London, 1998).
13 Simon Hattenstone, 'A Sad Hurrah', *Guardian Weekend*, 1 July 2000, p. 31.
14 All quotations from *The Waste Land* will be taken from *Collected Poems 1909–1962* (London, 1974).

for *Crave*. Eliot believed, 'The ideal medium for poetry, to my mind … is the theatre', and that when working at its most sublime would stimulate, 'the more musically sensitive [with] the rhythm, [while] for auditors of greater sensitiveness and understanding a meaning [will] reveal itself gradually'.[15]

Textually, the influence between Eliot's poem and Kane's play is an obvious one; where certain memorable lines from *The Waste Land* such as, 'Hurry up please its time', and 'Give, sympathise, control',[16] find their way directly into *Crave*. Kane also uses Eliot's device of introducing foreign words and phrases, and at times even mischievously plays with the convention, such as translating Eliot's line, 'In the mountains, there you feel free' (17), back into its native German.

The Waste Land is also very much the precursor for the twentieth-century preoccupation with *intertextuality*: here fragments of literary or religious quotation, and even snatches of popular song, are jumbled together with Eliot's original ideas for the poem. *Crave* adopts the same approach. The actress Ingrid Craigie, who played the role of 'M' in both British productions felt that these numerous literary and cultural references in the play were designed to have a particular effect upon an audience:

> Sarah had lots of quotations and references in the play … but you have to forget those and turn them into a piece of work. So you can clearly see this might be a line from *The Waste Land*, or this is a quotation from a song. Sarah is transforming them to create a completely new piece of art. So, the references and quotations add layers and a texture to the play that is extraordinary and thrilling. So, you can find them throughout from the Bible, Camus, *Prozac Nation*, Buddhism, Chekov, Shakespeare, Herman Hesse, Aleister Crowley, David Edgar.[17]

The use of such allusions make *Crave* a demanding play, and one that constantly eludes a definitive interpretation, becoming like 'the private iconography' that the character M 'cannot decipher' (31). However, Kane did not want to repeat the mistake of T.S. Eliot, who by including a set of presumably explanatory notes (although one can detect in the pedantic erudition of some of the entries, a sense of mischief making), to aid an understanding of the poem instead, 'stimulated the wrong kind of critical approach, the goose-chase after definitive sources, if not the Grail itself':[18]

15 T.S. Eliot, *The Uses of Poetry* (London, 1933), pp. 152–3.
16 Translated in Eliot's poem as, 'Datta, dayadhvam, damyata'.
17 Josephine Machon, interview with Ingrid Craigie, November 1999.
18 Helen Williams, *T.S. Eliot: The Waste Land*, 2nd edn (London, 1979), p. 50.

The play is quite obviously very heavily based and influenced on *The Waste Land*, and I had a choice of did I write a set of notes to go with the play to explain it: but what happened to T.S. Eliot – poor bastard, and I bet he regretted it forever, was that everyone got more interested in the notes than the poem because how can you understand the poem without them? And I really didn't want that to happen. Also I knew that the notes section would be longer than the script which would just be ridiculous. So I thought it's a very simple choice – either I explain everything, which means going into enormous detail about my own life, which I didn't really want to do, or I explain nothing.[19]

Eliot's original title for *The Waste Land* was to have been *He do the Police in Different Voices*, a quotation taken from a minor episode in Charles Dickens's novel *Our Mutual Friend*, (1864–65), and this informs the structure of both Eliot's poem and Kane's play. Both act as medium for the unidentified voices who, 'pour out their souls in a torrent of emotions, ideas, memories and desires'.[20] Just as we are unsure of the *personas* (as Eliot called them), in *The Waste Land*, Kane (directly influenced after reading Rainer Werner Fassbinder's play *Pre-Paradise Sorry Now*), does not give the characters in *Crave* specific names, but denotes identity by the letters A, B, C and M. The characters stand for specific *archetypes*:

To me A was always an older man. M was always an older woman. B was always a younger man and C was always a young woman … A, B, C and M do have specific meanings which I am prepared to tell you. A is many things which is The Author, Abuser (because they're the same thing Author and Abuser); Aleister – as in Aleister Crowley who wrote some interesting books … and Antichrist. My brother came up with Arse-Hole which I thought was quite good. It was also the actor who I originally wrote it for who's called Andrew. M was simply Mother, B was Boy and C was Child, but I didn't want to write those things down because then I thought they'd get fixed in those things forever and nothing would ever change.[21]

This blurring of character and narrative put some critics in mind of Samuel Beckett's wireless plays and later work for the theatre. And while Kane's characters are reminiscent of his 'men and women talking to

19 Rebellato, 'Brief Encounter'. See Vicky Featherstone's (pp. 129–30) and Phylllis Nagy's (p. 155) comments about Eliot's poem in relation to *Crave*.
20 Aleks Sierz, Review of *Crave*, *Tribune*, 25 September 1998.
21 Rebellato, 'Brief Encounter'. The name of the actor referred to is Andrew Maud, who played the roles of Doctor, Priest and Theseus in the British premiere of *Phaedra's Love*. Aleister Crowley belonged to a group called the Order of the Golden Dawn who practised Cabalistic magic. Crowley was also a diabolist who claimed to be the Beast from the Book of Revelation. In *Crave* 'A' quotes the central philosophy from Crowley's *Book of the Law*, 'Do what thou wilt shall be the whole of the law' (47).

themselves',[22] the four people in *Crave* are far more interconnected with each other – and the feelings they evoke in the audience are far more personal than the voices in a Beckett wireless play like *Cascando* (1962) – or indeed *The Waste Land* itself.

Kane's 'voices' are also gender specific, both in the writing itself and subsequently through the performance of each actor embodying an individual character:

> I thought there were always things that the characters said that made it very clear. For example, it would've been very odd if a man had said 'when I wake I think my period must have started'. It would also be very strange if a man kept talking about how much he wanted a baby. But on the other hand, yes it could be done. I'm sure I'll see a production in Germany where this is done![23]

Despite the fact that, 'with *Crave* the narrative strands are not chronological … the people say the most bizarre things in strange situations',[24] and while recognising (and welcoming) that the play will be open to an infinite number of different interpretations, Kane's own intentions in the writing were prescriptive:

> In some ways for me *Crave* has very fixed and specific meanings in my mind which no one else could ever possibly know unless I told them. For example, who knows what 199714424 (188) means? I'm the only person who knows – and the actors – and I have no intention of telling anyone what it means. So I can't ever possibly expect to see the same production of the play twice thank God.[25]

Crave, despite its experimental nature still has several narrative strands. We learn for instance that M is an older woman who craves a child from the younger man B, but does not love him. In contrast, B's initial callousness towards M is replaced by his growing dependency on her, which she mockingly rejects by turning around one of his earlier rebuttals – 'It's just. Not. Me' (163). There is also a relationship between the older man A and the young girl C. In the first British production C was played by a young black actress,[26] with the casting possibly referring to A's allusion about the 'small dark girl' (157) in his story. There appears to be a relationship of sorts between the pair, but one which is unequal, unreciprocated and possibly abusive. In some respects the dynamics between A and C refer back to the relationship between Ian and Cate in

22 Fletcher and Spurling, *Beckett: A Study of his Plays* (London, 1972), p. 37.
23 Rebellato, 'Brief Encounter'.
24 Thielemans, *Rehearsing the Future*, p. 12.
25 Rebellato, 'Brief Encounter'.
26 Sharon Duncan-Brewster.

Blasted. Kane believes there to be a 'very clear line from *Blasted* to *Phaedra's Love* to *Cleansed* to *Crave*'.[27] Echoes with *Blasted* arise from incidents such as A's account of checking into a hotel, possibly with the young girl C, 'pretending we weren't going to have sex' (178), to lines reminiscent of Ian's nihilistic sense of humour: 'M. Why do you drink so much? / B. The fags aren't killing me fast enough' (181). We are also reminded of Ian's fate of dying and returning to earth in a chant by three of the characters: 'Keep coming back / Again and again / The eternal return' (195).

Comparison of *Crave* to a wireless play rather than performance drama was raised by several critics in their reviews. However, as Michael Billington pointed out, *Crave* was far more than 'a one-man show for four voices',[28] and had an inherent theatricality of its own which came from the physical presence of the four actors themselves; and despite the fact that they are seated throughout the performance, the actor's bodies brought a particular visual dynamic to their speaking voices. Billington for instance, describes C's reaction to A's long 'love speech' as she 'twists and writhes like a trapped snake', while the other actors avert their faces throughout this episode, returning to normal after A has finished speaking. At another point in the play, C moves away from her seated position next to A to swap places with the older woman M. Billington concludes that even small physical movements such as these make the play far more than an exercise in dramatic poetry: 'on the radio, the play could easily be abstract music: in the theatre it is full of neurotic tension'.[29]

Aspects in the dramatic construction of *Crave* reveal, 'Beckett's gaunt shadow'[30] – most notably the experimentation with rhythm. For instance, the following lines are cited by Michael Billington, in which he believes, 'you can actually hear the rhythms of [*Waiting for*] *Godot*':[31]

A. Life happens.
B. Like flowers,
C. Like sunshine,
A. Like nightfall
C. A motion away,
B. Not a motion towards. (39)

The other feature, common to both *Crave* and *Waiting for Godot*, is the use of a character sustaining an uninterrupted and prolonged speech lasting several pages. Such an outpouring of words is unusual because Beckett

27 Rebellato, 'Brief Encounter'.
28 Irving Wardle, *Sunday Telegraph*, 13 August 1998. See Mel Kenyon's (p. 150) and Vicky Featherstone's (p. 132) comments on *Crave's* suitability for the medium of wireless.
29 Billington, *Guardian*, 15 August 1998.
30 *Ibid*.

and Kane share an attitude to language which seems to be one of, 'reduction, intensification and simplification'.[32] Whereas in *Waiting for Godot* Lucky breaks his mute silence to deliver a rambling and frequently incoherent speech containing the remnants of religious and humanist philosophy, A's speech in *Crave* is a carefully constructed rhythmical outpouring of overwhelming love and desire directed at C. David Greig believes that as a piece of writing, it will be considered, 'if not now famous then [will] certainly grow in fame'. What Greig points out about the speech, and what perhaps makes it so remarkable is that despite, 'precise physical details', such as A's recollection of going 'to Florent [to] drink coffee at midnight'(169), the audience are prevented from seeing the speech as something autobiographical, concerning either the character of A or the dramatist. Instead, Greig believes the audience place themselves into the account, 'because of its very precision it opens itself up to you me or anybody who has felt desire or felt those similar words. You don't have to know the name of the coffee shop … [it] allows you to bring your own detail to it.'[33]

While this notable speech is undoubtedly touching, with its suffused longing for another person, Kane underscored it with an equal sense of darkness. For instance, throughout the speech C constantly repeats '*under her breath*' (170), 'this has to stop'; and if A is the abuser Kane spoke of, then this powerful declaration of love is simultaneously a form of debasement.

This section illustrates a concern that Michael Billington believes manifests itself from *Blasted* onwards in which, 'love [is seen as a] source of obsession, corruption, ownership and breakdown, and that [Kane] seems to say that [for] any two people who form a relationship some kind of colonisation is bound to take place – someone will be abused, power structures will come into play'.[34] This is also true of the characters in *The Waste Land* where, 'sadly, the only alternative to the human world of thwarted and degraded desires, loss, change and compulsion is a barren waste'.[35] Yet *Crave*, along with Kane's earlier work also exhibits a cor-

---

31 It is likely that Billington is thinking of the following exchange from *Waiting for Godot*:
VLADIMIR. They make a noise like wings.
ESTRAGON. Like leaves.
VLADIMIR. Like sand
ESTRAGON. Like leaves.
    [*Silence.*]
VLADIMIR. They all speak together. (58)
32 Charles Lyons, *Samuel Beckett* (Basingstoke, 1983), p. 3.
33 *Nightwaves*. See Phyllis Nagy's comments on locale, p. 158.
34 *Ibid.*
35 Harriet Davidson, 'Reading The Wasteland' in Moody, David (ed.), *The Cambridge Companion to T.S. Eliot* (Cambridge, 1994), p. 123.

responding, 'yearning and a longing for relationships to work and the forces that stop these relationships working'. The same is also true of *The Waste Land* in which its exploration of the myths of regeneration and desolation speak of, 'a longing for renewal of life and growth but at the same time a longing to escape it'.[36]

This last sentiment also gives both works a shared sense of despair and nihilism. Vicky Featherstone's comment that *Crave* was 'absolutely rooted in twentieth century pain',[37] echoes Eliot's poem where the voices declare, 'We who are living are now dying / With a little patience' (V.329–30). Written after Eliot was recovering from a nervous breakdown, and Europe was slowing rebuilding itself from the cataclysm of the First World War, *The Waste Land*'s 'images are those of the end of the natural cycle',[38] and that ultimately, 'at the centre of its spiral movement … is "the abyss" [and] the terror of the unknown which cannot finally be evaded'.[39]

With the very opening words of *Crave* 'You're dead to me', and the use of phrases such as 'I feel nothing' (156), and 'nothing to be done'[40] (182), Kane was somewhat perplexed that some critics saw the absence of staged violence in *Crave* as evidence of it being a more hopeful work:

> I actually think *Crave* – where there is no physical violence whatsoever, it's a very silent play – is the most despairing of the things I've written so far. At some point somebody says in it, 'something has lifted', and from that moment on it becomes apparently more and more hopeful. But actually the characters have all given up. It's the first one of my plays in which people go, 'fuck this, I'm out of here'. Probably one of my disconnections with *Cleansed* is because it is about continuing to love and how love can save you. Whereas *Crave* was written during a process of ceasing to have faith in love.[41]

It is easy to take such false comfort as the end of the play approaches. For instance, partial quotations from the Bible such as Philippians (4:7), '[And the peace of God] which passeth all understanding' (198), alongside the voices coming together, 'Free-falling / Into the light / Bright white light' (200) – seem to offer hope; yet this benevolent light is in fact the characters collectively embracing the comfort of death. This image of annihilating light becomes a central image in Kane's last play *4.48 Psychosis,* and in many ways follows on from the themes and obsessions of *Crave.*

36   Elizabeth Drew, *T.S. Eliot: The Design of his Poetry* (London, 1950), p. 90.
37   Thielemans, *Rehearsing the Future*, p. 12.
38   Northrop Frye, *T.S. Eliot: An Introduction* (Chicago, 1981), p. 64.
39   Helen Gardner, *The Art of T.S. Eliot* (London, 1949), p. 49.
40   A borrowing Kane took from the opening line of Beckett's *Waiting for Godot.*
41   Kane, interview with Nils Tabert.

'Remember the light and believe in the light': *4.48 Psychosis*

If she really is – as it appears – trying to kill herself, then surely our presence here makes us mere voyeurs in Bedlam …

But why not? Why shouldn't it be / 'a performance'?

Exactly – it becomes a kind / of theatre.

It's theatre – that's right – for a world in which theatre itself has died. Instead of the outmoded conventions of dialogue and so-called characters lumbering towards the embarrassing dénouements of the *theatre*, Anne is offering us a pure dialogue of objects: of leather and glass, of Vaseline and steel; of blood, saliva and chocolate. She's offering us no less than the spectacle of her own existence, the radical *pornography* – if I may use that overrated word – of her own broken and abused – almost *Christ*-like-body. (Martin Crimp, *Attempts on Her Life*)

The scene above concerns a group of art critics who attempt to make sense of, and place in context, an art work by an anonymous woman called Anne. The piece consists of the 'various objects associated with the artist's attempts to kill herself over the past few months' (11:45), and it is perhaps Martin Crimp's *Attempts on Her Life* that provides the most useful starting point from which to discuss Sarah Kane's last play *4.48 Psychosis*. For instance, on the level of satire, the attempt to say something clever or profound about a work that tries to represent or comment upon intense human despair is pertinent to the task of the theatre critic coming to *4.48 Psychosis*, a drama whose main theme is suicide, written by a dramatist who took her own life after completing it. Michael Billington, in his review of *4.48 Psychosis* looked at another artistic precedent – namely the poet Sylvia Plath and one of her last pieces of work *Edge* (1963), which in its opening line, 'The woman is perfected / Her dead body wears the smile of accomplishment',[1] seemed to Billington a case of, 'the writer recording the act she is about to perform'.[2]

In some respects this was the obvious critical path to take, and indeed, when faced with the difficult task of reviewing the play, what most critics chose to do. By following the line of least resistance and seeing the play 'as a declaration of suicide,'[3] and a '75-minute suicide note',[4] critics were to some extent on safe ground. By interpreting lines literally such as 'I have resigned myself to death this year' (208), the play might appear to be given over to a tract that deals exclusively with the consolations of death. It is also undeniable that this last work was also the most clearly biographical and personally driven. Kane's agent Mel Kenyon, speaking about *4.48 Psychosis* outlines the problems and ambivalent attitude that prevailed during its writing:

> She has gone deeper into her own psyche and I think she knew she was delving deeper, and she did have – not problems with the play – but emotionally she had a very strong reaction to the play. She would ring up one week and say, 'Oh I really like this – this is going to be good', and the next week she'd ring up and say she hated it and that she was going to burn it. So, I think there was a kind of love hate relationship with this play and she knew that she was exhausting a certain reserve in herself while she wrote it.[5]

At the same time, thinking of *4.48 Psychosis* as little more than a suicide note also risks impoverishing the play: moreover, such a commentary runs the risk of providing too reductive a reading, both of the play's content and its themes. For instance, if *4.48 Psychosis* is to be seen exclusively in these terms, then the interpretation of suicide as an all encompassing theme could equally be applied to *all* Kane's work, as without exception every one of the plays, and even her short film *Skin*, contain someone who either attempts or succeeds in taking their own life. Of course, the opposite is also true, and that in denying the theme of suicide

1 Sylvia Plath, *Collected Poems*. Edited and Introduced by Ted Hughes (London, 1981), p. 272.
2 Michael Billington, 'How do you Judge a 75-Minute Suicide Note?', *Guardian*, 30 June 2000, p. 5.
3 Susannah Clapp, 'Blessed are the Bleak', *Observer Review*, 2 July 2000, p. 9.
4 Billington, *Guardian*, 30 June 2000.
5 *Nightwaves*.

in *4.48 Psychosis,* the critic can end up imposing a false aesthetic against the original intentions of the writer.

Suicide notes by their nature are brief, and only ever partly articulate what they want to say. One of the crucial things that must be stressed about Sarah Kane's last play is that it was not hastily written like a suicide note. In fact, there is evidence to suggest that she had begun preliminary work on it from January 1998 onwards, and it is as carefully crafted as anything Kane had worked on before.

The influence of Martin Crimp's *Attempts on Her Life* plays an important formal role in the development of both *Crave* and *4.48 Psychosis.* Kane is on record in believing Crimp to be 'one of the few genuine formal innovators writing for the stage',[6] and ideas from the structure and dramatic form of *Attempts on her Life* find its way into both *Crave* and *4.48 Psychosis* – not only through its rejection of stage directions relating to specifics such as scenography or the actors' appearance or movement – but in the move away from formal methods of characterisation. In *Attempts on Her Life* we are given no indication of how many actors are required for the play, or who is speaking at any given moment. Whereas in *Crave,* character is designated to four people through the letters assigned to them, *4.48 Psychosis* is far closer to Crimp's play in bringing together a myriad of unidentified and unnumbered voices to the drama.

It is evident from the early stages of writing that *4.48 Psychosis* was to be a continuation of the themes and ideas explored in *Crave.* In February 1998 Kane commented:

> It was strange – when I finished *Crave* I thought I don't know where to go now, because it seemed to me, this has become so minimal and so much about language – where could my writing possibly go? But when I started this new one [*4:48 Psychosis*] just a few weeks ago, I suddenly realised that it goes further. I mean the new one at the moment doesn't even have characters, all there is are language and images. But all the images are within language rather than visualised. I don't even know how many people there are ...[7]

By November of that year the play was much more fully realised, even down to specifics like the title:

> I'm writing a play called *4.48 Psychosis* and it's got similarities with *Crave,* but it's different. It's about a psychotic breakdown and what happens to a person's mind when the barriers which distinguish between reality and different forms of imagination completely disappear, so that you no longer

6   Sarah Kane, 'The Playwright's Playwright', *Guardian,* 21 September 1998, p. 13.
7   Sarah Kane, interview with Nils Tabert.

know the difference between your waking life and your dream life. And also you no longer know where you stop, and the world starts. So, for example, if I were psychotic I would literally not know the difference between myself, this table and Dan [Rebellato, the person sitting next to her]. They would all somehow be part of a continuum, and various boundaries begin to collapse. Formally I'm trying to collapse a few boundaries as well; to carry on with making form and content one. That's proving extremely difficult, and I'm not going to tell anyone how I'm doing it because if they get there first I'll be furious! But whatever it is that began in *Crave* it's going a step further – where it goes after that I'm not quite sure.[8]

The development of certain ideas and themes from *Crave* is evident in a number of respects in *4.48 Psychosis*. For instance, the tale that C recounts about being hospitalised in 'ES3' (187), with its clinical procedures where, 'They switch on my light every hour to check I'm breathing' (188), is a precaution taken for patients at risk of taking their own lives, and becomes a central theme in *4.48 Psychosis*.

However, the play is not simply a companion piece to *Crave*, and in her attempt to try and express abstract ideas such as different states of reality, Kane yet again moves onto a new dramatic form. Edward Bond comments that in coming to an understanding of *4.48 Psychosis*, 'it is important that the structure is used in the [theatre] direction: it has to become a window through which you see the play'.[9] The form this takes is through the division of the play into a series of *discourses*. The term is a slippery one, and has been appropriated by everyone from linguists to literary and cultural theorists to signify meaning as diverse as, 'language as a form of social interaction and power' or 'a distinctive way of seeing and saying the world' to, 'dialogue in general … [and] conversation in particular'.[10]

In *4.48 Psychosis* these discourses are used as a way of making language attempt to express the boundaries between reality, fantasy and different mental states – the forms used range from monologues; doctor – patient conversations; the language of medical questionnaires and clinical case histories; material taken from popular 'self-help' psychology books; apocalyptic visions derived and inspired by the Book of Revelations, as well as disembodied text and numbers that the characters do not speak. These instead provide a *meta-discourse* – unbounded by conventional language, and relying on theatrical imagery to take on the task of communicating emotions and ideas to the audience.

---

  8 Rebellato, 'Brief Encounter'.
  9 Bond, Letter to Graham Saunders, 27 May 2000.
 10 Cited in Rob Pope, *The English Studies Book* (London, 1998), pp. 45–6.

At times, Kane plays with these discourses, sometimes in a bleakly humorous way. For instance, in the case history sequence (223–5), where the patient's medication and reactions are monitored, Kane parodies the medical language used by reporting a suicide attempt in the same manner: '100 aspirin and one bottle of Bulgarian Cabernet Sauvignon, 1986. Patient woke in a pool of vomit and said "sleep with the dog and rise full of fleas". Severe stomach pain. No other reaction' (225).

4.48 Psychosis also takes up the other principal theme in *Crave* concerning the fragility of love, and in particular goes on to explore and develop the implications of C's comment, 'You've fallen in love with someone that doesn't exist' (158). Here, one of the speakers talks of going out 'at six in the morning [to] start my search for you' (214); and at one point echoes the sentiments of the love between Rod and Carl in *Cleansed*, when the speaker professes, 'I would rather have lost my legs / pulled out my teeth / gouged out my eyes / than lost my love' (230). At one point a speaker thinks they have found the 'cathected Other' (235) in one of the doctors, but it seems as if the lover referred to is destined to remain perpetually unknowable, and in the first two Royal Court productions the same speaker curses God, 'for making me love a person who does not exist' (215).

However, it is almost the last line of the play – 'It is myself I have never met, whose face is pasted on the underside of my mind' (245) – that sets up the implication of not only all the voices belonging to one person, but that the 'awful physical aching fucking longing' (214), in fact constitutes the search for self-hood. In the early stages of writing, Kane saw *4.48 Psychosis* as 'yet another play, which is about the split between one's consciousness and one's physical being. For me that's what madness is about'.[11] One of the speakers asserts, 'Body and soul can never be married' (212), while in *Crave* 'C' asserts, 'I want to feel physically like I feel emotionally' (179). In this respect both plays resemble Samuel Beckett's later drama in which he also attempts to articulate, 'the image of a mind, alienated from its body'.[12] For Kane however, 'the only way back to any kind of sanity is to connect physically with who you are emotionally, spiritually and mentally'.[13] The disturbing aspect of Kane's work is that often the only way that characters such as the Soldier, Hippolytus, Phaedra, or the voices in *Crave* ever achieve this connection is in the brief span of seconds before their own oblivion.

It is no different in *4.48 Psychosis*. Even on a lesser scale, one of the

11 Sarah Kane, interview with Nils Tabert.
12 Lyons, *Samuel Beckett*, p. 4.
13 Sarah Kane, interview with Nils Tabert.

speakers toys with the process through self-mutilation. In the first two Royal Court productions, the actor Daniel Evans had carved scars on his arm (which are not mentioned in the script), which spell out 'Yes / No'.[14] On being asked why he acts in such a manner the speaker replies, 'Because it feels great. Because it feels fucking amazing' (217).While such behaviour may seem pathological, it is paradoxically shown to be at least a temporary way of connecting mind and body together. The impetus for the scene seemed to be based on someone Kane knew:

> I just met someone who has taken God knows how many overdoses and has attempted suicide in almost every imaginable way. She has a huge scar round here [points to her throat] and scars round here [points to her wrists]. But actually she's more connected with herself than most people I know. I think in that moment when she slashes herself, when she takes an overdose suddenly she's connected and then wants to live. And so she takes herself to hospital. Her life is an ongoing stream of suicide attempts which she then revokes. And yes, there's something really awful about that but I can understand it very well. It makes sense to me.[15]

Kane was aware of the danger in playing with this 'connection', and *4.48 Psychosis* also explores the other alternative, of trying to reconcile this perceived separation between mind and body through the use of prescribed medication. However, Kane also understood that this course of action is at best palliative, and brings about a crucial loss of self-hood: 'I think to a certain degree you have to deaden your ability to feel and perceive. In order to function you have to cut out at least one part of your mind. Otherwise you'd be chronically sane in a society which is chronically insane. I mean, look at Artaud. That's your choice: Go mad and die, or function but be insane'.[16] In *4.48 Psychosis* one of the speakers finally calls for medication in a gesture of last resort: 'Okay, let's do it, let's do the drugs, let's do the chemical lobotomy, let's shut down the higher functions of my brain and perhaps I'll be a bit more fucking capable of living' (221). However, an earlier speaker believes, 'There's not a drug on earth can make life meaningful' (220), when placed beside the 'pathological grief' (223), that comes from the search for a lover 'who was never born' (218).

Kane also revisits the imagery from *Crave*, where death is visualised as a bright engulfing light that finally snuffs out its speakers. In *4.48 Psychosis* we are reminded twice to 'Remember the light and believe in the

---

14 For an account of the decision made behind this choice, see the conversation with Daniel Evans, p. 176.
15 Sarah Kane, interview with Nils Tabert.
16 *Ibid.*

light / An instant of clarity before eternal light' (206), as well as the repeated phrase – four times in all – 'Hatch opens / stark light'. These images occupy the dark centre of this final play, including the time of 4.48 in the morning, 'when sanity visits' (229); yet it is also the moment when the voice, 'shall not speak again' (213).

Crave and *4.48 Psychosis* are also both notable in their disregard of setting. Whereas in all her previous plays Kane had been very particular about providing details of location, such as the 'expensive hotel room in Leeds' (1:3), in which *Blasted* takes place – or 'inside the perimeter fence of a university' (1:107) of *Cleansed* – the places which *Crave* and *4.48 Psychosis* inhabit more closely resemble mindscapes which the director and / or designer are free to conjure with. For instance, Vicky Featherstone's two productions of *Crave* took 'place on a stage disconcertingly clean and precise', and consisted solely of 'four sensibly designed modern chairs … symmetrically arranged behind two small tables, on which two glass tumblers are symmetrically placed beside a water *carafe*'.[17] The set helped to articulate the isolation of the individuals concerned, each inhabiting their own space, while the cultural resonances thrown off, somewhere between 'chat-show style',[18] and the wireless programme *'In the Psychiatrist's Chair'*,[19] gave a sense of the audience eaves-dropping on a confessional.

The set of *4.48 Psychosis* for its London premiere was deceptively simple, but in its design attempted to suggest the other states of consciousness that Kane was attempting to explore. The designer was Jeremy Herbert, who had worked on the ambitious stage design of *Cleansed*, and despite the first production of *4.48 Psychosis* taking place in the much smaller Jerwood Theatre Upstairs, the concept was no less ingenious.[20] While the stage props of table and chairs were functional to the point of being anonymous, the intriguing feature that dominated the set was a mirror slanted at a 45 degree angle, cutting off the back of the set so that it resembled a small attic room. The mirror's presence meant that the audience could simultaneously see the drama on two planes, so that they could both witness the actors playing in front and above their heads. Audience members seated further back could also observe a vertical view of the first two rows of their fellow theatre-goers. This extreme use of perspective was also used in *Cleansed*, and provided one of the more notable features of that production, in which the audience could 'look down on

17 Jeremy Kingston, 'What Becomes of the Broken Hearted'? *The Times*, 15 September 1998.

18 Georgina Brown, *Mail on Sunday*, 23 August 1998.

19 Aleks Sierz, 'Stains on a Polaroid', *Tribune*, 25 August 1998.

20 Herbert's set subsequently won the 2000 Barclays New Stages award for best design.

the characters as if they [were] animals under experimentation'.[21] At one point in *4.48 Psychosis* the actors lie on the floor in different positions, and in the reflection given out by the mirror, one critic felt they resembled, 'insects trapped on a flypaper or people spread-eagled at a fairground wall of death'.[22]

The use of the mirror also directly commented on the different states of consciousness that the speakers inhabit in the play, especially the concerns about separation of mind from body. When one of the actors says, 'Here am I / and there is my body / dancing on glass' (230), the mirror was able to help visualise this dissociation of self-hood as the audience witnessed everything carried out on two separate planes: dual perspective also mimicked the state of clinical depression, where patients frequently talk of feeling as if they are trapped observers looking down on themselves and everyday reality carrying on outside themselves. The mirror as well as the table were also used as mediums on which to realise sections of the written text into theatrical images. For instance, the set of numbers in multiples of seven (232),[23] is visualised in performance through one of the speakers writing them on the table back to front which are then unscrambled by the mirror and reflected back to the audience. Also, at one point, the ghostly letters 'RSVP' appear on the mirror, to which one of the speakers replies by launching a paper plane across the stage (214).

The mirror was also used as medium in which (and upon) different states of mind were given expression. For instance, to complement the idea that the mirror was a vehicle for the separation of mind and body, video images were projected onto it showing a window in which people pass outside. The effect served as a reminder that the speakers in the play, and indeed the audience themselves were trapped behind this vista, unable to participate in the outside world.

The play's ending in the first Royal Court production was a memorable one, and puts into practice a comment Edward Bond made about *4.48 Psychosis*, refuting the interpretation of simply seeing it as a suicide coda. Bond believes the play, 'changes from a painful suicide note about death and loss and waste – into a sort of treatise about living consciously, and this is even more painful'.[24] The Royal Court production seemed to bring together Bond's sentiments by introducing a devised action separate from the text. The last lines of the play are 'please open the curtains' (245), and this was followed by the actors moving to the side of

---

21 Georgina Brown, *Mail on Sunday*, 24 May 1998.
22 Clapp, *Observer Review*, 2 July 2000, p. 9.
23 For the significance of these numbers, see the conversation with Daniel Evans, pp. 175–6.
24 Letter to Graham Saunders, 27 May 2000. Also, see Daniel Evans, pp. 174–5 and James Macdonald, p. 125.

the stage, opening the shutters to the windows, and summoning in the light and sounds of the London street outside. The experience was simple and yet profoundly moving. As one reviewer put it, 'the effect is strangely uplifting, like watching the final release of a turbulent spirit'.[25]

Mel Kenyon perhaps sums up the overall positive personal experiences that can be taken from *4.48 Psychosis*, as well as its merits as an artistic achievement:

> In many ways it's beautifully wrought so the fact that she could do it and try and communicate this, for me it gives an enormous sense of hope that she still had this gift and that she still wanted to communicate and she has done it with great dignity and eloquence and humour. So I hope that people won't kind of sit there with their head in their hands saying, 'oh poor girl'.[26]

To attempt to assess the contribution and significance of Sarah Kane's impact on theatre is a difficult task, although I have attempted to outline the distinctive features in her drama in the introduction. The reputation and reception of Kane's work will inevitably evolve and undergo a process of reassessment as the plays are read, discussed and performed. It is also tempting in the light of Kane's death to eulogise and mythologise their importance.

Taking the most pessimistic scenario, and assuming her work and reputation fall into neglect in years to come, *Blasted* will still be remembered as – if nothing else – a landmark in theatre history, in much the same way as Osborne's *Look Back in Anger* in the 1950s defined a new strand of British writing.

It is also true to point out that Kane was a writer who never stood still, and from *Blasted* onwards made bold new experimental inroads into dramatic form. James Macdonald, believes Kane's legacy as a dramatist was to have produced, 'a brave, angry, poetic body of work quite unlike anything else … At a time when much new writing was content to inhabit received dramatic form, each new play found a new structure to contain its ideas and feelings'.[27] David Greig shares these sentiments, adding that Kane's work, 'pushed recklessly at the naturalistic boundaries of British theatre'.[28]

Yet, it is elements of Artaud's conception of the function theatre should occupy that perhaps comes closest to the intention behind much of Kane's writing. In one of his influential essays, Artaud envisaged a theatre that would make gestures to its audience in the same way as those

---

25 Paul Taylor, 'A Suicide Note that is Extraordinarily Vital', *Independent*, 30 June 2000, p. 11.
26 *Nightwaves*.
27 James Macdonald, 'They Never Got Her', *Observer Review*, 28 February 1999.
28 David Greig, *Complete Plays*, p. ix.

about to be burnt at the stake. As conflagration approached, the victims made signs and gestures to the spectators who witnessed their agonies. Nils Tabert, the German translator of *Cleansed* and *Crave* found this to be one of the central themes in all Kane's work:

> Sarah's plays can't be limited to this but they are desperately making signs to society – not cries for help, but saying 'this is what the world is like from my point of view'. And it makes you very uncomfortable towards the world ... And I think that was one of the things Sarah was working for – that we have to get back in touch with our feelings – even if this is very risky.[29]

While David Greig is right to point out that, 'Kane mapped the darkest and most unforgiving internal landscapes: landscapes of violation ... loneliness ... power ... mental collapse ... and most consistently, the landscape of love',[30] the dramatist Howard Barker, echoing the comments of Artaud's figures at the stake believes, 'the most appropriate art for a culture on the edge of extinction is one that stimulates pain'.[31] In this way the bleak themes and stark, sometimes shocking imagery in Kane's plays (yet almost always underscored with a sense of hope) function as a stimulus by which to restore a sense of compassion and humanity to its audience.

29 Kane, interview with Nils Tabert, 16 July 2000.
30 Greig, *Complete Plays*, p. ix.
31 Barker, *Arguments for a Theatre*, 3rd edn (Manchester, 1999), pp. 18–19.

PART II Conversations

7

Conversation
with James Macdonald
8 August 2000

James Macdonald has been associate director of the Royal Court Theatre since 1992. His work there includes *Peaches* (1994); *Simpatico* (1995); *Blasted* (1995, 2001); *Cleansed* (1998); *Real Classy Affair* (1998); *4.48 Psychosis* (2000, 2001) and *Hard Fruit* (2000). For the RSC, *Roberto Zucco* (1997) and *The Tempest* (2000).

GRAHAM SAUNDERS Looking back at your work on *Blasted*, *Cleansed* and *4.48 Psychosis*, what aspects of progression strike you in Sarah Kane's work.

JAMES MACDONALD Well, the plays certainly got progressively more abstract as Sarah became more interested in removing the conventional signposts of psychological realism. And perhaps you could say that was a conscious agenda when she started writing *Cleansed*. I think that partly in response to the press reception of *Blasted* she wanted to write something that no one could possibly mistake for realism. Then with *Crave* she made another jump forward into an abstraction of character, and with *4.48 Psychosis* she realised she could go further – beyond Beckett even.

GS When you started work on *Cleansed* did you feel you had to re-assess Sarah as writer?

JM It didn't happen quite like that because Sarah had told me what she was writing about while we were rehearsing *Blasted*. I remember her saying when she finally gave it to me, 'don't read it late at night because you won't sleep'. In both plays she was very concerned to tell a story through images, but *Cleansed* confirmed for me that the images are there to tell the story more powerfully and immediately than the text. On the first day of rehearsal the play took half an hour to read, whereas finally it took ninety minutes to perform, so you could say there is an hour of imagery in *Cleansed*. Her work always seeks to engage an audience emotionally by the most direct route possible.

GS   Had Sarah spoken to you about directing *Cleansed* after the hiatus of *Phaedra's Love*?

JM   I think so. As I remember it, she asked me to do *Phaedra's Love* but I couldn't. Also, once she'd submitted *Cleansed* there was another gap because I couldn't do it immediately, and she got very cross!

GS   Sarah's spoken about the idea of rain in the second half of *Blasted* coming from you, and in the second edition of the play she amended the stage directions to include Autumn, Winter and Summer rain. We also get the startling image of water dripping onto Ian's head once he's inside the baby's grave. What gave you the initial idea?

JM   The rain on Ian's head was in the original script. It's very beautiful where it comes – both comical and cleansing. The rain in between the scenes may have come partly from looking at photographs of Bosnia at that time, because as you know much of the play is rooted in that conflict. I can remember saying to Sarah, 'listen, we're going to need some kind of sound to get from A to B to C, and cover us running around in the dark'. And she said, 'I'm not having bloody theatre music in my play'![1] So then the onus was on me to come up with something!

GS   The use of specifying rain through a spectrum of different seasons seems to give the play a further surreal quality – of time slowing down like one of Cate's fits.

JM   That sense of altering the time scale also relates to the use of alternating darkness and light once Ian has been blinded. The sense of time becoming compressed or subjective was all there anyway in those stage directions. It was just a case of realizing it on stage.

GS   With the work from *Blasted* up until *Cleansed* there seem to be two ways of interpretation in so far as the violence is depicted – either ritualise and abstract, or in the case say of the Hamburg production of *Blasted*, go for a more realistic approach to the violence. Are both approaches equally valid?

---

1   The production of *Blasted* at La Colline Theatre France in 2000 used such musical effects in the scene after Ian had been blinded.

JM For the audience, the most provocative thing might very well be to do a completely detailed and realistic production – I'm sure that can be argued. But I think in the end, the more different productions the better; it would be awful for there to be an authorised way of doing anyone's plays.

GS The Theatre Museum in London has included *Cleansed* in its education pack on Artaud as a modern example of 'total theatre'. Were you aware in your realisation of the play that you wanted to incorporate elements of The Theatre of Cruelty.

JM I don't quite know what 'total theatre' is to be honest. I remember as a student finding Artaud's theatre rather impenetrable. I only looked at him again when we were working on *4.48 Psychosis*, because she had said she'd gone back to his work when she was writing it. I loved the early letters to Jacques Riviere – they're extraordinary and very interesting in relation to her philosophy – that there's nothing you can't write about. And Artaud encountered the same problem of having to fight against very conservative notions of form in theatre. There's one particular letter where he says he needed his writing to take a form on the page which reflected directly what was happening inside his head. That's exactly what Sarah was doing with *4.48 Psychosis*. But 'total theatre' as it relates to *Cleansed*, I don't know – we were just trying to translate that extraordinary imagery into a consistent theatrical language. I think it's clear the moment you look at *Cleansed* there's no way you can do it realistically – it would be lethal to perform and unbearable to watch.

GS I'd like to ask you about *4.48 Psychosis* if I could. I gather you had seven weeks rehearsal for the play?

JM I did a couple of workshops on it. Little three day workshops before we programmed the play – and I did these to work out how many people were going to be in it. Because you literally can't rehearse it until you've decided how many people to do it with. Once I'd made that decision then we did six weeks in all.

GS How did the rehearsal process progress?

JM It was an unusual process in the sense that basically there is only one voice in the piece – or one central voice, although there is also the doctor / lover voice. What was fascinating, and very liberating for the actors, was to have three people sharing responsibility for one character. We spent a long time excavating meaning section by section and line by line. And as so often in Sarah's work, lines have multiple meanings. Then we played as many different versions of each section as we could think of, probably far more than we would have done had she been in the room. The central acting question was to be specific about who each voice is talking to. And we didn't decide who was going to speak which line until maybe the end of the fourth week – so the actors all had to have responsibility for the whole thing.

GS Daniel Evans mentions that a short section of the 'apocalyptic' section, where the voices quote from the Book of Revelations, was kept free each night for any one of the actors to speak those lines. Why did you keep that section free while the remainder of the play had traditionally assigned lines?

JM During rehearsals we used that technique a lot – the actors were free to say whichever lines they wanted. It meant that quite often you got two or three people saying a particular line. But if you used it in performance too many of the lines would end up being voiced by more than one actor, which would feel self-indulgent and get in the way of the text. It did feel completely right for the prophet section though, because the tone there is both choric and ironic. It was also a helpful thing at the point we were allocating lines, as a way of seeing who related to which line.

GS How did the final set and the use of the mirror come about?

JM We went through a number of production ideas before settling on the mirror. Distorted perspectives were something we had used in *Cleansed*, and Jeremy [Herbert] has always been interested in mirrors. So when he suggested it, we saw that it would help to realise the mind / body divide which is at the centre of the text; and also it would solve the problem of how to talk to the audience without addressing them directly.

GS Did the projections that came onto the mirror follow on from that?

JM It's something that interests both of us, and we spotted that you would get an extraordinary double image, like a rorschach test, which was video projected through a mirror onto a white floor and then reflected back through the mirror. We didn't actually finalise what we were going to project until quite late in rehearsal, so that it could develop from the contexts we settled on for each particular section. The text itself is chock-full of images so it was important that projection was used discretely – mostly as a light source which created specific atmospheres rather than in an imagistic way

GS How useful were the outside advisers you brought in to rehearsals to talk about mental health with the actors?

JM Extremely helpful actually. Each had a quite different perspective on their profession. I don't think any of them had much time to read the play before meeting us, although there was one person who had been right through it marking the bits they didn't agree with, which we found very amusing. But I think depression is a daunting subject initially if you've never suffered from it, so all the different technical viewpoints were fascinating and instructive. In retrospect I think we should have talked to more actual sufferers than we did, although it's an incredibly hard condition to describe from the inside – which is one of the things that makes the play so extraordinary.

GS   Edward Bond has commented that *4.48 Psychosis* should be seen as an affirmation to live rather than a suicide note. The actors opening the windows at the end seemed a fitting action to the last line of dialogue in the play – 'please open the curtains'. How did the idea arise in rehearsals?

JM   It's obviously a difficult play to end. That last line is very beautiful but if you had a conventional theatrical ending I think it would feel melodramatic. So we were looking for a way to release both actors and audience, which is what Sarah seemed to me to be doing, not only with that last line but also in the generosity and detachment of the last section. As for the suicide note question, Sarah wrote the play over quite a long period of time, and I think it wasn't necessarily going to be a play that described a path that led to suicide, although in the end that was how she chose to structure it. I think she set out simply to describe her 'illness' experientially – and to find a theatrical form which would mirror this experience. As to whether the play is affirmative – I do think it is, curiously, maybe because there's such life and passion in that voice, even though she's telling you how she arrived at a point where she couldn't find a reason to live.

GS   The penultimate line of *4.48 Psychosis*, 'It is myself I have never met, whose face is pasted on the underside of my mind', brings to mind the search that begins in *Blasted* onwards for all the characters – this search for love and self-recognition. Is this how the plays strike you?

JM   Love is in all the plays isn't it? And in context one of the possible meanings of that line at the end of *4.48 Psychosis* is that in order to live, the person you have to love is yourself. Looking back, a lot of her work dramatises contradictory impulses within her own nature, which is perhaps how she managed to have such understanding and compassion for all her characters.

GS   The humour in her plays never really got picked up. Did you find that frustrating?

JM   Of course – but it's very dry her humour isn't it? In my experience some audiences pick up on it and others don't. That was certainly true for the [first] run of *4.48 Psychosis*, around which there was a considerable level of tension because everyone in the audience knew that the writer had killed herself. And on press nights too there was obviously tension. Her work was admittedly hard to review because the plays demand that you experience them emotionally in the moment rather than intellectually. Which is perhaps antithetical to the fine art of criticism ...

GS Has your approach to directing been influenced in any way from exposure to Sarah Kane's work?

JM I'd say she taught me a lot about using language precisely in theatre, especially about punctuation. Her telling of a story through images – I think that has influenced the way I now work on plays. Also her courage – in that she stuck to her vision of what she wanted to see on stage.

GS Did she ever have to compromise?

JM I think it's fair to say that there were images in the [first] production of *Blasted* that were compromised by the limitations of the Theatre Upstairs, both financial and spatial. That was our fault though, not hers.

GS Looking back at *Blasted*, would you have changed your approach to it as a director in any way?

JM Inevitably I think so now, just because it's six years since we did it.[2] The main thing would be to do the bomb properly – it's the thing that unites the play and makes the second half of it possible, so it has to be fully realised, which we struggled with in the Theatre Upstairs. And led up to properly – the world explodes because of what happens in the first half of the play.

GS It was like the stage direction of Ian dying and coming back to life. How do you realise a thing like that?

JM I'm not sure we solved that one! Which was a pity, because it's a very good gag, and nothing more than Ian's just deserts.

GS Do you tend to do much background research on the plays?

JM With *Blasted* I did as much research as I could on Bosnia. With *Cleansed* I read or re-read quite a lot of the Holocaust literature. Sarah knew that literature well and in some ways it shadows the play, which isn't about the Holocaust specifically, but does ask large questions about what people will do under that level of extreme suffering. And of course there's that famous Barthes quote. With *4.48 Psychosis*, I looked at as much as I could on depression, and was shocked by how little I knew about such a large subject, especially considering that I'd known Sarah for six years – and also that statistically at least 50 per cent of women and 25 per cent of men in this country suffer from it at some point in their lives. I was completely ignorant about

---

2 James Macdonald directed the second production of *Blasted* at The Royal Court in April, 2001.

what causes it, how it's treated and what it does to people. And obviously, one felt a great weight of responsibility to excavate the truth of that play because she wasn't around to give you answers when you got stuck.

GS   Had Sarah left notes to the play?

JM   There were only various early drafts of it, which were much less structured. I think she was just writing it down as it came to her, and then developing it through collage as she did *Crave*. Gradually she found a structure to unify it from within the material.

8

Conversation with Vicky Featherstone

12 December 2000

Vicky Featherstone is Artistic Director of Paines Plough Theatre Company. In 1998 and 2001 she directed the British productions of *Crave*. Her other work includes *Sleeping Around* (1998); *The Cosmonaut's Last Message to the Woman he once Loved in the Former Soviet Union* (1999); *Crazy Gary's Mobile Disco* (2001).

GRAHAM SAUNDERS The first thing I'd like to ask you is about Sarah's involvement in Paines Plough, working with other writers as well as being resident dramatist.

VICKY FEATHERSTONE I think above everything else Sarah was a writer. And everything that came out was from that point of view. However, she was incredibly literate in all aspects of theatre, and so her interest in other writers came out of that. She had an extraordinary ability to help other writers develop work. And even though she had a very strong voice in her own writing it was interesting that she could make that voice secondary to what other people wanted to say. Her work on scripts came at an early stage of her career to try and earn money as a script reader.

GS *Crave* was a remarkable departure in style and form from the first three plays. How did it come about? And was it worked on by actors throughout the writing process?

VF Sarah was our writer in residence, and she had selected a group of six writers who she was interested in doing workshops in development with. We have this thing called Word Lunch on a Friday, and we asked the writers to do a short piece for that. And the last writer, Rebecca Prichard, had her play commissioned by the Royal Court so was unable to do it. So Sarah and I talked, and rather jokingly – as it took Sarah an incredibly long time to write a play – I persuaded her to write something for this lunch-time reading in front of an audience. So what she decided to do was come up with a title and chose four actors whose voices she was interested in. Then she went off and wrote the first twenty minutes of *Crave* over three days. Doing the extracts for a lunch-time reading really freed her up, and the fact that she used a pseudonym meant she was released from the pressure of this being a 'Sarah Kane play'. We rehearsed the material with the actors and then I asked if she thought there was a longer play there. She agreed it wasn't finished as it stood so I commissioned her to write *Crave*. From that original twenty minutes only about six lines were ever changed. But then it took a further year to write the rest of the play. There was never actually any conventional workshop development of the script as there is with other writers. When we sat down and discussed the play what she wanted to do was to find out if you could arrive at meaning through rhythm and whether language could become arbitrary. And that's something that we came back to when we were trying to understand the play – and that was to realise that it was written for its rhythm rather than meaning through the juxtaposition of the lines.

GS The influence of T.S. Eliot's *The Wasteland* looms throughout *Crave*. Did you use the poem as a way of attempting to understand the play?

VF Not at all. I know *The Wasteland* quite well through doing it at 'A' Level. And Sarah had studied it in similar detail, and it's one of those poems that if you study it at that level then the meaning of lines becomes quite a part of you. So that's something that I didn't feel I had to return to in any way because when we approached *Crave* we weren't looking at it to find an ultimate meaning in the bookish way critics did with Eliot's poem. Besides, *Crave* is full of deliberate paradoxes. I also had Sarah with me throughout rehearsal, so I never needed to go elsewhere. I was more concerned with finding ways in which to effectively present *Crave* to an audience. Is it going to be theatrical? This was the constant question I had in my head. What's interesting about *The Wasteland* is that the themes are so intrinsic that you don't have to return to it in order to understand *Crave*. Both the play and the poem share some of these themes such as the emptiness of the urban landscape. So visual metaphors in *Crave*, such as the glow of the city with people standing outside and not being able to escape are very much connected. *Crave* is definitely born out of the city, with the idea of the loneliness of the person isolated in this massive population. But if anything about *The Wasteland* informed me about *Crave*, it would be the ability of the poet or dramatist to move around at will into areas that suit their purpose and allowing their audience to follow them.

GS I know Sarah didn't want to repeat what she thought was Eliot's mistake of explaining individual lines in *The Wasteland*. However, she did provide translations for some of the foreign phrases.

VF Even if we don't understand where something has come from we understand the language which is used, so we can express that with meaning.

GS Is that for the actors or audience?

VF I think it's important to know what those lines mean. If you take a line like, 'a balloon of milk' (177) – If you don't know where that's come from, but you understand the words, you understand the image it evokes. Now of course, if that's spoken in another language you don't even get the image. And of course the actors playing *Crave* have to give each line meaning. It's impossible to play it without. It's a meaning which they own but they don't have to necessarily share that with the rest of the company or with me or Sarah. And I found that very exciting. There were so many possibilities about who people were speaking to at any one time. We played every single option but in the end we came back to where we were in the beginning because the play was so strongly written. What was fascinating about rehearsal was the way that the play was written fed into the way we played it. We rehearsed *Crave* incredibly intensely, but after we'd had our initial discussions about it things were the least pinned down than anything I'd ever worked on. Yet it was also in some ways the most rooted. It was a bizarre process really.

GS I found that to be very much the case with the long speech of A's. It's absolutely grounded in the use of rhythm, but in terms of the context in which it's spoken and the subject to whom it's being addressed is wide open to interpretation.

VF Absolutely. What was interesting about it is that there's one change in the final draft after we performed it. And Simon [Sarah Kane's brother], asked me why she might have changed it, and I looked up the original and it's clear to me now that it was completely guided by rhythm. And much of the way we worked in rehearsal was that if something wasn't right it would literally be a case of too many syllables. One of the conversations I've had with some people about the production was that they felt it was too fast and that they needed more space to ponder the language. But in a way it was deliberately so, and the whole point of the play as Sarah wrote it. Now of course, there have been other productions of the play, but the first production is always the writer's vision – it has to be. And it was absolutely about creating the rhythm through the communication of the lines to the next person. It wasn't about a member of the audience being able to ponder the meaning of each individual line. I think *Crave* was really exciting for Sarah because she'd been able to move into an area that'd been interesting her in terms of writing style. And when it pays off – when it's actually working – then it's incredibly liberating. And I know it sounds odd, but I think with *Crave* Sarah felt that it was quite perfect. And so do I. I really do. In terms of what it is as a piece of writing, it's the most perfect thing I've ever worked on. And I don't think I'll ever work on another piece of writing as perfect as that again. I never thought I'd ever imagine saying that, which is an extraordinary thing. And I think the actors felt that too, in that once we'd found it – it was there for us to find. Structurally, the thing that is interesting is the movement through it, where the voices separate and then come together. I've always had this image in my head of what I'd like to do – and don't get me wrong I never will – but I would almost like to direct a film of *Crave* where I'd be able to show where all the voices were; and where they came together and their location, which I'd be really interested in seeing what that did to it.

GS That image of the voices coming together as a chorus at the end of *Crave* was developed much further in *4.48 Psychosis*. There was also the use of video there too.

VF Which I thought worked really well. It was a fantastic production anyway.

GS Could video be used in the same way in *Crave*?

VF I don't know why you'd use it. One thing – and we'd probably never have done it – was an idea Sarah had in the very early stages, and that was she wanted it to be completely in the dark. It literally at one point was going to be just the voices. However, I don't think it is just all about voices.

GS How far then is *Crave* amenable and flexible to other performance styles, say physical theatre for instance?

VF Well, I don't think it would work at all because I worked with it using Sarah's original intentions, which was absolutely an examination of the rhythm of voices. It wasn't examining the use of text to give another visual form. However, I bet if I knew nothing about it, and just picked up the script I would think of other things to do with it. Nevertheless, I don't think other methods of presenting it would be as good when it's done like that, because you might as well take a piece of poetry by Ted Hughes and perform it in the theatre. And I don't think *Crave* is a piece of poetry that should have a physical side to it – they are four voices in the darkness – and they only exist to speak because people will listen to their sorrow. And this is why I think it's such a perfect piece of writing because it's so pure.

GS Beckett has been mentioned as a strong shaping influence on *Crave*. Did Sarah speak to you about Beckett regarding *Crave*?

VF Yes she did. But you are only ever the sum of people who have influenced you. I think Beckett fascinated her because of his challenge to dramatic form. And Sarah was so hungry to do the same. But it wasn't conscious. I'm sure you know this, but Martin Crimp's *Attempts on Her Life* was a huge influence. I don't think she saw the production but was fascinated by the play, and she spent an afternoon here reading it before writing *Crave*. She was fascinated by that play's use of voice, and the way the voices kept coming in and out. The other thing that interested her was Fassbinder's *Pre-paradise Sorry Now*, which is something I'd always wanted to direct, and it was sitting on the bookshelf here. The thing that comes through from that into *Crave* is the whole liturgy thing of fluidly moving from one person to another.

GS How did the idea of the chat show format as a location come about?

VF When I say it's a play about voices you don't need to show the physical action of what people are doing to each other – it's the emotional action that's coming forward. So there's no way it can be a radio play – absolutely it can't be a radio play with voices coming out of a box. It's about voices in front of you in a theatre. The theatre could be in the dark but you have to be there, and they only exist because of that. My question, along with Georgina Sion's [the designer] was, 'why are they talking?' Can you go to the theatre, and do people just exist? Or do we need to answer the question about why they talk? And one of the things we both felt really strongly about was the massive themes of psychiatry and psychology that were running through it. So when 'C' is talking to 'M' for instance, is she her psychiatrist or has that relationship changed? And we felt that we lived in a society that invites us to unburden our emotional baggage – yet what happens when we do that? Do we take responsibility for that? And we felt that in most cases we didn't, but culture in the West was desperate to encourage people to do this unburdening without taking responsibility. So this was why we went for the idea of a chat show but without making it explicit – so there were the four chairs and why were they there? So if there is any question of the setting it would be only because we want to sit and look at them. So we have to take some responsibility for the fact that they are telling you these stories. It also forces the audience to be active in that process, so if you are a chat show audience you are far more active than a theatre audience. So this is why much of the dialogue was addressed straight to the audience. And the other thing I thought about was the freedom of that format, having four people in front of you. Yet two people are supposedly allied – and that's something you get from the chat show format that gets you going. You can change your allegiances. So this is why the characters move chairs.[1]

GS   'B' and 'M' do that from time to time. They are more in conflict with each other in terms of straight forward argument than 'A' and 'C'.

VF   Yes. They have a story which is played out in front of us whereas 'A' and 'C' have a history where we get the repercussions.

GS   'A' also seems to be the audience's guide.

VF   Yes, sort of. When we started rehearsals we saw him as the chat show host, but we never wanted that to become literal so we got rid of it. So while it was all of their stories he has a massive realisation through all of it, especially about the damage he's inflicted on 'C'. In his head it was done for all the right reasons, but the repercussions of it were so wrong. So when Sarah says 'A' stands for Author and Abuser she would see it as both. That is a paradox – that is a given.

GS   When you saw *4.48 Psychosis* what did you feel were the main connections between the two plays?

VF   There are a lot of image connections. I certainly felt it to be a stage further on from *Crave* in that Sarah had allowed her writing to become totally personal and direct. It was almost a direct address from her which *Crave* is not. And whereas *Crave* was an experiment in rhythm and meaning through rhythm, she didn't need to explore that anymore. She'd now moved on, and was using it for another purpose which was a direct address to the audience. I think that when we were working on *Crave*, we felt it could be really interesting and not that trite nonsense about it being one person – which is so limited. Where you could think of *Crave* possibly being an examination of the psyche, you realised that it hadn't been that at all. Then you saw *4.48 Psychosis* because it gave you an absolute insight into that moment of insanity, which I felt was an extraordinary thing, which takes it away form being a suicide play. And I don't think *Crave* was either, although when we were working on it we thought it was. The last twenty-five minutes of *Crave* when it ends certainly seems to pick up on elements that expand on themselves in *4.48 Psychosis*.

1   In the second British production Featherstone directed in 2001, the characters remained seated throughout the performance.

9

Conversation
with Nils Tabert

16 July 2000

Nils Tabert collaborated on the German translations of *Cleansed* and *Crave*. He is associate at the play agency Rowohlt Theater Verlag who represents Sarah Kane's work in Germany, Austria and German-speaking Switzerland.

GRAHAM SAUNDERS The first question I'd like to ask is how has Sarah Kane's reputation in Germany evolved from 1995 to where we are now? How has her reputation changed or progressed?

NILS TABERT Well, I think by now you can say that in Germany she's considered to be the most important British playwright of the 1990s, definitely the most radical, and also the most well known which started at a rather early stage in her career. When *Blasted* first opened at Hamburg in 1996 it didn't provoke the scandalous reviews it received in England – instead the play was even regarded by some as the arrival of a major talent. Probably Sarah's final 'break-through' moment was when Peter Zadek announced he would direct the first German production of *Cleansed* in 1998. And although at that stage the German critics might not necessarily have started to embrace her plays, from then on most people started to take them very seriously. Of course, this doesn't mean there weren't voices who said, 'these plays are disgusting, preposterous, violence for the sake of violence, pornography etcetera'. But in general most people were quite impressed by her work, and most critics gave her plays glowing reviews. From an early stage they realised their poetic, metaphorical impact. Cynical as it sounds, her death kind of verified that she was absolutely serious, and that it wasn't just effects for effects sake but a disquieting reflection of society and life. But even before her death, when the English production of *Crave* played for three performances in Berlin, most of the formerly 'anti-Kane' critics re-evaluated *Blasted* and *Cleansed*. *Crave* didn't have any violence whatsoever – it was a complete surprise. Every single German review mentioned that this time no babies were eaten or limbs chopped off. They saw it as a very quiet, very desperate, melancholic and elegiac play. So, this re-evaluation happened regardless. It wasn't necessarily because of her suicide – *Crave* showed a new Sarah Kane. Sarah saw this herself. I remember she called from Edinburgh at some stage saying, 'I'm past violence – I'm really sick of it. It's become like *Trainspotting* with film – so marketable and boring and I don't want to deal with it anymore.'

One of the other things that allows her reputation to be reassessed constantly in Germany is our repertoire system, where you don't have this focus on one single production like you do in Britain. Instead, ideally there are lots of competing productions of the same play in different cities. For instance, in 1997 they did *Blasted* in Düsseldorf a couple of months after the Hamburg production, which had an interesting approach with the Soldier being black, which is even more brutal, with Ian being raped by someone from the Third World. Sarah quite liked this idea.

GS   What was the main conclusion drawn in Germany by the ending of *Blasted*? Edward Bond makes a perceptive point when he says the end of *Blasted* should not be about two individuals left stranded in a hotel room but the collapse of a whole world.

NT   That's exactly how a lot of critics saw it, but it was easier for them because they knew about the reactions to *Blasted* in Britain. Besides, most of them had already read the play, because we'd sent out the script a week before the opening in Hamburg. Also, Sarah came over to do an extensive press conference and in a way we had made sure that it wasn't the scandalous nature of *Blasted* which would be the centre of attention, but rather let people see the play as a piece of art, as a drama about war, about gender and a dysfunctional society. *Blasted* had a huge impact on them, and there were some extremely astute and bright reviews, realising that this wasn't necessarily a naturalistic well made play. Although, to be more precise, it is to a certain degree, up to the point where the Soldier enters. And then it starts to turn into a nightmare – a surreal and uncomfortably real nightmare.

So basically it was a good start for Sarah in Germany, and it became almost a ritual with the follow-up productions of *Blasted* – a majority of very good reviews, and two or three nasty ones. It was only *Phaedra's Love* which didn't have a spectacular German premiere; the circumstances of the production were rather unfortunate – the director fell ill during the process of rehearsal, so somebody else had to take over.

GS How did that production look at the end?

NT Very understated and stylised. They had a fantastic Hippolytus, and a great Phaedra, and the long scene between Phaedra and Hippolytus in the middle of the play was wonderful – very funny and quite shocking and brutal on an emotional level. But they kind of avoided facing the formal challenges which *Phaedra's Love* confronts you with. Because until the very last scene it's a chamber piece – there are only two people on stage and then suddenly it's loads of people coming on for Hippolytus' execution. Instead, at Schauspiel Bonn which first produced *Phaedra's Love* in 1998, they had Phaedra coming back on stage after her death, narrating the last scene, including the stage directions, like in a dream. The stage was bathed in a thin blue light, and it was all very simple and actually quite effective, but I thought there was a bit of cowardice in this concept of not dealing with this final monstrous scene.

GS Did Sarah see that production?

NT No she didn't. I told her about it, then asked whether she would like to come over and see it, but she didn't think it a good idea. She only saw three German productions – a run-through of the Hamburg production of *Blasted* in September 1996, the production of *Blasted* in Vienna in March 1998, and Zadek's production of *Cleansed* in December 1998.

GS Where does the fascination for her work come from in Germany? Is it a particular aspect of the plays?

NT Yes, it's mainly the plays. They really appeal to German theatre, especially since German theatre is obsessed with form, and one of the great aspects of Sarah's plays is that they do tell stories, which for a long time in Germany was looked down upon. They do connect with society; they are even highly political but in a formally challenging, very complex and poetic way. It's the heightened realism which makes her plays so fascinating to us, and they don't have 'messages' and they don't offer easy solutions. Also, of course, the powerful images and the fact they are so language driven, so very economical and precise in their plotting and characterisation are other strong points.

German theatre is not exactly fond of naturalism / realism or well-made plays in general, so the reaction to Sarah from the very beginning was quite enthusiastic because she seemed to 'deconstruct' these paradigms. She subverted them – there is very little psychology in her plays, they are never explicit, very little is explained. Things just happen and you have to make up your own mind what it means, like in poems. Characters are not analysing themselves, or give any explanation of themselves. They're just there and this is something which was considered to be, and still is considered to be, an important aspect of her work. And of course at the moment *Crave* is – with fifteen productions – one of the most popular plays currently produced in Germany by a European dramatist.

GS   Why *Crave* particularly, and not say *Phaedra's Love* or *Blasted*?

NT   Because German theatre is also a director's theatre. The author is not necessarily the sole centre of the production, unlike in Britain or America. To a certain extent in Germany the director becomes something like a second author. And *Crave* gives a lot of freedom to a director, because nothing is given; there are hardly any stage directions, only things like '*a beat*', or '*silence*'. So directors can let their imagination go, because you don't even have fixed characters in the conventional sense. This means that all the productions of *Crave* I've seen so far couldn't differ more from each other. I haven't seen all of them, but I've seen Thomas Ostermeiers's production for instance.

GS   What was it like?

NT   Very strict, very formal, with hardly any movement. There are four people on stage. It's the equivalent to the original production's cast of two men and two women – but even that isn't given in the script. They are on four separate huge pillars and within the pillars there are sometimes blurred video projections. Every now and then they are switched on and it's like the images of bodies floating in space, or embryos. But it's basically four people on pillars with microphones which they use on occasions. They are not talking to each other, but more or less to the audience or to themselves. It follows the script very conscientiously, without any changes or cuts. This is worth mentioning because most German directors tend to make cuts in scripts, but I don't think they can do it with *Crave*.

GS   This throws up a contradiction in Sarah's work, because her plays almost invite a 'director's theatre' approach, while she herself was very suspicious of people tampering with her work. I was surprised to learn for instance that she seemed to enjoy a Belgian production of *Blasted* where they made the baby the focus of the play.

NT I mean I can see why she didn't like the Hamburg production of *Blasted*. Again, this was a production that kept close to the script and had great actors. But it had this kind of Tarantino-like attitude, and she though this to be very cynical – a glossy and trendy approach to violence.

GS Were the sex scenes graphic?

NT The whole production was done a bit like a peep-show. The set was a realistic hotel room, but the audience was sitting around it, so there weren't any hidden angles or anything. The sex scenes were especially difficult for the actors – blocking them without showing too much, without being pornographic. And while I really admired them for how they did it, Sarah for understandable reasons thought it all wrong. It was too much 'in your face' – it lacked sensitivity, fragility and subtlety. It was more about the physical violence rather than the mental, emotional violence.

GS How did the production handle the baby eating scene?

NT Ian's shown eating a baby. I mean it was a prop of course – chicken or something. But he really ate the meat which was absolutely terrifying. A few people walked out at that moment. Some of them walked out earlier – not many actually, but for some people that finally did it. You had this subtle sound of tiny bones being broken which was horrible. But you know, even that in Germany didn't cause a scandal, because most people are used to German theatre being quite extreme. And for most critics, again it was more of an image which some of them hated, but most of them were – I won't say at ease with it – but they didn't react as if this mustn't be shown on stage.

GS Has Sarah influenced the current generation of German dramatists?

NT I think she has. Together with Mark Ravenhill, Sarah is quite influential. As said earlier, Sarah has reintroduced to German theatre the idea that you can be challenging in a formal way, but not forget about content in the process – or forget about so called social reality. She reminded German dramatists that you can do both: that you can write politically like in *Blasted*, *Phaedra's Love* or even *Cleansed* without dealing with reality in a journalistic way – that you can work it into some kind of poetry or work of art. I think that's basically what she introduced, or reintroduced into the theatre.

It was rather encouraging for young German playwrights, of not having to shy away from telling stories, of being allowed again to have some kind of narrative, which was in a way out of fashion in the early to mid-1990s in Germany, when theatre had become formal to the extent of being almost inaccessible.

GS I wanted to speak about the translation of *Cleansed*. Walter Benjamin said that a translation shouldn't be a literal copy of a work, but should try to reproduce the effect of the original. Were you happy that your translation did that at the end with *Cleansed*?

NT I have to say that most of the translation of *Cleansed* was done by Elisabeth Plessen and Peter Zadek. I had made a rather literal translation of the script which I then gave to Elisabeth and Zadek, and they reworked it completely. Elisabeth is a renowned writer in Germany and they dared to move away from the literal translation, to save the images and to save the rhythm because Sarah is so very precise with words. And they did a wonderful job with it.

I hadn't dared to get too far away from the original, especially since there are so many parallels and references in the script – recurring echoes for instance with the word 'clean'. In English the same word can mean so many things – like clean from drugs, cleansed in a religious sense or cleansed as in ethnic cleansing.

So at first, I tried to translate it with the same word which ended up sounding totally clumsy. And then Zadek and Elisabeth rightly said, 'well, on an academic level this is fine, but theatrically it just doesn't work. It sounds stilted and over-constructed'. So they had the courage and the competence to decide that you have to change the word sometimes, to save the atmosphere of the scene and to capture the poetry. So in the end, and as little as possible, we varied between *Gesäubert*, which became the German title of the play and also alludes more to ethnic cleansing. *Gereinigt* leans more to the religious context, and 'clean' as in free from drugs. Of course, Sarah was involved in this process and we also discussed at length the choice of word for the German title.

GS Were there any specific examples where the language barrier was a real problem?

NT It always is with Sarah's plays. I mean, it was very difficult to translate *Blasted*. For instance, there were elliptical phrases where you had to be very careful, especially with the missing subject. In English, instead of, 'I don't want to', it's 'Don't want to' etcetera. And if you do that in German too often it sounds very dull and unappealing. So that was a delicate balance between a) putting the subject back in sometimes, because otherwise it would reduce the characters to stupid cartoon figures or b) skipping them at other moments when the German language would allow.

GS So, in *Blasted* for example, the waiter is black. Was that kept in the German translation?

NT Yes, he was. That wasn't a problem at all. You do have a lot of racism in Germany too, so words like 'wog' which are used in *Blasted* have many German equivalents – that was the easy bit. The problem is more with tiny little phrases like, 'save me' in *Cleansed*. Again, it means 'save me from this terrible situation', and 'save me' in the religious sense. And again, it's different words in German. It's *rette mich* and *erlöse mich*, and both have different contexts.

GS Were there problems in preserving the rhythm of her language?

NT Well, we did our very best in trying to solve them. You have to be as brief and precise as possible, and sometimes it's even like counting syllables, working to musical patterns. And sometimes you don't succeed and a line becomes a little bit longer, so you just have to use one more word.

GS When you were translating *Blasted* did Sarah collaborate much in the process?

NT Well I could phone her whenever I needed her, and she would phone when there were further changes. And she would answer questions very patiently and extensively. The titles of the plays were always a bit of a problem, not only with *Cleansed* where, after discussing this with Sarah, we finally went for the meaning of ethnic cleansing, *Gesäubert*, mainly because it sounded better. *Gereinigt*, the religious aspect, in German would also have references to dry cleaning which would have been rather awkward!

Sarah was worried at one stage about the German title of *Phaedra's Love* which for her means Hippolytus. It's more the object of Phaedra's love which she wanted to underline rather than the emotion itself. In Germany the play is called *Phaidra's Liebe* which, when you first hear it, is more about the emotion of love. But then I think it's the same in English when hearing *Phaedra's Love*.

Whenever questions like these would arise, or questions concerning details of the script, you could phone her. She even agreed to changing the order of two lines in the meeting with Hippolytus and the Priest – it just sounded better in German. The good thing is that she could read German to a certain extent – not that she understood everything, but she had some sense of the language and this was important because brevity and precision of expression were important to her. With *Cleansed* she once said, 'I've finished the script and now I'm chopping away the unimportant bits'.

GS One question that always puzzles me in *Cleansed* concerns the woman in the booth. Everybody has a different interpretation of her role. Did Sarah explain her function during the translation process?

NT No, she never gave an explanation of the second Grace.

GS Is she the second Grace?

NT No. She is not. I remember Zadek asking Sarah at one stage whether she should be played by the same actress, and Sarah said absolutely not – they are two different women.

GS Did the Hamburg production of *Cleansed* keep the same songs?

NT Yes they did. And they also did the same dances. The only thing they didn't keep was the rats, because Zadek did a very literal, very realistic production of the script, and within that concept the only logical solution would have been to have real rats. Not stylised rats like they had in London, but real rats. That was Zadek's original aim. They even wanted to hire a rat trainer but he told them that rats couldn't carry these heavy items offstage such as a human hand. Then they thought of having real-looking mechanical rats instead but quickly abandoned the idea, since everybody would have noticed this as a special effect. So in the end Sarah agreed to having the rats cut. It's a shame really. I would have liked to see the rats. It's such a strong image. It's like the apocalypse – the only surviving creatures. Like cockroaches rats are hard to eradicate …

GS Your interview with Sarah was fascinating[1] because it solved a lot of problems with her sources for *Cleansed* – things like *Woyzeck*, Orwell's *Nineteen Eighty-Four*, Strindberg's *The Ghost Sonata* and Kafka's *The Trial*. Did the German productions produce echoes of those sources?

NT I don't know whether Zadek used any additional material to the play in the rehearsal process, but he definitely didn't in the final performance. He only kept asking Sarah questions about the relationship of the characters and the meaning of individual lines. The only thing the production added was using a 'Brechtian curtain' in the set. They didn't have the individual rooms, only the lighting changed according to the colours given in the script. Sometimes for scene changes, and the scenes with Rod and Carl inside the perimeter fence a curtain would be drawn. For Zadek, constantly changing the set would have meant having longer intervals between the scenes which would have destroyed the rhythm of the show.

GS One of the other revealing things in your interview with Sarah was a comment she made about all her dramatic characters being misunderstood – that they're Romantic figures in the tradition of Keats and Shelley, or Goethe and Schiller. Do you recognize these similarities?

NT I do. They're extreme in their desire, their longing and commitment as far as love and relationships are concerned. It's like *Die Leiden des jungen Werthers* by Goethe.[2]

---

1 See 'Gespräch mit Sarah Kane' in Nils Tabert (ed.), *Playspotting. Die Londoner Theaterszene der 90er* (Reinbeck, 1998), pp. 8-21.
2 *The Sorrows of Young Werther.*

GS Which has been said to have been a source for *4.48 Psychosis*.[3]

NT I think you can see traces of Werther. It's this never ending longing
    and the rejection of society where there is no real place for emotions
    like that. His feelings are so extreme, so strong and overwhelming.
    Which is also a very beautiful, painful and frightening, but absolutely
    Romantic. An individual hands themselves over to another individ-
    ual and this Other becomes themselves – they forget about them-
    selves because they are so lost in the other person. I think the
    characters in *Cleansed* do this too – Grace with her brother for
    instance. It's very difficult to see where the separating line is between
    them. And it's also there with Rod and Carl.

GS *Cleansed* has been described as an Artaudian play. Has that been
    picked up in Germany?

NT Not in a literal sense, but Artaud's concept of Total Theatre is almost
    a paradigm in German theatre. Not in this cliched sense of scream-
    ing and shouting all the time, or being extremely physical and going
    berserk, but that theatre should appeal to all the senses, and that it
    requires actors to act without a safety net. I think Sarah's plays –
    among other things – have the same quality. They are risky and
    exhausting for actors and directors, but at the same time very enrich-
    ing.

---

3 Sarah Kane's agent Mel Kenyon maintains that *4.48 Psychosis* as a play was already
   being written when Nick Philippou from the Actor's Touring Company suggested a
   direct adaptation of Goethe's epistolary novel, and while the theme of suicide is
   common to both, the play shares no direct influences from the novel. See Simon
   Hattenstone's article in *Guardian Weekend*, 1 July 2000.

10

Conversation with Mel Kenyon

13 November 2000

Mel Kenyon is Sarah Kane's agent.

GRAHAM SAUNDERS The first question I'd like to ask is what is the state of play with Sarah Kane's drama? For instance, I saw a review for a play by Joanna Laurens at the Gate Theatre[1] and it was talking about the similarities between this young playwright and Sarah Kane. Do you see a legacy emerging whereby young writers are taking themes and ideas form her work?

MEL KENYON No. I think it's critical shorthand. I know the Joanna Laurens play and it doesn't resemble Sarah's work in any way, shape or form at all. So it's a form of critical short-hand because it's based on the Philomela myth. So because the play's on at the Gate, like *Phaedra's Love*, and because Joanna, like Sarah, is a young woman, the critics make a literal connection. Such criticism also elevates the play. It kind of imbues it with longevity. To date, none of the writers I know of have consciously sought out the work of Sarah Kane and copied it. Of course, that may happen over time. All writers who are any good know their theatre history: what has gone before. They absorb everything. Use everything. However, any writer who is any good will also be unique. So if there are spare, derivative little plays

1   *The Three Birds,* November 2000.

– and I'm sure there will be – they'll probably be rather bad. If Sarah's work eventually does influence other talented writers, the influence will be oblique and tangential and we probably won't make an obvious connection between the new play and Sarah Kane's work. Even so, it's a testament to Sarah as a playwright that the work is being performed all the time. The only problem now is that with her death people can be attracted to the work for the wrong reasons. One tries to steer clear of granting rights to productions where the only relationship the producers / directors have with the work is one of subjective emotion – a depressive empathy. I don't want to see people doing Sarah's work who see it solely as an articulation of their own despair. So, on the one hand, the work is being reassessed in good faith, and on the other, it is being elevated out of a kind of wilful despair. Someone said to me, 'well of course everyone loves a dead girl, especially if she was talented'. And it's true, Sarah has no right of reply anymore.

GS   What do you take from the positive reassessment?

MK   It allows you an intellectual overview of the work you normally don't get in quite the same way dealing with the writer on a day to day basis. For instance, recently David Greig wrote a very sensible introduction to her collected plays. His reassessment of the work is warm but also very incisive and objective. When we talked he spoke about her use of disembodiment and sense of fragmentation, the use of the authorial voice etcetera. For me that's quite a positive thing. It allowed me to look at the work from a different perspective. I can now examine the body of work and see recurrent motifs, her particular use of imagery and so on. I think if that happens it's only to the good.

GS   One of the things that surprises me about the plays in Britain is that after a period of five years there hasn't been a major revival of say Blasted or Phaedra's Love.[2]

MK   I think there are two things going on. One, the work is very much associated with the Royal Court and James Macdonald. And two, I think the work is quite difficult to produce in the regions. And one has to be quite ruthless with oneself about who her audience actually was and how finite the numbers were. A mythology can grow up. Sarah was an extraordinary talented woman. However, one could never claim she was a populist writer. She was a popular writer in that she had a cult following who would come back and see her work

---

2   Blasted, Crave and 4.48 Psychosis, together with rehearsed readings of Phaedra's Love and Cleansed, were part of a Sarah Kane season at the Royal Court Theatre which ran from April to June 2001.

more than once, but that particular audience is finite. I do think one has to be rational about things now she's dead. For instance, *Cleansed* was produced by the English Stage Company (a.k.a the Royal Court) at the Duke of York's Theatre but it did not attract big houses. She was a particular kind of writer, and there are a lot of people, who have worked a twelve hour day in a difficult job and are stressed out, who may not want to sit through *Cleansed* or *Blasted*. I don't admire them but I can't blame them – the plays are gruelling.

So, in terms of major revivals I'm not sure I know what that means. I think students will study the work, and academics will write about the work and I'm sure the work will now be remembered. Sarah said in her last letter, 'these are not museum pieces. I want these plays performed'. So I don't want to get too precious. Sarah was a theatre animal. The plays are visceral in every sense of the word. So Simon [*Sarah Kane's brother*] and I want to keep promoting the work for theatrical performance. Sarah would have hated to have become an academic's darling.

GS I'd like to talk about the beginning of your relationship with Sarah Kane. We both saw the first production of *Blasted* at the Allardyce Nicoll Studio in Birmingham back in 1993. It was an extraordinary powerful performance. I was wondering if you could say something about that process of seeing the work for the first time and the eventual debut of the full play at the Royal Court in January 1995.

MK Yep. I saw the first half and thought the writing was absolutely terrific. Even talking about it now the hair on my arms stands up which is always a good sign. A physical response to something unique. After the first half finished you could hear a pin drop. Sarah then got up and passionately defended the play from the detractors in the audience. I thought, 'God she's talented but she's going to be a handful'. After leaving Birmingham that first half of *Blasted* would not leave my head – the writing was exquisite, passionate, spare, raw, truthful and the relationship between Cate and Ian was extraordinary. Sarah's use of the space and silence was brilliant. In fact it was her use of silence that was the most extraordinary thing.

So, I wrote to her and asked if I could see the second half. The play duly arrived and as we now know the hotel room explodes and the socio-realistic becomes increasingly surreal. It was an odd experience reading it for the first time because in a strange sort of way the play is both beautifully controlled and yet completely uncontrolled. This mirrors the way she combines her linguistic spareness with an energy and anger which feeds it.

I couldn't ignore the play so I rang her. Typically Sarah said, 'I'm talking to Leah Schimdt so you'd better get a move on.' I then asked her to meet me. So, she sauntered in. And she was sort of hunched up in the corner. We had this strange exchange about the play, but I got the feeling that Sarah was the real thing. By this I mean when I start talking with playwrights I soon get the sense of whether they are the real thing or not because of the way they talk about theatre. And I knew we were going to have a tempestuous but very fruitful relationship. So I was pleasantly surprised when she rang up and went, 'Alright then. I'll come to you'. I then said, 'actually there's only one place we can take this play to which is the Royal Court, and only one man there who could do it justice which is James Macdonald'. Although James is very quiet and ruminative, I'd been at script meetings with him and I knew the way he reacted to particular types of work. So then the Court read the play and acquired the rights relatively quickly but kept not programming it. Sarah and I got quite distressed because we increasingly got the feeling there was some kind of dissent in the building. The Court committed to Judy Upton and Nick Grosso and Joe Penhall. I kept thinking that we were going further back in the queue. The Court then did a reading of the whole play with Sam Kelly playing Ian. Again I remember having a physical response to it. I almost felt I couldn't stand up properly at the end. I felt I'd been through a fight and you've come out the other end. And I remember thinking, 'if they don't do this they're insane'. However, there wasn't a battle with them to do this play – there was just this delay.

Then they programmed it for January [1995]. And I had said to Sarah, 'you know the critics might hate this?' However, I also said, 'they may hate this but none of them can deny the quality of the writing'. So what surprised me was not that the critics didn't universally hail the play, but the unanimity and foolishness and the specious nature of their critique. Michael Coveney was intelligent and I think Paul Taylor was quite bright about it. As for the rest, I just couldn't understand how they could take such umbrage – that they couldn't see line by line how gifted Sarah was. Then the media machine started rolling. Remember, she was very young and so I felt incredibly protective. I'm not sure that the Court quite knew what they had on their hands. But I'm sure they hadn't prefigured that response.

On the Press night critics didn't get the play from the outset; it wasn't entirely their fault because the set was not how Sarah had envisaged it. It was supposed to be one of the most opulent hotel rooms in the world and it actually looked like a bed-sit. So Ian's first line, 'I've shat in better places than this', which should immediately set up the play's black sense of humour and the ironic counterpoint between what you see and what you hear, simply didn't work. If that line is taken literally then the play has a completely different tone right from the start. That night the play lost its sense of humour. So, although I still can't forgive the critics their reaction I do, to some extent understand their misreading of the play. If you strip the work of its humour you deprive it of much of its charm.

Sarah had this wonderful gallows sense of humour, and now she's dead it would be awful if directors start doing laboured, self-important productions. Sarah was very funny and very vivacious and her work was a reflection of every aspect of her being. Even *4.48 Psychosis* is hilariously funny in parts.

GS Going back to the debut of *Blasted* – I saw the early drafts of the play from Birmingham, and there were small but significant differences to the final production at the Royal Court such as Cate sucking her thumb and explicit references to the Yugoslavian war. How much work did Sarah do on *Blasted* from 1993 to the beginning of 1995?

MK Often I give very specific notes to writers but every single writer is different. And while Sarah always wanted to have my opinion, whether she actually welcomed criticism is something else entirely. I always had to be very careful in the way I responded to her work because I knew I could hurt her. So, on the one hand, she desperately wanted my opinion, and on the other, she didn't want any adverse criticism. I had to be very measured and careful. So, as far as I was concerned, the writing and rewriting process was very private to her. Even though she would show me every draft and ask me for comments, I can't pretend to have had the open dialogue about the work in the way I have with others. She wanted me to respond more to the spirit of the work and give very broad comments. She didn't want a line by line or scene by scene breakdown. She was also one of the most private writers I know. She often wrote at night – she wouldn't ring me until midday because she hadn't got up, or she'd ring up and sound really tired because she'd been up all night writing and smoking.

As to her writing process, I think she fully informed herself – she wrote and rewrote. She'd ring up and say, 'this is a fucking brilliant play I'm writing now', then she'd ring up two weeks later and say, 'It's shit – it's utter shit and it's going in the bin'. I wouldn't have seen any of this new play at that point. And then eight, ten, twelve weeks later she'd come in with a package. Sarah was a woman who compartmentalised her life, so she only showed you certain aspects of herself.

I wonder who got to see the whole Sarah. I probably knew eight tenths of her and you respect that. We often spoke about everything under the sun except writing – most often about sex – sex and sadness.

GS Which is most often what her plays come down to in the end.

MK She was a romantic – an incredible romantic. My theory, although I could be wrong here, is that she had this overwhelming feeling for romantic love, and that there were two ways of looking at it. She craved a fulfilling and successful relationship, but was torn by the thought that in giving yourself fully to another you have to negate yourself in some way; and in doing so you literally disappear. She didn't know if this was a good thing or a bad thing. She questioned whether there was a power thing going on in all relationships, and would punishment necessarily be a part of it? I think she was trying to look for equality in relationships, and a lot of the relationships in her plays are about inequality. In her own life and her work she was striving for total honesty, but she always asked the question that if one person is totally honest with another aren't they going to risk being brutal? There's that wonderful speech between Carl and Rod in *Cleansed*, 'I love you *now*. I'm with you *now*. I'll do my best moment to moment not to betray you. Now. That's it. No more. Don't make me lie to you.' It's extraordinary but also quite cruel. It's saying, 'don't ask me for anything else. This is it.' She had a very complex response to it, but most of the work in some way, shape or form is about love.

GS Yet they are impossible loves. So for instance there's the line in *4.48 Psychosis*, 'Body and soul can never be married' (212).

MK It doesn't surprise me that there's increasing disembodiment. If you look at the series of plays there's an increasing sense of fragmentation which started very early on – both physically and psychologically. It's a linear progression in the work. And I think that was what she was doing – trying to get closer to the particular conflict that she felt very acutely. Most of us are at war with ourselves but Sarah made it manifest in her work. She discussed every aspect of her inner conflict. She realised her perception of the world and asked how can anyone live in it. Let's face it, most plays are about how one can survive in this world.

GS That conflict seems to be most manifest with *Crave*. Were you surprised at the sudden change in style?

MK Remember that *Crave* was written under a pseudonym, and she did a typical Sarah thing. We were going to the reading at Paines Plough. She walked into my office and she said, 'I've written it under a pseudonym so whatever you say afterwards, whatever you think; just say you liked it then we'll talk about it afterwards. But I think they'll fucking hate it.' And of course she knew damn well that I wouldn't hate it. I sat through it and thought it was absolutely extraordinary. In an odd sort of way she may have been liberated by disposing of her own name and the identity that went with it. So it didn't really surprise me that it came about under those circumstances. *Crave* is one play that, in the first instance, she wrote very quickly. However, she went back to it repeatedly. And even though it marks some change, and is linguistically different it still has the same obsessions. By the end of the play she had disembodied herself as the author. The fact that it is a play for voices makes perfect sense as the fact that *4.48 Psychosis* comes immediately afterwards. *Crave* is also different because it came out of a new professional relationship with Vicky Featherstone. I know Sarah was very happy at Paines Plough, and they provided her with a kind of comfort zone. She was also helping other writers. And although it was a difficult period for her at that time she had a lot of material to draw upon. In a strange sort of way she was returning to previous methodology. The very early work pre-*Blasted* mainly took the form of monologues. They were very good but adolescent. So there was a strange symmetry.[3]

GS I'd like to backtrack a little and ask you something of the genesis of *Phaedra's Love*. How did it come about, and was it a way of breaking the association of Sarah becoming 'a Royal Court dramatist'?

MK If I can remember correctly, the Gate rang us and asked Sarah if she'd like to do an adaptation of a classical drama. I encouraged her to do it because after *Blasted* she was very exhausted and upset. Second plays are notoriously difficult to write anyway. So I thought it would be a good experience – she'd flex different writing muscles. I also saw it as a way of keeping her going as a writer – and I don't just mean financially. With Paines Plough, Mark Ravenhill was still literary manager, and he came in and said they needed a writer in residence. And I laughed and said, 'you know what Paines Plough needs? They need Sarah Kane'. And he went away and came back and said, 'yes, it's a brilliant idea'. By that time Vicky had taken over as Artistic Director. It all worked out extraordinarily well. A writer's life is quite solitary and one tries to give them a sense of security, so they can go back to their room to write the plays that must be written.

---

3 In August 1991 Sarah Kane performed *Comic Monologue*, part of piece called *Dreams / Screams*, with Vincent O'Connell (*Sore Throats Theatre Company*) in a double-bill with David Greig, at the Edinburgh Festival Fringe. In August 1992 Kane performed two further monologues, *Starved* and *What She Said*, with Vincent O'Connell, again at Edinburgh.

So there wasn't a plan to get her away from the Court – they'd been wonderful to her. It was more a case of keeping her writing and bringing in some money so she could keep body and soul together. She also made some forays into television, but she was so unhappy with that working process I was not surprised she gave up on it.

GS What sort of projects was she involved in?

MK She wrote an embryonic screenplay which I liked.

GS What was that about?

MK Oh, two girls ... and some of it was actually very moving, and some of it hilariously funny. And she wrote *Skin* of course.

GS Was the actual writing of *Skin* conceived before *Blasted* made its debut?

MK No, as far as I know, it was written after *Blasted*. I didn't instigate the project. Again, I remember reading the first draft and finding it very funny. It subsequently got less funny, although it would've probably been difficult to capture that sort of humour on-screen. The first draft was 16–20 minutes long, and they had to cut it down to 11 minutes. Sarah has also made it clear that none of the plays must ever be reproduced in any other media whatsoever. I think that says something both about Sarah and her relationship to the other media.

GS Even wireless?

MK No. They wanted to do *Crave* for the radio but she was adamant and quite clear.

GS That's a shame because I think it would work perfectly as a play for the wireless.

MK So do I, but in a strange kind of way, I do quite like the way Sarah won't let it happen. The character's physical presence is so entirely necessary.

GS Were there any partly realised or unfinished stage projects outstanding at the time of her death?

MK There were the very early monologues.[4] She saw them as juvenilia and reminded me that I turned them down when I was working at the Royal Court. And then as I said, for the screen there was this teleplay she never really completed. She'd been very clear with the producers beforehand. She told them exactly what she was going to do. The fact that the viewers would never see the protagonist – you would just see fragments of her. The play was to be about anorexia, and it was all going to be from her point of view. So, if the character were to open a cupboard you they would just see her hand. When she

---

4 Sarah Kane made known that the monologues were not to be performed after her death.

had written the first draft the producers got cold feet. And I suppose her reaction to them underscored why we got on so well. I remember at that time she went into a script meeting with these people and they said, 'we don't think we can do the script in the way you've written it'. And she said, 'but I told you this is what I was going to do. You were thrilled with the idea and now I've executed the idea'. And she had done it very well, so it was a case of, 'why don't you want to do it'? So, the producers rang me and I said, 'she was absolutely clear with you about what she was going to do. If you're too scared and frightened to take it any further that's fine'. And that's why working in television and film was alien to her.

She had also been commissioned by the RSC to write a new play and by Sphinx Theatre to do an adaptation of *Medea* which would have been exciting if she had been able to realise it.

GS Absolutely! Going back to *Cleansed*, was that a difficult project to realise, also in terms of interesting the Royal Court? It was not only her first production on the main stage but also a very ambitious project.

MK I think emotionally it was a play that cost her quite a lot. And I do remember the first time I read it, lying on the bed in my old flat. It was one of the only times I had real difficulty in knowing what to say about a play. I do remember just crying, and I don't know why it was with that particular play. I rang her and said, 'I'm not going to give you any notes on this. I'm not sure I can.' And she came back, 'well, that means you hated it'. And I replied, 'No I didn't, but I think I'm going to have a very difficult relationship with this play'. She did and I did.

GS It certainly took her a long time to write. Did she start writing *Cleansed* immediately after *Blasted* - even before taking up the commission for *Phaedra's Love*?

MK Well, she was going to write a trilogy, the third one of which hasn't been realised. I think *Cleansed* was a slow burner. We spoke about it relatively early on, shortly after *Blasted* came out. She did have a strange relationship with that play. For instance she'd say, 'It's crap isn't it? I know it's crap.' And then in the next breath she'd say, 'It's my best play ever'. So her relationship to *Cleansed* was volatile. And while I admired it, I'm not sure I fell in love with it ever. I felt there was a lot of Sarah's writing peccadilloes and personal obsessions woven into it, and at times I find it incredibly powerful and at other times I think, 'no, you've done this once too often. Don't make us go through this again. Don't put yourself through this again.'

Anyway we took it to the Court who commissioned it quite quickly, although again it took them a long time to put it on – in fact it took them so long they had to renew the rights after twelve months. Then I got a call from Ian Rickson who'd just taken over as Artistic Director, who said, 'you're going to be very pleased with me. I'm putting *Cleansed* on Downstairs at the Duke of York's Theatre.' My feelings were a mixture of elation and fear. I wanted to ask, 'Are you sure? Is that space too big? Will it work? Will it find the audience?' I should've been ecstatically happy, and in a way I suppose I was, but there is always this kind of wariness in me around *Cleansed*.

GS So there was always an assumption that it would be done in a far smaller space?

MK Yes. I'd always assumed it was going to go to the Ambassadors Theatre which is actually quite a nice space with two hundred or so seats, so I kind of envisaged it there. Obviously if we had tried to do it in the old Royal Court Theatre Upstairs it would've looked cramped.

I'm being really honest about the play. I had a difficult relationship with it, but so did Sarah. She was trying something very novel in terms of its image structure. I remember having a long conversation with her about the notion of setting the play in a university and whether it would make sense in a literal as well as metaphorical way. I was sure the metaphor of the play would work, but I was never quite sure if all the elements were there to convey the literal sense of the play. Sometimes I still think that's the case. However, the more I know about the play, the more the emotional journeys the characters make connects with me. Sometimes I think that the iconography is too private to Sarah. Yet, I also find the play incredibly generous because there is that space and that openness to interpretation. Perhaps that's what has made it so successful on the continent. Even so, I think she imagined every moment very clearly.

GS Which comes through I suppose in her interest for directing things such as *Phaedra's Love* and *Woyzeck*.

MK I actually thought she was a very good director. If I was going to put my hand on my heart I'd say she was a far better director than she was an actress.

GS Which she herself has also admitted. What was her method of directing like? Did you ever sit in on rehearsals.

MK No, but I think she had a very clear idea of how things would look and how they would work. And certainly with the *Woyzeck* she had a crystal clear vision of how it would look. It was rendered very straightforward and true, and I wish a little more people would direct with such a sense of purpose. It was like her writing – seemingly simple but intellectually complex and emotionally very wrought. With *Phaedra's Love* someone else had been directing it but

Sarah and she fell out with each other. I think Sarah found it a very difficult experience watching someone else do the work when she knew how it was to be done.

GS And finally *4.48 Psychosis* ...

MK Yes. What can I say? She gave me a first draft shortly before she died. She rang and rang the same afternoon and was desperate for notes. A response. It was unlike her to be like that. So I read it overnight and we talked the next day, on a Saturday afternoon. She actually demanded close reading of *4.48*. She wanted notes in a way that she hadn't before. It now makes perfect sense. We looked at some particular passages and then we discussed the role of the doctor and lovers, and the music of the play, and whether the play was for three voices; and the sex, or sense of sex of the characters; and how oblique and obscure she could afford to be and still render the play meaningful to people in general; and how funny she should be and so on. And within days she had made her first suicide attempt. It was on a Tuesday. She left a package, and the play – revised – was in the package. I was asked to go and see her in hospital, and I did, and we laughed about everything; and she was very calm and very serene. Two days later she was dead. I then received *4.48* and couldn't read it for a while. When I did, it was very difficult to be objective. But over time it became easier. I remember James [Macdonald] coming in to see me when he read the play, and we spent a few hours talking about it; and it reminded me of why I had liked Sarah's work so much: the humour, the potent imagery, her incredible use of language and her emotional rawness. It made it much easier to accept what had happened even though I'm still angry that she felt she had to dig so deep to write the last play that she couldn't find another way out.

11

Conversation
with Phyllis Nagy
17 July 2000

Phyllis Nagy's plays include *Weldon Rising* (Royal Court Theatre / Liverpool Play-house, 1992); *Butterfly Kiss* (Almeida Theatre, 1994); *Disappeared* (Leiceister Haymarket / UK Tour / Royal Court Theatre, 1995); *The Strip* (Royal Court Theatre, 1995); *Never Land* (Royal Court Theatre, 1998); *The Talented Mr Ripley* (Palace Theatre Watford, 1998).

GRAHAM SAUNDERS Sarah Kane has been described as a theatrical magpie, in that you can find bits of Samuel Beckett, John Webster and Shakespeare in her work. Was this something you recognised in her work?

PHYLLIS NAGY I would not call her a theatrical magpie. It's one of the peculiar characteristics of British and American theatre criticism to describe all new plays in relation to work that's preceded them – reviewers do this in an effort to try to describe what is sometimes indescribable – they say, 'this is like that'. And the moment that any writer admits, 'well, yes once I read x play, or while I was writing this play I read x poem', critics seize on it and they don't let go – whether or not it was relevant. I don't think that any truly talented writer sits down to write with such conscious references to other work in their heads. It would be impossible to write anything that wasn't hugely derivative of anything else. On the other hand – all good writers do carry such references around with them – like pocket change, to be used whenever and however they suit. There's nothing wrong with that, and to describe it as magpie behaviour seems a bit unfair.

GS The one play where I suppose the borrowing is most apparent comes in *Crave* where on several occasions direct quotations are used from T.S. Eliot's *The Wasteland*.

PN It might be fair to say she's borrowed some of the thematic concerns of *The Wasteland* – but who hasn't, from time to time? She certainly hasn't borrowed its structure. *The Wasteland* is a poem, of course, and there is a definite and quite relentless attempt to create a sense of roundness – a circularity – in *The Wasteland*, and I think Sarah is doing something vastly different in *Crave*. If I hadn't known, or if Sarah hadn't said, 'I was influenced by *The Wasteland*' – apart from the direct line references in *Crave* I would never have connected the two pieces. Whereas in *Blasted* I would say there is an enormous debt of gratitude owed to Howard Barker – particularly in the second act. That is not to say that it's derivative. Sometimes people borrow directly and overtly and make no secret of it. This is a device I think Sarah employed occasionally in her work. Other writers are more oblique in their references to other writers' work because it is simply their way.

GS From *Crave* onwards several critics, and indeed Sarah herself felt that her work was moving closer towards poetry than theatre. Did you find this to be the case?

PN No, I can't say that I do see her work moving towards a poetic structure. Again, I think critics tend towards the facile when they say that if work appears to be 'language' based it is more poetic than theatrical. And that's a mistake because poetry has as discrete and rigorous a form as drama. The language of poetry tends to work not only metaphorically but also imagistically, viscerally. And it is an intensely specific language. I think this construct becomes less viable in Sarah's later plays. Those plays are quite blunt emotive appeals which describe various states of being – 'I am not loved. Love is not possible' – They sometimes become cryptic, or obscure. And although that is not a criticism of the plays, I do not equate their structures or metaphors with poetical structures or use of metaphor. The impulse towards poetry is something quite other – and while its language seeks to distil, it does not necessarily seek to 'abstract'. Sarah seemed to me to be moving towards abstraction, not away from it.

GS Do you think that was what Beckett was trying to do in his later plays?

PN Perhaps he became increasingly bored! No, seriously – Beckett's stripping down, his 'closing in' seemed deeply connected to his sense of mortality. One sees this often in the work of writers who live long lives. Shakespeare is one of the few who became more expansive with age. He did not 'close in'.

GS Do you think that was also what Sarah's last works were doing – closing in on themselves?

PN Yes, I do. Beginning with *Cleansed* she became the subject of her work – often in a very liberating and surprising manner, and sometimes in a very dangerous manner – and I'm not talking about the literal facts of her life – I'm talking about the direction her work took. There's a point at which its insularity can lead only to the point of departure – and it becomes impossible to actually 'get' anywhere. Great risk brings great reward and – at times – failure. What compels me about those three plays is their zealotry, their absolute singular vision. There's something so rigid about this work – rigid in the best pos-sible sense. You can see the fire and brimstone behind the writing – again, a great advantage and a great disadvantage because what one sacrifices is the writer's sense of objectivity. Not that I think any writing is objective, but there can be a sense of self-awareness about how well one's work might communicate its point of view to an *audience*. For me, some of the later work lacked this sense of self-awareness.

GS Your phrase about the writing having a zealot's drive finds its way to my mind through her male characters especially – figures such as Ian, Hippolytus and Tinker who seem to have this joyless sense of obsession – which makes them essentially tragic.

PN Yes, joyless is a very good word. Again, this was part of a risk she took, and I'm sure she was aware that the renunciation of love would generally lead to a feeling of nihilism that would then beg the question, 'why have I sat through this?' Now, in *Blasted* I think she answers that question very well. And there is a sense of redemption – not religious redemption but a soaring metaphorical redemption, which is tied to the image structure of the play. And it informs the dramatic action – the act of Ian looking up at the rain, for example. And the metaphor is woven into the play's narrative structure, so it is extremely satisfying. But in some of the other work, the renunciation of love is more uncomfortable, if not more unsettling. I suppose the denial of the possibility for change did not sit well with me, and stripped the work of its political potency in my opinion. David Greig once said that he felt truly political writing offered the possibility for change – not happy endings, not love-conquers-all scenarios – but the very *possibility* for change. And this, to me, is radical. I do not look for a way out of the utter hopelessness, but I do look for a crack in the surface that tells me I *might* find my way.

GS People like Phaedra and Rod in *Cleansed* also tend to sacrifice themselves for love. Her characters all seem to function in this extreme manner.

PN You mustn't forget it's also a function of youth, this notion of extreme behaviour which both imprisons and liberates. Not to be at all flippant, but Sarah was young and her youth worked exuberantly in her favour much of the time. Hers is an extremely eighteenth-century vision of Romantic love. Even when there's sexual consummation in her plays it is not so much consummation as conflagration – and the act itself appears to be relatively unimportant. The primary pleasure is in the build up, in the foreplay. Of course, without consummation, there is the possibility that one might abdicate responsibility for setting off a chain of events that stops just short of the act. I believe she was very interested in exploring this notion – both in the content of her plays and in their formal concerns.

GS Do any specific examples of that come to mind?

PN The most vivid example of this is Cate's rape in *Blasted*, which occurs when she's in the throes of a fit. How can she implicate him when she wasn't a witness to it – or even a conscious participant? Ian is oddly abdicated of responsibility because Cate wasn't really *there*. Again, I find this terribly interesting and terribly Romantic.

GS She calls Ian one of her Romantics who yearns for love despite being this monster.

PN What's also interesting and rather disturbing is that the monsters are the ones who are redeemed. It's never the 'good' people, it's the 'monsters'. They have the last word. Now, I can't begin to guess what's behind that. Maybe she's very simply stating, 'the fuckers win'. I don't know.

GS These extremes of behaviour in her characters and these monstrous men somehow being given a second chance seem to mark out Sarah Kane's work from that of her so called contemporaries such as Mark Ravenhill and Rebecca Prichard.

PN Yes, she is dealing in extremes and in much broader brush-strokes than either of the two dramatists you mention. And she is an insular writer. That is important to consider. When I say that her subject is herself, I do not make a value judgement. But it is undeniable that she is her own best source material. Both Ravenhill and Prichard are writers who look outward, who do not make themselves the subject of their work. Theirs is an interest in other people – in 'the other' in general. And as much as I admire Sarah's work, I do not think she shares this interest with her contemporaries. But extremes are seductive, and I dare say tempting to engage with. I have done it myself, and continue to do so. The larger-than-life often defines life. The dramatist's struggle becomes to keep the larger-than-life earthbound. And I admire Sarah's ability to abandon, quite bravely, that struggle.

GS What you say also seems to have taken place so swiftly. If you look at *Blasted* for instance. What begins as an Ibsenite well-made first half is suddenly jettisoned like the lunar capsule. And it seemed that once she'd played with traditional structure for a short while in this first play then she kissed it goodbye for forever and we go on this strange journey.

PN Yes, we do. I don't know if I would call the first half of *Blasted* Ibsenite, but I would call it well structured. However, it is also decidedly non naturalistic – no matter how 'well-made' it is, no matter how logical it is in terms of the two - people - in - a - room - who - are - doing - things - we - might - not - like - but - recognise - nonetheless - structure, and it is a very great achievement. It looks easy, like Pete Sampras playing tennis, but it's anything but easy. As we move through her work, however, we begin to find an absence of character, and sometimes characters are stripped of their identities – literally – and given 'letters' instead of names, for instance. These characters begin to speak into a void. This is what I find somewhat problematic. Because the technique tends to render an audience morally passive. One either cannot or is not required to respond to characters who float in a void. It might be argued, on the other hand, that this lack of specificity, the absence of definition, allows an audience to respond more personally – this could be 'you' or 'me', instead of 'A' or 'B'. However, I do feel that the increasing lack of reference to the world we mutually inhabit – rather than the world she exclusively inhabited – was not necessarily a strength. She was at her formidable best when she paid a great deal of attention to the specifics of place, of setting.

GS I certainly get a strong sense of place in her work. Even in *Crave* the city weaves its way strongly into the things the characters speak about.

PN Absolutely. There are direct references to New York in that play, of course. Ghostly references to actual places, such as, 'we'll go to Florent and drink coffee at midnight' (169). And this was – although I've not been there for years – a very popular restaurant, open 24-hours-a-day, in the meat-packing district.

GS The playwright David Greig said that it also makes the audience locate that restaurant into their personal lives, as if the dramatist is speaking to them directly.

PN Yes. The ability to make oneself the subject of one's work and to make the audience who watch that work feel as if they, too, are its subject is difficult and admirable. But it requires a further immersion in one's 'self' as a writer, which can be tricky. There is another way to achieve such complicity with an audience, which involves challenging the audience into self-awareness by disguising that self-awareness – that is to say, to present a scenario of what it *might* be like as someone 'other'. I suppose this is the argument which suggests that people learn to walk in another's shoes in order to gain self-awareness. I find this very compelling because it is dangerous – the risk of an audience rejecting such an invitation is high. Both approaches work and are valid. Sarah chose, in the later work, an immersion in self. And when we get to *4.48 Psychosis* the insularity reaches a point where it becomes, despite its other elements, a suicide note. There's no way of avoiding that – its sense of undiluted anger and desire to apportion blame.

GS Yes, it is a very angry play. It also places the audience in a strange position where we are not actually a theatre audience anymore but rather taking on the role of bearing witness.

PN I believe that process began with *Cleansed* – there's a sense that we – the audience – are not necessary. We don't have to be there. Which again I find fascinating, yet it goes against every instinct I have about how drama communicates.

GS Sarah Kane's drama has also been called Absurdist.

PN When I think of Absurdists I think of Ionesco and other such playwrights. I find there's no point of connection between their work and Sarah's work. Existential perhaps, but not Absurdist. I think she has more in common with the Existentialists than the Absurdists – but that's just me.

GS So do the last two plays become something else in that they are less plays in the received sense, and more texts for performance?

PN This notion of moving towards a 'text for performance' is a tricky one. What does that mean, precisely? Aren't all theatre texts written for performance? I think what does happen in the last two plays is a movement towards a literary, rather than a purely theatrical form. And by this time, she had clearly abandoned any sense of character. There is only one character in both of those plays, despite the number of voices present. Narrative hasn't been abandoned. There is a narrative both in *Crave* and in *4.48 Psychosis*, but there is not really what I would call 'character'. When you abandon character you abandon drama, so for me she has effectively abandoned drama. Not even Martin Crimp's *Attempts on Her Life* abandons character. There are distinct characters present – they are mutable, but fully grounded. There are no attempts to ground character in *Crave* and

4.48 Psychosis. Something else I think we must remember is that Sarah did not call these works of 'performance art'. They are plays, and she wrote them as such. The strength of her talent as a writer carries her through these works, regardless of my questions about her formal choices. I personally question where lines should or must be drawn in the matter of dramatic fluidity – is it a good thing or bad thing that some plays can be performed by two or five actors? Is it possible for a play to be so open-ended that it defies any meaningful critical interpretation? I don't know. But what I do believe is that there is a diminishment of dramatically viable image structure in both of the last two plays, which renders them, for me, viable works of experimental literature rather than viable works of drama.

GS Yet her argument was in relation to things like impossible stage directions, or no particular image structure, was to give an example from Shakespeare's *A Winter's Tale* and the stage direction 'exit pursued by a bear'. So if Shakespeare can do that then I can too.

PN But that's a very different thing. You can realise that image. You put a man in a bear costume and it works. And again, however much of a *non sequitur* it appears to be – because it ties in with the statue and many other specific images in that play – it's a perfect image. But you cannot ask for a stage of rats in *Cleansed* and think that's going to work. And I know she was disappointed with the vultures in *Phaedra's Love*, and flirted with using a shadow and a mechanical contraption, and debated these issues at length. Also there was discussion about the use of fire, which ultimately was realised with the sound of fire and a glow of some sort. There was an attempt to visualise a fire, but it was a long way from being a funeral pyre. Not that you could necessarily get that on the stage of The National Theatre, mind you, as I imagine fire regulations would prevail. One of the great things about Sarah was that she disregarded all of that. But on the other hand one does think at some point, 'no, this is the medium you work in. You have to be damned sure that you can get as close as you mean to get to realising your vision in order to integrate the image and word'.

GS Yes, and it's interesting that up until *Cleansed* there was a distinct image structure like the rats that were solely language based.

PN That's why I keep going back to *Blasted* and its sublime image structure. Even in the second act, where certain critics overreacted to the atrocities, the image structure is created through the language and the characters' actions. In subsequent plays, the images are created, mostly, through the stage directions which is a very different thing – much more a cinematic than a theatrical technique. Again it works, and that's fine. But I find it interesting and ironic that she basically transformed herself from a language based playwright into something quite other. I believe most people would tend to think of her making the opposite transformation. For me, if a play is firing on all cylinders, its image structure is generated by the language, the behaviour of the characters and its metaphor working together. Seamlessly. Imagine King Lear's heath speeches. And in the middle of a speech, Shakespeare inserts a stage direction which says, 'a toy car spins circles around Lear throughout'. It seems clear that such images tend to be disassociated from the action of the play.[1]

GS I see. So in *Blasted* say it's the action of Ian digging up the baby rather than the explicit stage direction telling the actor to carry out a specific action?

PN Yes, it's fully integrated into the fabric of the drama.

GS And it's a play that's clearly rooted in the real world.

PN Yes, it is. One can also say that Sarah's private world *was* her real world – who is anyone to say anything different? There is surely validity in that. This was the world she lived in so this was the world she wrote. On the other hand, there is a reason playwrights are playwrights and not essayists, say. There's a reason why Sarah wasn't a novelist or a poet – and part of the reason involved the desire to communicate in a particular way. In a public and immediate way. It does seem to require the desire to actively debate sets of ideas or emotions with a live audience.

GS Sarah also acted in *Cleansed* and *Crave* and directed *Phaedra's Love*, as well as a production of *Woyzeck*; so in some ways she remained rooted to the theatrical form.

PN With *Phaedra's Love* she came in and replaced the director. That's what generally happens when playwrights direct their own work. That's why I ended up directing *Disappeared*. I think when plays are very new the last thing most of us would want to think about is directing our own work. I could direct a production of *Never Land* now, but I could not have directed its first production. One also knows that the perspective of a director one likes, trusts and admires is necessary.

GS It's often been said that the most successful dramatists are the ones who enter into a fruitful partnership with a director who shares aspects of the writers vision, and who also channels something of their own creativity into the plays. I'm thinking of Arnold Wesker and John Dexter or Caryl Churchill and Max-Stafford Clark. I think

---

1 A reference to the stage direction in *Phaedra's Love* (4:74).

that happened with Sarah Kane and James Macdonald, although I know she worked with Vicky Featherstone and found that to be a successful partnership as well.

PN   I think that's probably true, and I think Sarah probably knew that however one might disagree with a director on a day to day basis, there exists in the finest directors the ability to empathise with one's writing, and an ability to translate what one writes to a group of actors. This is crucial. A lot of playwrights allow ambition to override common sense and hop from director to director in the misguided belief that if you find a good working relationship with one director you can find an equally good one with another. It is possible, but not likely. Simpatico is never easily found. I think Sarah realised that James was good for her work. There was a strong emotional bond between them. James once told me that he loved it when he would say to Sarah in rehearsal, 'what do you mean by this'? And she would reply, 'I don't know'. James has an ability to puzzle through her work and the results are pretty magnificent.

GS   Sarah Kane's theatre has been called both excessive and chaste. And certainly that seems to occur at times in the language where the carefully controlled minimalist style suddenly gives away to huge outpourings of extravagant language such as A's 'love speech' in *Crave*.

PN   Well, it's a theatre of emotional excess certainly, as opera can be emotionally excessive – the structure of opera suits emotional excess. There is a little box into which you can put such extravagant and emotional flamboyance. But I think the critics who talked about this excess were referring to what they saw as the atrocities depicted in Sarah's work. And what I have to say to that is that all playwrights have their pacifiers and favourite blankets – the little things they fall back on. I think it's fair to say that Sarah fell back onto one too many blow-jobs, so to speak. And yes, I think that was a fault. But we all have such faults. One has to be able to write through those things in order to access the grace and beauty which might follow.

12

Conversation with Kate Ashfield

19 July 2000

Kate Ashfield is an actress who appeared in some of the major new plays by British dramatists during the mid 1990s. Her work for theatre includes *Peaches* (Royal Court, 1994); *Blasted* (Royal Court, 1995); *Three Sisters / The Break of Day* (Out of Joint, Touring Production, 1995); *Woyzeck* (Gate Theatre, 1997, directed by Sarah Kane) *The Positive Hour* (Out of Joint and Hampstead Theatre, 1997) and *Closer* (Lyric, 1997).

GRAHAM SAUNDERS Going back to the very beginning, when you received the script for *Blasted*, what were your first impressions when you read it?

KATE ASHFIELD Well, I remember reading it on the bus and getting to certain bits and going 'urgh'! And I was wondering how would these things work? I'd worked with James Macdonald [the director of *Blasted*] on Nick Grosso's *Peaches*, and at this point we were still performing the play when I went to meet him. So I knew that it was somehow alright, and that he would know what to do with it. I just remember having a lot of questions when I went to meet him.

GS Were your questions answered? Or were you left to work things out for yourself?

KA Yes, there were some things like that. But I remember at that first meeting with Sarah, a lot of my questions were way off the mark. You know about plot, and what was happening with Cate's brother and things like that. And Sarah filled all of that in. But when it came to rehearsal, there were some things that were just not answered. In particular I remember, why does Cate give Ian that blow job, at that point in the play? I was trying to think of a reason, but that wasn't answered so we made up our own reasoning for it (2:30). However, I asked Sarah on the last night, and she said, 'I didn't know what to do at that point in the play, and I remember Joe Orton saying something about if you didn't know what to do at a given moment in writing, then shock your audience – that's why I put that in'.[1]

GS   I'd like to ask about the sudden change in both theme and dramatic form we encounter in *Blasted*. There're almost two parts to the play in that it seems to begin as a domestic drama of two people trapped together in a hotel room. Then you've got the second part of the play where Ian's meeting with the Soldier produces devastating consequences. Once you reappear in the second half of the play how much had you to change as a character? Did you feel that you had to adopt a completely different persona to take into account everything that Cate had gone through at that point?

KA   You knew things happened to her, that she comes back with a baby. It was because of the way Cate's character was anyway – that she always seemed to be living in the moment. She wasn't analysing the things that were happening around her in any way. It was almost as if she had gone out and come back, and because of what she had seen, it wasn't a shock to see Ian blinded and sitting in the baby's grave. Earlier, when she was just dealing with the baby, and the reality of that situation she moved on with the play's reality. So no, it didn't seem like I had to adopt a different acting style – I never thought of it like that actually.

GS   I've heard Sarah say that Cate is simultaneously the most intelligent person in the play, and at the same time absolutely stupid to walk into that hotel with Ian, because she knows what's going to happen. Did you see her as this kind of person who is in actual fact going to survive the war zone?

KA   Yes, I did. She does seem very strong and weak at the same time. You get this real sense the morning after when Ian and Cate wake up, when she's about to leave and stops to pick up the jacket … a lot of people who saw it said to me that they thought at the time, 'get out!' The frustration of the audience at that point arises from the fact that they know, having learnt so much about Ian that she should really leave. However, a weaker person would run out but her anger makes her stay to hurt Ian.

---

1   Evidence from early drafts of the script point towards Cate's seduction of Ian being used as a ploy to extract information about his activities in a secret organisation.

GS In some ways they are the eternal couple who can never escape from one another.

KA They become bound together. And at the end you know, that's not even her fault. She's managed to get through the war and it's a case of back to basics.

GS It's a hopeful ending, that's the way it felt to me. When we've looked at *Blasted* in classes students have come down on two sides. Some of them say it's awful and really depressing, and some think its uplifting and optimistic.

KA Yes, I felt it was more optimistic because Cate's kind of looking after him, and they've got this kind of truce at the end.

GS One of the most disturbing things about Cate are the catatonic states she slips into at various times, especially when under stress. Did you have to research that, because Sarah spoke about knowing someone who went into such fits.

KA Yes she told me about that as well, and the whole stuttering thing. I had to work on that when the voice coach came in.

GS That's almost the opposite thing you'd imagine a voice coach would do!

KA Yes, it didn't really work out because the voice coach was trying to work in a completely different way to me. The way I found to do it in the end was to really work on the sounds alone – both of someone laughing and crying. You don't have to be really emotionally involved that way.

GS Cate seems to have learning difficulties in the play which Ian is ruthless at exploiting. Was a decision made about her mental age in rehearsals?

KA Well I always thought it was twelve. I don't know where I got that from, but that's what I've got in my head, a mental age of twelve.

GS How did you react to all the furore that blew up about the play in the press?

KA It just went mad. Everyone wanted to see it and were talking about it. People were queuing around the block to see this 'disgusting play'. But on our part there was just a desire to perform the play properly.

GS *Blasted* only ran for about three weeks. Was there a feeling that the play was only just beginning to be explored?

KA Well apparently the Royal Court had the option of it playing at the Criterion Theatre for five weeks, but I was going straight to the Hampstead Theatre to do another play, and they would've had to transfer straight away. So they said that they weren't going to recast me, because that would mean another three weeks delay. I also think they had come to the decision at the Court as well, that it wasn't designed for a West End show. Once you put it on in the West End, you take it out of its context, and you shouldn't really do that, because then people come for the wrong reasons.

GS I wanted to ask you about the sex scenes in *Blasted*. In the first German production the sex scenes were done very realistically with full nudity, whereas in the Royal Court production they were performed in a low key way. Was that the conception originally, that it was going to be done without the sensational depiction?

KA Yes I think so. I remember having a discussion about the blow-job, because we did that under the bed clothes, and it worked better than a scene we'd rehearsed where more was exposed, and it also made Cate seem to be more young and vulnerable. You also avoid people looking to see if they can actually see anything. That's always made worse in the Theatre Upstairs because it's such a small space.

GS Cate's Christian faith seems to sustain her throughout the play. Did this become an issue in rehearsals?[2]

KA Not really. I think with Cate she wasn't a practising Christian, in that she wouldn't go to church. She just knew that Jesus loved her. Something along the lines of Jesus wants me for a sunbeam! That was how I thought of her in my mind.

GS You've appeared in some of the major plays of the mid-1990s by the so called New Brutalists such as *Shopping and Fucking, Peaches* and *Closer*. Do you feel these plays share similar concerns?

KA I don't see them as in any way similar. *Blasted* is so different to *Peaches*, and I think that *Closer* is different again. There are some similarities between them in the language that's used, but that's about all.

GS After *Blasted* you worked with Sarah again when she directed Büchner's *Woyzeck* at the Gate Theatre. Did Sarah approach you for the part?

KA Yes, she approached me through my agent, and then I went and read with her and Mike Shannon who was playing *Woyzeck*. We went to the Gate and she gave me a piece of one speech to read. And I read this bit and I thought, 'I can't do this'. It seemed too abstract to me. I didn't know what I was talking about.

GS What did she do with the play?

KA It was a real ensemble piece. We sometimes used musical instruments too. The sets were very small and the stage was in the middle, and right next to it around the edges there would be actors, and at the

2 In James Macdonald's second 2001 production of the play at the Royal Court, during the opening scene where Cate explores the hotel room she finds a Gideon Bible in one of the drawers which she reads from briefly.

back we'd be banging drums and the audience were all around us. The set had things that pull out, like a chair that would come out of what was otherwise a solid wooden floor, and at the end we all went underneath the stage. We did so many different things in rehearsal; lots of exercises with Sarah, and then with the whole cast. We all went through these exercises; getting up in the morning and going through what you would do as your character, then you mimed it out in front of the cast. Then you'd go to bed at night, get up again in the morning, and you'd do it again, and try to get some sort of idea of what those characters' lives would be like. In a way the language in *Woyzeck* is similar to *Blasted* – there's no extra language, there's nothing you don't need.

13

Conversation with Daniel Evans

19 July 2000

Daniel Evans is an actor who appeared in both *Cleansed* (Royal Court, 1998) and *4.48 Psychosis* (Royal Court, 2000 and 2001). Other theatre work includes *Henry V*, *Coriolanus* and *A Midsummer Night's Dream* (RSC, 1994); *Troilus and Cressida* and *Candide* (National Theatre, 1999) and *Merrily we Roll along* (Donmar Warehouse, 2001).

GRAHAM SAUNDERS I want to talk to you first if I could about *Cleansed*. When you received the script for the play what were your first impressions?

DANIEL EVANS Literally the first thing was that I couldn't wait to turn the pages. It's a really easy read – very short, and there's a lot of stage directions. I read it in about ten minutes to quarter of an hour. I just couldn't wait to get to the end of it, and when I eventually put it down I said to myself, 'I must do it'. Of course I had an audition to get through, but that was my initial thinking. I knew that there was something big going on.

GS Were you aware of *Blasted* and *Phaedra's Love*?

DE I didn't see *Blasted* but I was aware of what had happened with it because I was in Stratford at the time, and I remember reading Edward Bond's article about it in the newspaper. And also I actually did a reading for *Blasted*. I was in an RSC new play festival, which is at the Young Vic. We just got three actors from the company, and I played the Soldier.

GS   What was the rehearsal period like for *Cleansed* as opposed to *4.48 Psychosis*?

DE   They were two very different processes for me. To begin with we had four weeks on *Cleansed*, and seven on *4.48 Psychosis* – a significant difference in the theatre. And of course in *Cleansed* we had the playwright in the room with us when we wanted her help, although sometimes she refused to help us!

GS   She once said that every line in *Cleansed* has many different meanings.

DE   Well James Macdonald will probably tell you this, but I remember distinctly the day we were discussing something, and it was to do with Stuart McQuarrie who was playing Tinker. There's one word – just 'no'. We went around and we discovered five different possible meanings for it, so we turned to the playwright and said, 'so which one?' And she said, 'all of them, play them all'. Which of course is impossible, but you just leave it open.

GS   I don't want to ask too many specific questions about meaning, because like you say the play is so complex and open to endless interpretations. However, for me the most puzzling episode in *Cleansed* was when you as Robin go into the booth and see the woman dancing.

DE   And why do I cry?

GS   Yes. And why do you go there in the first place? To me the woman in the booth is also the most mysterious figure in the play. Does she have some connection with Grace?

DE   Well, in a way she's sort of like Grace's other side. You remember Tinker calls her Grace?

GS   Yes.

DE   So, in a way she becomes Grace. And I think the reason why Robin cries is for many reasons. It's to do with shame – sexual shame – as well as pity and love probably.

GS   Was Robin in Tinker's institution for any specific reason?

DE   Well you know Robin is a schizophrenic?

GS   The voices he hears?

DE   Yes, he hears voices. I think that's what we decided. I mean it could be anything but I think that was what we decided – that he's probably there because they think he's ill.

GS   Sarah has spoken in interview about the large number of different literary sources informing *Cleansed*. Did she speak to you about these sources?

DE   Yes she did. *Twelfth Night* was one, which is interesting isn't it? It became very classical at times. I also think *Twelfth Night* extends to the incest motif in *Cleansed* with brother and sister.

GS And Büchner's *Woyzeck*.

DE With *Woyzeck* she took it as a structural blueprint. I think there are twenty scenes in *Woyzeck* and twenty scenes in *Cleansed*.

GS Orwell's *Nineteen Eighty-Four* also informs *Cleansed*.

DE I remember talking about *Nineteen Eighty-Four* for obvious reasons. I think the links are quite apparent there. I also think that *Nineteen-Eighty Four* comes into *4.48 Psychosis* with the idea of 'newspeak'. Somehow the language becomes a tool, or a weapon.

GS Can you say more about that?

DE It came up in rehearsals quite a bit. I'm trying to remember where. The main point is the section where I'm on the floor, which we called 'the palsy', where I'm saying the lines – 'unpleasant, unacceptable, uninspiring, impenetrable' (221). For me there was a desperate grappling to hold onto language, because your mind has been deadened by all of those drugs and the overdose you've just taken with some Bulgarian Cabernet Sauvignon. There's this thing that's completely cold, and your mind is desperately trying to hang on to these words – you're trying to play a game with words. That reminds me of *Nineteen Eighty-Four*.

GS The rats in *Cleansed* are another reference I suppose to the part they play in *Nineteen Eighty-Four*. Did Sarah mean them as a theatrical joke, as she's implied, designed to test the designer or the director?

DE Absolutely not! You've read the end of *Phaedra's Love*, in those stage directions where the genitalia is cut off and thrown to a dog, and then the vultures come down and eat it? So no, far from it, I don't think it's a joke at all. I think it's something very real which she sees – it's nevertheless a supreme challenge to realise that into a stage image. James was adamant that it should be in no way naturalistic, just as the cutting off of limbs shouldn't be naturalistic. Whether that's the right way to do it or not, is something that I'm not actually sure about. When I was in it I was always saying, the way to do this is to be as naturalistic as possible, to try and see the tongue cutting, which is what I gather they did in the German production. But again I heard that didn't work either, because the sex scenes were like being in a porn cinema.

GS I've heard that Robin in *Cleansed* is based on a character from the South African prison of Roben Island. Is this true?

DE Absolutely true. Nelson Mandela taught this black boy to read and write and count, and he counted how many days he had left of his sentence and hanged himself. It's unspeakably terrible. I think that monologue Robin has is fantastic, when he's counting out the beads.

GS Did Sarah do much rewriting during rehearsals for *Cleansed*?

DE She was always cutting. That was her main thing to cut, to make the text as spare as possible. I think that she was constantly revising stuff as well. You know there's going to be a complete works published? I know she went back to the first three plays and revised them. Simon, her brother told me.

GS Many of your scenes with Grace in *Cleansed* are perhaps the most optimistic and life affirming in the play, such as when she's teaching Robin to write.

DE I also had the most horrible scene as well. I think the scene where I'm made to eat the entire box of chocolates is one of the most disturbing in the whole play.

GS The sceneography in *Cleansed* was one of the other remarkable things about the Royal Court production. Did you work with the sets very much from the beginning?

DE No.

GS So was that a problem when you actually had to go in and you had this huge hydraulic apparatus to contend with?

DE To be frank it was a problem. Sometimes the set got in the way of the text. For instance, they had to cut things like the electric fence – the perimeter fence that Sarah describes in the play. That used to take such a long time to bring down onto the stage that they decided to cut it altogether. When we saw the model we all fell in love with it, and thought it was fantastic. But of course doing it in practice is a different thing altogether. There were brilliant things however like the concept of the white room, because it was so stark and sanitised. I also thought the show booth/shower room was equally stunning.

GS Jeremy Herbert was also the designer for *4.48 Psychosis*, and although a much simpler set there's still the strange use of perspective.

DE Yes.

GS Like the use of the mirror showing the action occurring from several perspectives. In the rehearsal process were you aware that your acting was going to be witnessed by the audience from several different planes.

DE We had a mirror.

GS All the way through?

DE No, but for the last three weeks we had a mirror.

GS Were you told at the beginning that this was going to occur?

DE It was proposed as an idea yes, but nothing was absolutely fixed.

GS To me it also conveyed the idea of altered states. When you're depressed I've heard people describe it as sometimes hearing yourself talking outside the body.

DE   That's exactly it for me. People have come to see it and have said lots of different things that I've found fascinating. But as you say, depressed people feel they are watching their own drama. Not that we ever looked at ourselves in the mirror ...

GS   Did you not?

DE   Well I never did.

GS   Because sometimes you seemed to be staring directly up at yourself when lying on the floor.

DE   I'm just looking at the roof of the theatre. I never looked at myself in the mirror. I didn't like to. Obviously altered states and different planes inform the whole play, but I think for me the main thing was being able to look outside of yourself.

GS   Were your movements under the mirror choreographed in any way?

DE   No.

GS   You say there were seven weeks rehearsal for *4.48 Psychosis*. That's an intense period for a very short play. I gather from reading the theatre programme that you had psychiatrists and other professionals at rehearsals. Were they useful?

DE   Absolutely essential. We had Louis Wolpert who was actually a famous embryologist and also suffers from depression. One of the most helpful people was an actress and poet called Poppy Hands who suffered from depression, but who's well now. She had many failed suicide attempts, and was really helpful. We went to the Maudesley Hospital where Sarah had been. We didn't go to her ward, though I had been there whilst we were doing *Cleansed*. Just to see the Maudesley was a thing in itself, because it's fucking horrible! Oh the wards that we were on, God alive! From the colours of the walls, to the ... I mean the nurses were great. The nurse who spoke to us was brilliant. But they were obviously under so much pressure from bureaucracy, that how anyone can get better in that atmosphere is beyond me.

GS   Did you learn about the drugs that they used?

DE   Absolutely. Going to the Maudesley for me showed and justified absolutely the anger that flows through *4.48 Psychosis*, against the way the medical profession treat people when they fall ill.

GS   There does seem to be one doctor in the play who seems to understand, or at least says he does.

DE   Or she.

GS   Yes, sorry.

DE   I don't want to speak out of turn, but I think that this was something very real in Sarah's life. I think she did have a very good relationship with a specific doctor, who in the play becomes everything to her.

GS You know there's that line, 'you're my last hope' (236). Then there're those speeches that Jo McInnes did – 'sometimes I catch the smell of you and I cannot go on, I cannot fucking go on' (214), and then her later cursing God for making her love someone who doesn't exist (215). This seems to happen again and again in Sarah Kane's work – this incredible craving to find the beloved. In *Cleansed* it happens with Carl and Rod and Robin and Grace – this call for love to be reciprocated.

DE And when it doesn't come back, well that's the unbearable thing isn't it? There's that line in the monologue from *4.48 Psychosis* where he or she says – 'I cannot believe that I have all this love for you, and you feel nothing' (214). So she has all of this love, and all of these feelings, and they're not reciprocated. I also think its important to say that I think it's unconditional love, especially with Rod and Carl. Rod starts off saying, 'I love you now', (111) and of course at the end of the play he's transformed.

GS Again and again so many of the characters in her plays have to prove their love by actually killing themselves. Hippolytus does that too, when he sees that Phaedra his stepmother, has given her life for him.

DE But I suppose it's the ultimate sacrifice – would you die for someone? If the answer is yes, then I think that is Sarah's proof of unconditional love. It's back to Shakespeare again – *Romeo and Juliet.*

GS This is probably one of the interesting things about her plays that I think distinguishes her from dramatists she's been likened to such as Joe Penhall, who write very much in the moment, and whose plays relate to aspects of British society.

DE They're issue plays, whereas Sarah's plays are these huge things. I think there's a Jacobean element to her drama. All of her characters are these huge bubbling masses of emotion. You wouldn't have them sitting about talking of football. There's also that line in *4.48 Psychosis* – 'how can I return to form now my formal thought has gone' (213), and I think after *4.48* there was a definite feeling of, 'I shall not speak again'(205). And you think, 'well where would she go afterwards?' We had a playwright's evening during our previews. All of the playwrights came who the Court have either staged or encouraged – Joe Penhall, Mark Ravenhill and I think Nick Grosso came another night. They came and you couldn't help thinking, where do they fit in now? And I also think her death also just shows up the banality of a lot of the younger playwrights coming along. As actors in *4.48 Psychosis* all three of us have all received play scripts recently, and our reaction going through them – and I can speak for the other two – has been one of disgust. I can't be doing with that sort of thing, it's so terrible, it's so banal, so ridiculously television.

GS Speaking of dramatic form, both *Crave* and *4.48 Psychosis*, while both being very different plays do seem to owe a certain debt to Martin Crimp's *Attempts on her Life*.

DE Yes, we spoke about that in rehearsals. There seems to be these scenes you can play at any moment, but what is important is the whole picture, although I think she's obviously decided when to place the scenes. There's also a definite playing with form and not allocating lines on a specific level.

GS Were the lines strictly apportioned by the director or was it more democratic?

DE For the first five weeks of rehearsal we all learnt the play, and we did it in every which way you can imagine. Obviously in the doctor patient scenes, we tried seeing the doctor patient in a naturalistic way. It was terrible, needless to say. The multi-voice bits, we tried as monologues, and we tried them as dialogue. In the end we learnt all of them, and we came in as we wanted to.

GS That's a clever idea.

DE Whenever you felt like it you could say a line. But two weeks before we opened, James allocated specifically the dialogue bits. So he came in and said, 'in the first patient doctor scene you're the doctor'. Similarly, with the multi-voice bits, we just looked at them and read them around, and James said, 'okay that's how we're going to do it'. He had someone record who was saying what bit. But there was one section that we never allocated, so it was a free for all every night. It was the section beginning with the line, 'we are anathema, the pariahs of reason (228-9). It's remarkable in that it's the first time the characters use the pronoun 'we'. It's also the first time Sarah gets very religious.

GS It seems like the rehearsals were a real exploration. No one, including the director seemed to come with an agenda.

DE Absolutely. It was like doing a workshop. We had done a workshop in February 2000 on the play. Madeleine wasn't there but Jo and I were, and we had five other actors as well. It was like an extension of that, it really was. I can't imagine any other way of doing it, unless you're a director who's decided everything you want to do before you come in, which thank God James didn't. Otherwise it wouldn't have been half as rewarding as it was.

GS You mention the religious imagery. Where is most of that located?

DE The Book of Revelations.

GS There were no explicit stage directions in *4.48 Psychosis*, so for instance how did the ending with the cast opening the shutters of the theatre building come about?

DE Letting in all the light and noise outside in the street came about very late in rehearsals. We knew that there were windows, and it was an idea that James had in his mind that might happen. James does that, and he probably knows this, but he does like to leave things until very much the last minute – which is absolutely fine. We tried so many different ways to do the ending, because it's so extremely difficult without becoming an anti-climax or just fizzling out in embarrassed applause. Nothing seemed to work – it all seemed terrible and unremarkable. So when we got into the theatre, it was just perfect. I remember the three of us when we first opened the shutters. It was so moving, and then opening the window and hearing the noise – it was so very moving and poignant.

GS I remember one night there was the sound of workmen drilling, and the sound of people laughing in the street.

DE Fantastic! I remember the three of us saying how the hairs on the back of our necks were standing up.

GS What about the use of video?

DE That came late, although we had a bit of it in rehearsals, but very little. When people talk about video in theatre I normally go absolutely berserk, because it's like Robert Lepage at his worst. But in *4.48 Psychosis* when I saw how the window played on the surface of the mirror with the people walking across, I thought it was really effective.

GS And the three of you on stage are trapped inside.

DE Yes, we were all the same person, which is pretty unique in theatre. The three of us were playing the same person, on the same journey every night. That's bizarre, because you're normally working with people who have their own particular journey and you have your separate journey. And although we start and end up at the same place, you don't have any eye contact with each other, and you don't touch anyone – it was so bizarre.

GS There wasn't any eye contact?

DE None. It wasn't allowed.

GS I wanted to ask you about the use of numbers in *4.48 Psychosis*, and the multiples of seven.

DE Well, both numbers start at a hundred, and the first numbers are completely random. The second numbers come down from the hundred in regular sevens. Apparently it's an exercise that psychiatric nurses give patients to assess their level of concentration. Sometimes they count down from a hundred, or sometimes they do it from a thousand to get to seventeen, which is probably even harder. If you can do it regularly then your concentration is fine. So obviously on the first set of numbers she's way off.

GS   One interesting thing I noticed, was that you were writing the numbers back to front so we in the audience could see it reflected back at us.

DE   You've seen how it is in the script, the first set of numbers? Well we wanted to put that on the stage somehow, in the way Sarah set it out on the page. So we decided we would write the numbers on top of the table, so that the audience could see them. With the second set of numbers, I wrote them in a single line.

GS   You played a self-mutilator in that play, the scars almost saying that you were still alive.

DE   I think that's common.

GS   Was it a specific design etched into your arm?

DE   It was the words, 'yes' / 'no' backwards. So if you looked in the mirror they became the right way around.

GS   What did that mean?

DE   I came up with that. We'd seen pictures of people including Ritchie James, the guy from the Manic Street Preachers who disappeared. He was a self mutilator, and he'd written the word 'HEART' on his arm. It's a very common thing to do – you write messages, scraping them into your skin. We toyed with what I should write and I thought putting '4.48' was a bit pathetic. I then thought of just doing some lines, but that just seemed stupid, because I was drawing them with a pen. Then I thought I'd write 'YES/ NO' on my arm, this being a reference to a later line in the play which they chose to show as a piece of black and white film of, 'yes or no, yes or no'.

GS   Have you seen that short film Sarah wrote called *Skin*?

DE   Yes.

GS   Because the black woman there carves her name into the skinhead's back.

DE   And she scrapes off his tattoos.

GS   When the play ends have the characters given up hope as in *Crave*? Is the opening of the curtains a sort of exorcism?

DE   Well the opening of the curtains is definitely for us a release. I don't know, it's strange with hope isn't it? Because she says, 'no hope, no hope, no hope, no hope' (218), yet there's always love until the last moment. There are those final lines aren't there, 'in death you hold me, I'm never free. I have no desire for death, no suicide ever had' (244). Those are almost the very last lines, so I think that maybe hope has gone, and she does the deed ... it is done – then it goes onto something else. I think it's a release, into warm darkness.

GS   What about the long silence that starts the play? It seemed to vary in length on any given night.

DE   That was up to Madeleine [Potter]. You weren't there the night of the mobile phone were you?

GS   No.

DE   This mobile phone went off, five seconds into the play and someone shouted from the back, 'you fucking arsehole'! Then someone else, a friend of mine turned around and said, 'just sit on it'! So, the careful atmospheric opening was ruined and it became a different play. So that was a shame. But I felt the longer that initial silence was sustained the better. It just gave everyone a chance to settle. Sometimes people take ages and you think, 'come on, calm down. Its going to be an interesting evening, so you need to concentrate'. I love that.

GS   Sarah acted in the last few performances of *Cleansed*. What were your reactions to acting with the writer?

DE   She was brilliant – extraordinary and above all raw. I always said that she made us look like actors, because she was so raw. She wasn't acting in the accepted sense of that term and any acting next door to that just seems like huge acting.

GS   She actually made an interesting comment about the acting style she wanted in *Cleansed* by saying you shouldn't act – the key was not to play the characters in the sense of them being characters you'd meet in the street.

DE   I understand that because that's what we wanted for *4.48 Psychosis* – everyone living in the moment, like in the workshop and in rehearsals. But its terribly difficult, because you can't just do nothing. Any acting is acting, however small or real it is. There's such a fine delicate balance between what is and what isn't appropriate.

GS   One of the other most powerful things about *4.48 Psychosis* was the opportunity it gave audiences to really listen to the actor's voice. And especially the diversity of the three voices on stage individually and as a chorus. Did you do much voice work?

DE   Patsy Rodenburg worked with us and she did work on Greek choral speaking.

GS   Had you seen *Crave*?

DE   Yes, I was actually asked to be in it, but I couldn't.

GS   I assume you'd have been the younger chap 'B'.

DE   Yes. I don't think many people got *Crave*. There're many links which become apparent when you see *Crave* and then read *4.48 Psychosis*. That was also something we did in our rehearsal process, to read all of the other plays again. This involved everyone – all of the actors, director, stage management, everyone. We went around and played different parts, and that was so brilliant because I realised that they are all interlinked. But I think *Crave* and *4.48 Psychosis* are the most similar in terms of style and subject – they are all like one play. Things like the image of the light in *Crave* is a big thing, and it's even more significant in *4.48 Psychosis*.

GS Many critics chose to see *4.48 Psychosis* as a suicide note.

DE I hate that term for it, because I think it reduces the play. But I suppose that's what people think. I also think that in *4.48 Psychosis* she was sometimes having a joke with some of it.

GS Do you know when Sarah Kane began work on *4.48 Psychosis*?

DE Two years. She began it after *Cleansed*.

GS And *Crave*?

DE I was handed the copy of *Crave* to read during a performance of *Cleansed*. So it was finished and I think that's when she started working on *4.48 Psychosis*.

GS Was that copy very different from the final *Crave*?

DE No. Almost exact.

GS In *4.48 Psychosis* were there any literary sources that informed the play that you were aware of?

DE We read the books that Sarah was reading at the time of her death. So, we read [C. S Lewis'] *The Silver Chair*¹ and *The Myth Of Sisyphus* by [Albert] Camus. We read [Sylvia] Plath's *The Bell Jar*, and a book called *The Suicidal Mind*,² which is very key to *4.48 Psychosis*. She was reading it and using large sections of it for *4.48 Psychosis*. You remember the lists?

GS The sections that begin like a wish list? 'To achieve goals and ambitions..'.

DE Directly taken from it.

GS There was also the Goethe play, *The Sorrows Of Young Werther*.

DE Yes, but we didn't touch that.

GS For *Cleansed* was there much reading to do?

DE Just *Woyzeck* and *Twelfth Night* I remember reading, and there was one other. There was much more reading for *4.48 Psychosis*.

GS How did they know about this list of books which informed *4.48 Psychosis*? Was it from Sarah's notebooks?

---

1 In a later correspondence Daniel Evans comments, 'Yes, *The Silver Chair* does inform any reading of *4.48 Psychosis*. It tells the story of a Prince who is forced to live underground and has only an hour of true sanity every night. However, during this hour, everyone else underground thinks it is his only hour of madness … The parallels are wonderful.' Email from Daniel Evans to Graham Saunders, 4 February 2001.

2 Schreidman, Edwin, *The Suicidal Mind* (Oxford, 1996).

DE No, it was from her bedside. Her brother let us know about the read-
ing material. There were also loads of books on suicide, the play by
Phil Jameson and Lewis Wolpert's book *Anatomy of Despair* and
Prozac Nation.[3] There was a huge reading list we had just to dip into.

---

3 Elizabeth Wurtzel, *Prozac Nation: Young and Depressed in America: A Memoir*, rev.ed
(London, 1996).

14

Conversation with Stuart McQuarrie

28 October 2000

Stuart McQuarrie is an actor who played the part of Tinker in the 1998 Royal Court production of *Cleansed*. Other theatre work includes *Shining Souls* (Traverse Theatre and Old Vic, 1996–97); *The Government Inspector* (Almeida, 1997–98) and *The Taming of the Shrew* (RSC, 1999).

GRAHAM SAUNDERS *Cleansed* has been described as play almost impossible to realise on stage. Were these your first impressions once rehearsals got underway?

STUART MCQUARRIE It was complete confusion at first. I had no idea what is was about. It was very sparely written, and it hardly gave anything away about itself. I thought it could be a disaster, or it could be very exciting. I really wanted to know what the approach was going to be because *Cleansed* is very brutal, and the character I was playing was the most brutal of all, so all that was going round in my head. Principally, I thought it might well be impossible to do. I couldn't see any way that these things could be represented – the brutality, such as the mutilation of people's hands, feet and tongue. I knew it would be represented by some form of symbolism, but I wanted to know how graphic it would be.

GS During the rehearsal process was there a gradual move towards finding a style of representation for the action in *Cleansed*?

SM We had a brainstorming session where we discussed how symbolic some of the violence would be. And there was always going to be a strong element coming from design I suppose. So, instead of blood there were ribbons and red material. At the time I remember thinking I'd have preferred the violence to have been more graphic than it turned out to be. I remember the scene where Rod's hands are removed taking a long time to work out in rehearsals. And I thought the way around it at the time was to make the amputations more graphic.

GS How was it realised eventually in the production?

SM I pulled sections of his cuffs off, as if I'd ripped sections of his hands away – and attached to his cuffs was red silk material.

GS How was the removal of the tongue achieved technically?

SM I made a snipping sound with the shears, and there was a length of red rubber wound around a film canister that I had within my hand.

GS Tinker seems to be this strange mixture of brutality and tenderness. Did you feel there was a schizophrenic quality to the character?

SM That's not an issue as far as the character goes. The facets of the character alone are not difficult to do. But I think I can answer this in two ways, in that I never got to understand Tinker, yet it's impossible not to understand him. I know that sounds like a really stupid thing to say; because everyone can be very brutal or very tender depending on how they are at any given time – it's always comparative. For some people, their personality won't allow them to be that brutal, but they can exhibit this aggression in another way. So their plimsoll line if you like can be much lower, but nevertheless to them they are being just as brutal – the intent is there. Some people are emotionally brutal or physically brutal – or some people are both. And Tinker just had a different expression for his brutality. But he would be just as cruel physically as when someone else might have been abusive emotionally.

GS He also uses his brutality at times to get to the truth of things, or to test people.

SM I think that's a very strong aspect with him. It's almost as if he were scientifically testing out the boundaries of love. And I think with the gay couple, Carl and Rod, there was something that he perhaps found really very distasteful – perhaps less distasteful in that it was a gay relationship, and more the fact that it was unconditional love. And he couldn't understand how far it could go. Their relationship was so strong that it was disturbing to him – although he has the same unconditional love for Grace. He does the kindest thing he can think of which is extremely warped, in giving her a man's penis. He actually thinks he's doing her a huge service, giving her exactly what she wants. But he's destroying her and also creating an opportunity where he cannot have a resolution to his love because he is changing the woman he adores into a man. And by doing that he's disallowing himself any relationship with her – it's a place he can't go.

GS   Is that why he starts a relationship with the Woman in the dancing booth?

SM   That's interesting. He goes to see the Woman I think because it's a simple transaction. It's just guiltless sexual relief. He transposes the idea of Grace onto this woman who he can communicate with. He actually finds it very difficult to communicate with Grace, but through this third party he is able to do so.

GS   Was it decided in the production what Tinker's relationship with Grace's brother was going to be?

SM   Only really that he was going to be somebody in the regime. And also that there's a logical factor of guilt he feels to her brother, even though he's asked to die. But it was difficult to establish much of the relationship between the two because Tinker and Graham only have that brief opening scene together. The meeting of Tinker and Grace in the next scene is more important because she talks about her brother there, and Tinker's reaction is more significant as he decides there's something really interesting about her.

GS   There was a sense watching the Royal Court production that all this was taking place in some sort of late Strindbergian dreamscape. This institution had very little feel of existing in the real world.

SM   I think the script makes that happen. And I think Sarah was very keen that it was going to be a very difficult play. There was very stark dialogue, very few proper sentences and very staccato conversations. I think it was also the inability of people to express themselves. They have the need to do so but they don't have the language or vocabulary in which to achieve it properly. Everybody is tarnished and broken in some way. And this sounds pretentious, but after doing *The Taming of the Shrew* I found this to be a similarity between the two writers. What happens in both plays is that the issues are gigantic – utter extremes of emotions, but very often exercised by people who haven't got the wherewithal to express themselves coherently to one another; yet nevertheless feel what we all feel. And it's also Sarah's honesty. Her characters aren't imaginary. They're facets of herself – and she's so honest with herself that the characters all are too. Truly great writing is honest writing.

GS   This need to express strong emotion through the stark framework of the language must have been difficult to work on as actors.

SM   That was the most difficult thing to get around, and there was one scene in particular that I always found difficult, and that was the third meeting with the girl in the booth (Scene 14), because the play requires no emotion. It merely requires you to say the lines. And the connection with the characters on stage are left open for the audience to decide. But it's very difficult to do that particular scene without becoming angry and emotional because dramatically it seemed to work better. And we worked longer on that scene than any other because I tried it so many different ways and they all worked to a certain extent – but I think that's what I'd change now. I would try to find a way of doing the scene without strong emotions, because ultimately it forces the audience into thinking something that should be left up to themselves to decide. And again the actors had the problem of feeling that they hadn't anything to work with. You think it's too easy sometimes – you don't actually feel you're doing anything, but Sarah's done all the work in how the order of the scenes come about. I know that before the production she rearranged the order of the scenes to deliberately not try and tell a story, or to avoid telling a logical story.

GS   I suppose another point where you're required to show some emotion is at the end where the Woman is released from the booth and you embark on the beginnings of a relationship.

SM   That shows Tinker at his most honest and weakest. He has premature ejaculation for a start! And he says many tender things to her and he reveals himself in many respects to the Woman to be weak. And I think it's the only time you get a chink in the armour and see behind him to a certain degree. I think Tinker's a very difficult character to have sympathy for, but you do end up having a little sympathy for him, and I think that's one of the great things about the play that he has no saving grace – pardon the pun!

GS   The locale itself was something of a combination of the real and the world of dream. Did a rationale exist behind the kind of place Tinker was overseeing?

SM   I think it was similar to South America or Bosnia where they used football stadiums to incarcerate people – normal institutions which previously were used for other purposes such as a sports hall with a gymnasium, so the space becomes something different. This also comes out in costume, so Tinker's own thing was combat – that was how he expressed himself outwardly. His shell was a kind of homage to urban terrorists – that was how he liked to see himself. For the others their costumes consisted of heightened ideas of normal people – normal streetwear etcetera clashing with a completely different world.

GS   Tinker also constantly adopts these different roles. He's a drug dealer one minute, a doctor the next; he's a surgeon, an interrogator and a torturer. We don't seem to form a strong impression about him at any point in the play.

SM   Yes, it was difficult. We came to the idea that he was also incarcerated but was given certain powers within the institution. That often happens in prisons within harsh political regimes where they give someone a little bit of power and they do all the dirty work – and they feed them nonsense in order to keep them in control. Then again it's not absolutely stated so we felt there was someone up above who is higher than Tinker.

GS   Had you seen any of Sarah Kane's work before *Cleansed*?

SM   None. After I'd been given the role Sarah gave me *Blasted* and *Phaedra's Love* to read which I'm glad she did. They're completely different plays. I think *Phaedra's Love* is very funny, and *Blasted* has its moments as well. But *Blasted* is almost conventionally written while *Cleansed* isn't.

GS   Did you subsequently see *Crave* and *4.48 Psychosis*?

SM   I saw *4.48 Psychosis*. I found it very difficult to watch. I thought it was a fantastic production, and so revealing. I didn't know whether I was watching something that was literal. I hoped I wasn't, but I suspect I was.

GS   There's also the same overwhelming craving for love that Tinker also succumbs to in *Cleansed*.

SM   In one sense she talks about this figure of a doctor a great deal, and there were many doctors in that play. And one seems to have let her down very badly, and you don't know which one it was – there's no one to blame. Also there's this thing about giving up – that she's done it all and what's the point?

GS   Whereas in *Cleansed* Sarah has said that hope exists for the characters despite it appearing to end very bleakly. There certainly seems to be hope for Tinker.

SM   Yes, there certainly is hope for Tinker, although it's hope inside a disaster area as far as the audience is concerned. The world that the characters live in is so desolate and desperate that such hope wouldn't count in the normal world – but it is there.

GS   Yet Grace's last speech to me is an acceptance of defeat and descent into madness.

SM   I find it very desperate with Carl just existing as bits of a human being and in complete agony. And everything that gave him expression has been taken from him – his hands and his feet and his tongue and his genitals. He has absolutely nothing. And Grace has been given this new body of a man but it hasn't changed her life dramatically – she's just the same. Perhaps the most extraordinary thing was suddenly realising that *Cleansed* was a play about love, because at first it seems to be absolutely the opposite. It's about the extremes of emotions – about how people will do things for love, and involving people who don't seem in the least bit loving or gentle.

GS You spoke earlier about the problems of language. Was there much work done on the text is terms of breaking the language down almost to its linguistic nuts and bolts?

SM Not so much in that sense although Sarah was very particular about every word. When you do a play you ought to say exactly what the writer has written – that should be a given but it so often doesn't happen. You change one seemingly meaningless word or run some- thing on without having a full stop. And she was extremely particu- lar about that – you had to say *exactly* what was written. And I never had a problem with that. I remember coming up with an idea which I can't remember now, and asking if this was possibly what she were looking for; and it would've meant a word change like 'never' to 'ever'. And she said, 'no – it's how it's written'. And the next day she came in and said, 'well, actually we could do it the way you suggest'. And I'd gone away and thought about it and came back with the conclusion that it was fine in the first place!

GS One of the things that struck me about the production as a whole was its ambitiousness in terms of the highly technical stage design and the fact that such an experimental piece of theatre was playing on the main stage at the Royal Court.

SM I think there was no question that it was a brave decision to stage *Cleansed*. It was certainly a very difficult technical rehearsal because lots of things weren't ready until literally moments before the public saw it in the preview – the rats for instance! So we didn't get to work with the famous rats until the second or third preview. And they never really worked properly – sometimes they'd move about, but more often they wouldn't. But it was such a difficult thing to do – almost impossible. I think there's something about the designer [*Jeremy Herbert*] that makes him able to do the most amazing things. The sunflowers to me were extraordinary – using a backwards umbrella in a tube! And I remember first of all when I was reading the play thinking, 'how do you make a flower come up like that through the stage'? Not only was it beautiful but its ingenuity was breathtaking too.

GS The daffodils were equally stunning. How were they achieved?

SM There was an area of polystyrene in front of the backcloth. And they were literally tipped onto it – they were weighted and the ends of them were like darts with bits of wire inside them. They were heaviest at the wire end and so they fell like darts into this polythene.

GS   Were many of the theatrical effects worked on during rehearsals or were they fully realised beforehand?

SM   While we were rehearsing nothing was done beforehand. And it wasn't until about week two or three that we began to talk about specific effects – at least that's my impression of it. And some things took much longer to realise than others because technically they were very difficult to do.

GS   I gather *Cleansed* was not the most audience friendly of plays and sometimes got a hostile reaction.[1]

SM   God yes! We regularly got booed especially towards the end when they saw the sewed up penis on Grace. I remember one particular time – again right at the end of the performance and the audience was clapping when someone shouted out, 'boo! What's it all about?' And what I desperately wanted to do was climb down and go into the audience to find him and bring him up on stage and try to explain the play, but then I'm glad I didn't because it would've been a terrible thing to do, because I really respect that guy for making his feelings known when everyone else may be just clapping out of duty. There was another occasion when people were just uncontrollably laughing, and again I had to just try and get rid of the anger and just carry on, because when it happens during a show it's often not the real feelings of these people. In a way it's gratifying to get an effect – even if that effect is sometimes negative. I think many people came away form *Cleansed* thinking, 'what the fuck was that about. It was atrocious. It was awful'. I remember some friends of mine came to see it and they just couldn't say anything. They were friends of friends, and because they didn't know what to say they avoided the subject until my friend, who had come to see it purposely, said 'so what did you think of it?' And they just didn't know what to say.

GS   Yet, I feel that in ten years time *Cleansed* will be judged a landmark production in the Royal Court's history.

SM   Exactly. Critically we got mixed reviews. I don't think we got any appalling notices, although we got some that sat on the fence, and we got a few that were very good. And at the time I went to see a friend of mine who was working at the National Theatre. And they'd all just come off-stage for a drink and he introduced me to the other actors. And he said, 'this is Stuart and he's playing Tinker in *Cleansed*'. And they all turned round and looked at me in this patronising sympathy as if to say, 'Oh dear. Poor love'. And I was proud of it! And to

---

1   *Cleansed* played on average to 14 per cent houses.

actually have acted with Sarah when she took over for those last performances were some of the most extraordinary nights I'll ever have
in the theatre. Her delivery was just perfect. That's how we all ought
to have been doing it in – that was the way she wrote it. She couldn't
have done it in any other way just saying the lines.

AFTERWORD
Sarah Kane and theatre[1]
Edward Bond

Sarah Kane swallowed an overdose of pills. Her stomach was pumped clean in a hospital. She went home, but was taken back to hospital. There she took the laces from her shoes and hanged herself in the lavatory.

She had written four or five plays in about as many years. Press and radio violently attacked her play *Blasted*. Television did not mention it, though incidents of the sort in *Blasted* are regularly reported in TV news programmes. Television deals with events, not their meaning. It deals with 'culture' only when it can be made an anodyne consumer product.

There are two sorts of dramatists. The first sort play theatrical games with reality. Some do it badly, some well and their plays even remain interesting. The second sort of dramatists change reality. The Greeks and Shakespeare did it. Molière did it in his strangely modern, precariously balanced *Misanthrope*. Racine almost did it by confining rampaging passion in rigid structures – but passion must be released if it is to know itself. Büchner did it by seeing justice from the point of view of the scaffold. Half-way through watching *Blasted* in a small, cramped theatre, in an adequate production, I realised that reality had changed. I do not exaggerate. This century's horrors do not change reality, they merely draw its conclusions and we could go on as if we had learnt nothing from

1   This article, which has been subsequently revised by Edward Bond, originally appeared in *Theater der Zeit* May / June 1999.

them. *Blasted* changed reality because it changed the means we have of understanding ourselves. It showed us a new way in which to see reality, and when we do that reality is changed. Einstein changed natural reality – we understand it differently and so we make different bombs. Drama of the second sort changes human reality. It makes a demand on us. We must either respond to it or reject it and in doing so we define ourselves.

Drama of the second sort confronts the ultimate in human experience so that we can seek to understand what humans are and how they create humanity. In the past the ultimate was personalised. The Greeks bought their gods onto the stage. Shakespeare brought his ghosts and Jupiter. Racine depended on civic orderliness, but when the madness was too great he fled to God. Molière depended on the human. Büchner needed to enter the gap between science and romanticism, reason and imagination.

Drama shares its ultimate with religion. Religion is merely theatre claiming to be real. It does this in order to control reality more effectively. God is dead and we still live with his ghost. Faith is debased into fanaticism, superstition and diabolism because faith and reason can never again serve the same end. Is theatre also dead? If it is, the 'human' is dead.

We can no longer personalise the ultimate. No God, gods or spirits have watched over the twentieth century. The heaps of bodies are not martyred, they are the refuse of science and fanaticism. Could they be martyrs of reason? Not if drama is dead.

I was surprised to see how many of *my* characters commit suicide, often with some 'gesture' quite like Sarah Kane's shoelaces. We wear shoes to take journeys. On which journey do you hang from shoelaces in a lavatory, are cut down and burnt? It is the confrontation with the implacable.

Modern drama of the second sort must confront the implacable. It is the ultimate. It cannot be personalised as God or New Age spirit. It is not the Absurd, which merely reduces human purpose. It is not even our mortality, because that is only a tiny incident in history. It is not transcendental. It has no meaning. Its logic is absolute: 'Do *this* and *that* will follow.' And so in confronting it we are totally defined. We deny or assert our meaning. We are either corrupted by nihilism and its trivialities – or we create our humanness.

The purpose of drama is to confront the ultimate. Can our drama do this or is it corrupt? I find that my characters impose on themselves the confrontation with the implacable – as if, should I wish to avoid it, *they* will impose it on *me*. This is not paranormal, it is very simple. I began to write when great actors performed the classics in productions that had been rehearsed for two hundred years. The productions were not deadened by tradition, they were activated by our wars and revolutions and even by the triviality of most of the contemporary plays in which the actors also acted. The human still survived in the market place. Actors had not yet learnt how to trivialise the confrontation with the ultimate. Now there are even more good actors – but there are no great actors. They are not allowed to create their own epiphany. There is too much theatrical trickery and gimmickry, too great a commercial imperative. Artaud said no one can work in film without being ashamed. Television has made it worse. Television and film satirise and trivialise our lives – and increasingly trivialise our theatre. The market place has become corrupt. We no longer know what a play *is*.

Sarah Kane was a dramatist of the second sort. The confrontation with the implacable created her plays. Did she – the dramatist in her – know that she might not be able to go on confronting it in her plays? Our society and theatre are against it. We must consume to maintain the economy, to maintain the only life we bother to imagine. But the need to consume is not the desire to be human. The *desire* is the *need* to confront the implacable. It is the logic of the situation. If we do not confront it and find our humanity, it will confront us and destroy us. That is the logic of the twenty-first century.

At some time in that century everyone – alone or collectively – will confront the implacable. Without the elucidation of drama they will not know till too late – if at all – what is happening. This is not an over-grandiose claim to make for drama. We are in an age of science but our lives are saturated by the reductive, violent, sentimental, meaningless drama of the media. The media are self-important enough to want to deal with important problems, but they make them worse by trivialising them.

Sarah Kane had to confront the implacable. You can postpone the confrontation only when you are certain that at some time it will take place. Otherwise it will slip away. Everything Sarah Kane did had authority. If she thought that perhaps the confrontation could not take place in our theatre, because it is losing the understanding and the means – she could not risk waiting. Instead she staged it elsewhere. Her means to confront the implacable are death, a lavatory and shoelaces. They are her comment on the meaningless of our theatre and our lives, and on our false gods.

SELECT BIBLIOGRAPHY

Works by Sarah Kane

Blasted This version of the play is contained in a volume, *Frontline Intelligence: New Plays for the Nineties* (London, 1994), selected and introduced by Pamela Edwardes.

Blasted and *Phaedra's Love* (London, 1996). In this edition Sarah Kane made several small but significant changes to *Blasted*. These concerned cuts to the dialogue at the end and additions to stage directions indicating the changing seasons.

Skin Ten-minute film. Written summer 1995, filmed the following September, and broadcast by Channel Four on 17 June 1997. Cast: Ewen Bremner, Marcia Rose. Directed by Vincent O'Connell. Produced by Tapson Steel Films for Channel Four / British Screen.

Cleansed (London, 1998).

Crave (London, 1998).

4.48 Psychosis (London, 2000).

Sarah Kane: Complete Plays. Introduction by David Greig (London, 2001). This edition also contains the script of *Skin*. All of the plays, with the exception of *4.48 Psychosis*, underwent minor revisions by Sarah Kane shortly before her death.

The first British productions of *Blasted*, *Cleansed*, *Crave* and *4.48 Psychosis* exist as audio recordings by the British Library National Sound Archive. The recording of *Cleansed* is notable as one of the performances where Sarah Kane played the role of Grace. For details, see their catalogue:www.cadensa.bl.uk.

A performance of the first Royal Court production of *4.48 Psychosis* also exists on video and is available to view at the Theatre Museum London.

Secondary reading

Books

Ansorge, Peter, *From Liverpool to Los Angeles: On Writing for Theatre, Film and Television* (London, 1997).

Artaud, Antonin, *The Theatre and Its Double*, trans.Victor Corti (London, 1999).

Aston, Elaine and Reinelt, Janelle, *The Cambridge Companion to Modern British Women Playwrights* (Cambridge, 2000). Brief discussion of Kane's importance and her rejection of gender as female playwright.

Atkins, John, *George Orwell* (London, 1954).

Barker, Howard, *Arguments for a Theatre*, 3rd edn (Manchester, 1999).

Bate, Walter Jackson, *Coleridge* (New York, 1968).

Beauman, Sally, *The Royal Shakespeare Company: A History of Ten Decades* (Oxford, 1982).

Beckett, Samuel, *The Complete Dramatic Works* (London, 1990).

Berry, Ralph, *The Art of John Webster* (Oxford, 1972).

Blunt, Rosalind, 'Princess Diana: A Sign of the Times', in Jeffrey Richards, Scott Wilson and Linda Woodhead (eds), *Diana: The Making of a Media Saint* (London, 1999), pp. 20–39.

Boyle, A.J. (trans.), *Seneca's Phaedra* (Liverpool, 1987).

Bradley, A.C. *Shakespearean Tragedy* (London, 1967).

Bradwell, Mike (ed.), *The Bush Theatre Book: Frontline Drama 5* (London, 1997).

Braunmuller, A. and Hattaway, M. *The Cambridge Companion to English Renaissance Drama* (Cambridge, 1990).

Brecht, Bertolt, *Baal*, in *Plays 1*, trans. Peter Tegel, Ralph Manheim, John Willett and Steve Gooch (London, 1987).

Brecht, Bertolt, 'Emphasis on Sport' in John Willett (ed. and trans.), *Brecht on Theatre: The Development of an Aesthetic*, 2nd edn (London, 1992), pp. 6–9.

Brusberg-Kiermeier, Stefani, 'Re-writing Seneca: Sarah Kane's *Phaedra's Love*', in Bernard Reitz, and Alyce von Rothkirch (eds), *Crossing Borders: Intercultural Drama and Theatre at the Turn of the Millennium. Contemporary Drama in English 8* (Trier, 2001).

Camus, Albert, *The Stranger*, trans. Joseph Laredo (Harmondsworth, 1983).

Carlson, Harry, *Strindberg and the Poetry of Myth* (Berkeley and Los Angeles, 1982).

Charney, Maurice, *Titus Andronicus* (Hemel Hempstead, 1990).

Coe, Richard, *Beckett* (Edinburgh, London, 1964).

Cohn, Ruby, *Currents in Contemporary Drama* (Bloomington, 1969).

—— *Retreats From Realism in Recent English Drama* (Cambridge, 1991).

Crimp, Martin, *Attempts on her Life* (London, 1997).

Davidson, Harriet, 'Reading *The Wasteland*', in David Moody (ed.), *The Cambridge Companion to T.S. Eliot* (Cambridge, 1994).

Dollimore, Jonathan, *Radical Tragedy: Religion, Ideology and Power in the Drama of Shakespeare and his Contemporaries* (London, 1984).

Drew, Elizabeth, *T.S Eliot: The Design of his Poetry* (London, 1950).

Dromgoole, Dominic, *The Full Room: An A–Z of Contemporary Playwriting* (London, 2000). Contains a short anecdotal essay on Kane and a brief assessment of her work.

Edgar, David (ed.), *State of Play. Issue 1: Playwrights on Playwriting* (London, 1999).

Eliot, T.S., *Collected Poems 1909–1962* (London, 1974).

Esslin, Martin, *Artaud* (Glasgow, 1976).

Fassbinder, Rainer Werner, *Plays*, ed. and trans. Denis Calandra (Baltimore, 1992).

Fletcher, John, and Spurling, John, *Beckett: A Study of his Plays* (London, 1972).

Freedman, Gerald, *Titus Andronicus* (London, 1970).

Frye, Northrop, *Fools of Time: Studies*, in *Shakespearian Tragedy* (Oxford, 1967).

—— *T.S. Eliot: An Introduction* (Chicago, 1981).

Gardner, Helen, *The Art of T.S. Eliot* (London, 1949).

Gerard, Albert, *The Phaedra Syndrome: Of Shame and Grief in Drama* (Amsterdam, 1993).

Gielgud, John, *Early Stages* (London, 1953).

Gottlieb, Vera, 'Lukewarm Britain', in Colin Chambers and Vera Gottlieb (eds), *Theatre in a Cool Climate* (Oxford, 1999), pp. 201–12. A sceptical view taken on the 'New Brutalists'.

Greenblatt, Stephen, 'Fiction and Friction', in R.S. White (ed.), *New Casebooks: Twelfth Night* (Basingstoke, 1996), pp. 92–128.

Hansford, James, 'Sarah Kane', in Thomas Riggs (ed.), *Contemporary Dramatists*, 6th edn (Detroit, New York, 1999), pp. 348–9. Includes a brief synopsis and overview of the major themes and theatrical influences operating in each of the plays up to *Crave*.

Henn, T. *The Harvest of Tragedy* (London, 1956).

Hirst, David, *Edward Bond* (London, 1985).

Holdsworth, R. (ed.), *Webster: The White Devil and the Duchess of Malfi: A Casebook* (London, 1975).

Hollis, James, *Harold Pinter: The Poetics of Silence* (Illinois, 1970).

Hunter, G.K., *Dramatic Identities and Cultural Tradition: Studies in Shakespeare and his Contemporaries* (Liverpool, 1978).

Innes, Christopher, *Avant-Garde Theatre 1892–1992* (London, 1993).

Johnson, Samuel, *Johnson on Shakespeare*, Vol. II, ed. Bertrand H. Bronson (New Haven, 1968).

Kott, Jan, *Shakespeare our Contemporary*, trans. Boleslaw Taborski, rev. edn (London, 1967).

Langridge, Natasha and Stephenson, Heidi, *Rage and Reason: Women Playwrights on Playwriting* (London, 1997). Includes an interview with Sarah Kane.

Lappin, Lou, *The Art and Politics of Edward Bond* (New York, 1987).

Lesser, Wendy, *A Director Calls: Stephen Daldry and the Theatre* (London, 1997).

Lyons, Charles, *Samuel Beckett* (Basingstoke, 1983).

Mangen, Michael, *Edward Bond* (Plymouth, 1998).

Middleton, Thomas and Rowley, William, *The Changeling*, in Bryan Loughrey and Paul Taylor (eds), *Thomas Middleton: Five Plays* (Harmondsworth, 1988).

Muir, Kenneth (ed.), *King Lear: The Arden Shakespeare* (London, 1977).

Mulryne, J. 'Jacobean Drama', in *The Jacobean Theatre* (Stratford-upon-Avon, 1960).

Nightingale, Benedict, *The Future of Theatre* (London, 1998). Identifies and attempts to summarise shared themes and concerns of the young Royal Court writers of 1994–96 who are seen as a distinct movement in much the same way as the 'angry young men' of the late 1950s.

O'Brien, Conor Cruise, *Camus* (London, 1970).

Pankratz, Annette, 'Greek to Us? Appropriations of Myths in Contemporary British and Irish Drama', in *Crossing Borders: Intercultural Drama and Theatre at the Turn of the Millennium: Contemporary Drama in English 8* (Trier: 2001).

Pinnock, Winsome, 'Breaking Down the Door', in Colin Chambers and Vera Gottlieb, (eds) *Theatre in a Cool Climate* (Oxford, 1999), pp. 27–38.

Plath, Sylvia, *Collected Poems* (London, 1981).

Plunka, Gene (ed.), *Antonin Artaud and the Modern Theatre* (London, 1994).

Pope, Rob, *The English Studies Book* (London, 1998).

Roberts, Philip, *Bond on File* (London, 1985).

—— *The Royal Court and the Modern Stage* (Cambridge, 1999).

Sierz, Aleks, *In-yer-face Theatre: British Drama Today* (London, 2000). An indepth study of the new British dramatists who rose to prominence in the mid 1990s. Contains a chapter on Sarah Kane.

—— '"The Element that Most Outrages": Morality, Censorship and Sarah Kane's *Blasted*', in Edward Batley and David Bradby (eds), *Justice and Morality: Visions of Change in European Theatre* (Amsterdam, 2001).

Smith, Mal, *Antonin Artaud and his Legacy: Theatre Museum Education Pack* (London, 1999). Identifies Artaudian features in Sarah Kane's work. Includes a brief interview with Janette Smith, assistant director on the Royal Court productions of *Cleansed* and *4.48 Psychosis*.

Spiers, Ronald, 'Baal', in Siegfried Mews (ed.), *Critical Essays on Bertolt Brecht* (Boston, 1989), pp. 19–30.

Strindberg, August, *Miss Julie and Other Plays*, trans. Michael Robinson (Oxford, 1998).

Styan, J., *Modern Drama in Theory and Practice 1: Realism and Naturalism* (Cambridge, 1981).

—— *Modern Drama in Theory and Practice 2: Symbolism, Surrealism and the Absurd* (Cambridge, 1981).

Taylor, John Russell (ed.), *Look Back in Anger: A Casebook* (London, 1978).

Tonnquist, Egil, *Strindbergian Drama: Themes and Structure* (Stockholm, 1982).

Trussler, Simon, *Edward Bond* (Essex, 1976).

Voigts-Virchow, Eckart, 'Sarah Kane, a Late Modernist: Intertextuality and Montage in the Broken Images of *Crave*', in Bernhard Reitz and Heiko Stahl (eds), *What Revels Are In Hand: Assessments of Contemporary Drama in English in Honour of Wolfgang Lippke* (CDE-Studies 7. Trier, 2001).

Webster, John, *The Duchess of Malfi* (ed.), Elizabeth Brennan (London, 1983).

Wells, Stanley and Taylor, Gary (eds), *William Shakespeare: The Complete Works* (Oxford, 1988).

Williams, Helen, *T.S. Eliot: The Wasteland*, 2nd edn (London, 1979).

Williams, Raymond, *Modern Tragedy* (Stanford, 1966).

Zimmermann, Heiner, 'Theatrical Transgression in Totalitarian and Democratic Societies: Shakespeare as a Trojan Horse and the Scandal of Sarah Kane', in *Crossing Borders: Intercultural Drama and Theatre at the Turn of the Millennium. Contemporary Drama in English 8* (Trier, 2001).

Journals

Benecke, Patricia, 'Fixer, Monster und andere Traumgestalten', *Theatre heute*, July 1998, pp. 29–32.

—— 'Im weitesten Sinn', *Theater heute*, November, 1998, pp. 96–8.

Billington, Michael, 'Zwischen Triumph und Depression: Wir sind am Scheideweg', *Theater heute*, January 1997, pp. 37–40.

Engelhardt, Barbara, 'Auftritt: Wien: Blutige Rohkost', *Theater der Zeit*, March / April 1998, pp. 65–7.

Grund, Stefan, 'Sprachgewaltige Sehnsucht nach Friedfertigkeit' and 'Zerbombt'. *Theater der Zeit*, November, December 1996, pp. 86–98.

Kahle, Ulrike, 'Ein ekelerregendes Fest des Unflats? Sarah Kane: Zerbombt', *Theater heute*, November 1996, 54f.

Kralicek, Wolfgang, 'Write a Play', *Theater heute*, 4 May 1998, p. 70.

Morris, Peter, 'The Brand of Kane', *Arete*, 4 (2000), pp. 143–52. Provocative article, assessing Kane's posthumous reputation, and relating her work to a 'punk sensibility'.

Preusser, Gerhard, 'Sex gestrichen – Sprache ist Macht', *Theater heute*, June 1998, pp. 43–5.

Rebellato, Dan, 'Sarah Kane: An Appreciation', *New Theatre Quarterly*, 59 (1999), pp. 280–1. A personal tribute and assessment of her work. The article makes the point that *Cleansed* and *Crave* move away from a depiction of violence to concentrate on an examination of love, played out against a background of cruelty and despair.

Sellar, Tom, '"Truth and Dare", Sarah Kane's *Blasted*', *Theater* (1996), pp. 29–34. One of the earliest scholarly articles in which the British critical reaction to *Blasted* is discussed and closely related to Edward Bond's *Saved*.

Sierz, Aleks, 'Cool Britannia?' "In-yer-Face" Writing in the British Theatre Today', *New Theatre Quarterly*, 56 (1998), pp. 324–33. Makes an assessment of the impact and importance of writers such as Sarah Kane, Mark Ravenhill and Jez Butterworth, as well as identifying what he feels to be shared themes in their drama.

—— 'Shocking and Fumbling: Censorship and British Theatre Today', paper delivered at the European Theatre Justice and Morality International Conference at the University of London School of Advanced Study, Senate House, London, 17–19 June 1998.

Taylor, John Russell, 'British Dramatists: The New Arrivals: The Dark Fantastic', *Plays and Players*, 18 (1971), pp. 24–7.

Newspaper articles

Armitstead, Claire, 'No Pain, no Kane', *Guardian*, 29April 1998. Includes an interview with Sarah Kane in which she discusses *Cleansed* and talks about the development her work has taken in *Crave*.

Bayley, Clare, 'A Very Angry Young Woman', *Independent*, 23 January 1995. An early interview with Sarah Kane after the critical reception to *Blasted*. Kane discusses the morality underlying the play and influences on her work.

Benedict, David, 'Real Live Horror Show', *Independent*, 9 May 1998. A detailed review of *Cleansed* with an attempt to analyse some of its complex theatrical imagery.

Christopher, James, 'Rat with Hand Exits Stage Left', *Independent*, 4 May 1998. The article reviews *Cleansed* and includes an interview with director James Macdonald in which he discusses the theatricality and European sensibility which operate in Kane's work.

Egan, Caroline, 'The Playwright's Playwright', 21 September 1998, *Guardian*. Very brief 'sound-bite' interview, where Kane amongst a group of other playwrights talks about the other living dramatist she most admires – her choice is Martin Crimp. Rebecca Prichard talks about Sarah Kane's *Blasted*.

Gardner, Lyn, 'Obituary', *Guardian*, 23 February 1999.

—— 'Vicky's Odyssey', *Guardian*, 12 May. Profile and interview with the director of *Crave*, Vicky Featherstone.

Greig, David, 'Sarah Kane', *Herald*, 27 February 1999.

Hattenstone, Simon, 'A Sad Hurrah', *Guardian Weekend*, 1 July 2000. Substantial feature to coincide with the British premiere of *4.48 Psychosis*. Includes a discussion of Kane's work and personal reminiscences from friends and colleagues.

Heine, Mathias, 'Furcht und Elend der Neunziger', Die *Welt*, 26 February 1999.

Kane, Sarah, 'The Only Thing I Remember is ...' *Guardian*, 13 August 1998. Diary style article written during the Edinburgh Festival in which Kane lists memorable and formative theatrical and non-theatrical 'performances'.

—— 'Drama with Balls', *Guardian*, 20 August 1998. Diary style article written during the Edinburgh Festival. Kane writes of her frustrations about theatre when placed against other performative arts – notably football. She also talks about the rehearsal process for *Crave*.

Karasek, Hellmuth, 'Kein Skandal mehr!' *Der Tagesspiegel*, 14 December 1998.

Macdonald, James, 'They Never Got Her', *Observer Review*, 28 February 1999. Includes a personal tribute to Sarah Kane and brief assessment of her importance as dramatist prepared to use new theatrical forms.

Mortimer, John, 'Diary', *New Statesman*, 26 April 1999.

Ravenhill, Mark, 'Obituary', *Independent*, 23 February 1999.

Sierz, Aleks, 'The Short Life of Sarah Kane', *Daily Telegraph*, 27 May 2000.

—— (wrongly by-lined as Nick Smurthfield), 'Angriest of all', *The Stage*, 1 June 2000.

—— 'The Anniversary of the Death of Sarah Kane', *Real Time* 36, April / May 2000.

Stringer, Robin, 'Walk-outs at Royal Court "Atrocity" Play', *Evening Standard*, 19 January 1995.

Williams, Tessa, 'The Final Curtain', *Marie Claire*, February 2001, pp. 199–202.

Wilson, Snoo, 'Blasted metaphors', *New Statesman*, 3 February 1995.

Interviews

Machon, Josephine, Interview with Ingrid Craigie, November 1999.

Rebellato, Dan, 'Brief Encounter Platform', interview with Sarah Kane, Royal Holloway College, London, 3 November 1998.

Saunders, Graham, interview with Sarah Kane, Brixton, London, 12 June 1995.

Sierz, Aleks, interview with Greg Hobbs, 23 October 2000.
Stratton, Kate, 'Extreme measures', *Time Out*, 25 March–1 April 1998.
Tabert, Nils, 'Gespräch mit Sarah Kane', in Nils Tabert (ed.), *Playspotting: Die Londoner Theaterszene der 90er* (Reinbeck, 1998), pp 8–21.
Thielemans, Johan, interview with Sarah Kane and Vicky Featherstone, 'Rehearsing the Future': 4 European Directors Forum. Strategies for the Emerging Director in Europe (London, 1999), pp. 9–15.
Wolf, Sarah, interview with James Macdonald, The Royal Court London, 10 April 2000.

Radio and television

Discussion of *Blasted* on *Newsnight*, BBC2 Television, 19 January 1995.
Discussion of *Blasted* on *The Late Show*, BBC2 Television, 23 January 1995.
Sarah Kane and Dominic Dromgoole discuss Peter Ansorge's book *From Liverpool to Los Angeles: On Writing for Theatre, Film and Television. Kaleidoscope*, BBC Radio 4 (date unknown).
Kaleidoscope, 16 August 1999. Jude Kelly, Artistic Director of West Yorkshire Playhouse discusses the importance of *Blasted* as one of the defining plays of the 1990s.
Nightwaves, BBC Radio 3, 23 June 2000. Broadcast the day before the opening of *4.48 Psychosis*. Provides a short retrospective of Kane's work and influence as a dramatist including contributions from Edward Bond, Michael Billington, Vicky Featherstone and David Greig.

Internet sites

While there are numerous sites that make mention of Kane's work, the selection here is chosen on the basis of their indepth treatment of her work or ongoing scholarly interest.
In-Yer-Face-Theatre – http://www.inyerface-theatre.com/. Site maintained by Aleks Sierz that not only includes a section on Sarah Kane, but the other young British dramatists from the mid 1990s.
Contemporary Theatre and Drama in English – fb14.uni-mainz.de/projects/cde. Interest in Sarah Kane's work has always been keen in Germany, and this site maintains an up-to-date bibliography and details of conferences relating to Kane's work and other contemporary British dramatists.
Sarah Kane – www.iainfisher.com/kane.html. Site dedicated to Kane's work. Contains an archive, links, photographs and a discussion forum.

INDEX

Notes: Titles of works, including those by Kane, appear as subheadings under the writer's name. Footnotes are denoted by 'n'.

Absurdism, 159
Actor's Touing Company, 142n.
Ambassadors Theatre, 152
Ansorge, Peter, 51
Arden, John, 4
Aristotle's Unities, 41–2
Armitstead, Claire, 4, 10, 20
Artaud, Antonin
    Cleansed, 142
    film, 190
    Kane on, 16, 114
    theatre, 15–16, 40, 86–7, 91,
        117–18, 123, 142
Ashfield, Kate, 163–7

Barker, Howard, 15–16, 19, 23, 118,
    155
Barnes, Peter, 19
Barthes, Roland, A Lover's Discourse,
    93, 126
Beauman, Sally, 89n.

Beckett, Samuel, 54–5, 104, 106, 113,
    121, 154, 155
    Cascando, 105
    Endgame, 22, 23, 56, 59
    Kane's Blasted, 50, 54–5, 56, 58, 59,
        68
    Kane's Crave, 106–7, 132
    Waiting for Godot, 10, 54, 55, 56, 58,
        59, 68, 106–7
Benedict, David, 21
Benjamin, Walter, 139
Billington, Michael, 2, 5, 6, 29
    Kane's works
        4.48 Psychosis, 110
        Blasted, 9, 10, 11n., 40–1
        Cleansed, 12
        Crave, 102, 106, 107
        Phaedra's Love, 78
Birmingham, University of, 39
Blunt, Rosalind, 75n.
Bond, Edward, x

correspondence with Kane, 13,
    100
Kane compared to, 7, 24
Kane on, 27
Kane's *4.48 Psychosis*, 112, 116, 125
Kane's *Blasted*, 24–5, 37, 40, 48, 49,
    135, 168, 189–90
New Jacobeans, 19
on Kane, 189–91
Saved, 24, 37, 38
Boyle, A. J., 72n.
Boyle, Danny, viii
Bradley, A. C., 58, 61, 67
Brecht, Bertolt, 15, 54, 62
    Baal, 72, 73, 74, 77, 81
Brenton, Howard, 2, 19
    The Romans in Britain, 37
Bristol University, 39
Brit-pop, 6
Brook, Peter, 89, 90
Brown, Georgina, 89n.
Bruford, Bill, *Among Thugs*, 61
Büchner, Georg, 189, 190
    Woyzeck, 71, 152
        Ashfield, 166–7
        Gate Theatre, 13, 88
        illustrations, 82–3
        influence on *Cleansed*, 87, 141,
            170, 178
Bush Theatre, 11, 13, 41
Butterworth, Jez, ix, 4, 7, 34
    Mojo, 2, 3, 7, 8

Camus, Albert
    The Myth of Sisyphus, 178
    The Outsider, 73–4, 77
Carlson, Harry, 99
Cavendish, Dominic, 86
censorship, 14
Charney, Maurice, 89n.
Chekhov, Anton, 41
Churchill, Caryl, 25, 161
    Seneca's *Thyestes*, 72
Clapp, Susannah, 86n., 87, 88, 90,
    110
Clark, Alan, 79

Coe, Richard, 55n.
Cohn, Ruby, 71
Coleridge, Samuel Taylor, *The Rime of
    the Ancient Mariner*, 65–6
'Cool Britannia', viii, 4, 6
Coveney, Michael, 86n., 146
Craigie, Ingrid, 85, 103
Crimp, Martin, 25, 53n.
    Attempts on Her Life, 109, 111, 132,
        159
Crowley, Aleister, 104
Curtis, Nick, 23, 49

Daldry, Stephen, 1–3, 6, 9
Dexter, John, 161
Diana, Princess of Wales, 75
Dickens, Charles, *Our Mutual Friend*,
    104
Dollimore, John, 21
Donaghy, Pip, 64
Doughty, Louise, 23–4
Dromgoole, Dominic, 14
Duke of York's Theatre, 145, 152
Duncan-Brewster, Sharon, 105n., 85

Edgar, David, 7, 29, 39
Edinburgh Festival Fringe, 149n.
Eliot, T. S., *The Waste Land*, 100,
    102–4, 105, 107–8, 129–30,
    155
English Stage Company, 145
Euripides, 72
Evans, Daniel, 114, 124, 168–79
Existentialism, 159
Eyre, Richard, viii

Fassbinder, Rainer Werner, *Pre-
    Paradise Sorry Now*, 101, 104,
    132
Featherstone, Vicky, 102, 128–33, 162
    Crave, 100–1, 108, 115, 128–33,
        149
Fenton, James, 37n.
film, 14, 191
Ford, John, *'Tis Pity She's a Whore*,
    90n.

France, Kane's reputation in, viii

Gardner, Lyn, 5
Gate Theatre, 72, 73
    Büchner's *Woyzeck*, 13, 72, 83, 88,
        166
    Laurens' *The Three Birds*, 143
    Phaedra's Love, 13, 71, 72, 84, 149
Gerard, Albert, 75
Germany
    critical practice, 12
    Kane's reputation, viii, 134–5, 136
Gielgud, Sir John, 62
Gilliat, Penelope, 24
Godfrey, Paul, 25
Goethe, Johann Wolfgang von, *The
        Sorrows of Young Werther*,
        141–2, 178
Gottlieb, Vera, 6, 23, 54
Grassmarket Project, 18
Greenblatt, Stephen, 95
Greig, David, ix
    critical process, x
    Edinburgh Festival Fringe, 149n.
    on Kane, 117, 118, 144
        Blasted, 10, 37
        Crave, 107, 158
        non-realism, 10, 11
        political writing, 156
Gross, John, 11n.
Grosso, Nick, ix, 4, 146, 173
    Peaches, 163, 166

Hampstead Theatre, 165
Hands, Poppy, 172
Hansford, James, 15–16, 20, 32, 68
Hare, David, 2
Harkins, Cas, 84
Harvey, Marcus, 28
Hemming, Sarah, 20n.
Herbert, Jeremy
    4.48 Psychosis, 115, 124, 171
    Cleansed, 86, 115, 171, 185
Hewison, Robert, 6
Hickey, Paul Thomas, 85
Hindley, Myra, 28

Hirst, Damien, viii, 6
Holland, Patricia, 45, 52
Hollis, James, 57
Hughes, Ted, 132
humour, New Jacobeans, 19
Hunter, G. K., 61
Hytner, Nicholas, 6

Ibsen, Henrik, 41, 43, 44, 54
    A Doll's House, 43
    Ghosts, 37, 43
intertextuality, 103
Ionescu, Eugène, 159

James, Ritchie, 176
Jameson, Phil, 179
Jerwood Theatre Upstairs, 115
Jesus and Mary Chain, 17
Johnson, Samuel, 61
Jonson, Ben
    The Alchemist, 96
    Volpone, 96

Kafka, Franz, *The Trial*, 87, 141
Kane, Sarah
    4.48 Psychosis, 109–17
        comparisons with other works:
            Cleansed, 88, 113; *Crave*, 108,
            111–12, 113, 114, 115, 131,
            133; *Phaedra's Love*, 81
        conversations: Evans, 169, 170,
            171–8; Kenyon, 147, 148, 149,
            153; Macdonald, 121, 123–5,
            126–7; McQuarrie, 184; Nagy,
            159–60
        critical response, ix, 110
        discourses, 112–13
        humour, 113, 147, 153
        imagery, 124, 133, 153, 160: light,
            108, 114–15, 175, 178
        influences on, 54, 178: Crimp's
            Attempts on Her Life, 111, 174;
            Goethe's *The Sorrows of Young
            Werther*, 142, 178; Orwell's
            Nineteen Eighty-Four, 170
        non-realism, 121

rehearsals, 123–5, 169, 170, 171,
    172, 174, 177–8
setting, 115
silence, 177
stage set and effects, 115–17, 124,
    171–2, 175
themes: depression, 116, 124–5,
    126–7, 171–2; gender issues,
    30; love, 113, 125, 148, 173,
    176, 181–2, 184; religion, 174;
    self-mutilation, 113–14, 176;
    suicide, 110–11, 113, 114, 125,
    142n., 159, 178
writing of, 110, 127, 142n., 178
acting, 13, 152
Cleansed, 13, 88, 161, 177, 187
Crave, 13, 161
Blasted, 37–9
    audience, 14, 145, 158
    Bond on, 24–5, 37, 40, 48, 49,
        135, 168, 189–90
    comparisons with other works:
        Crave, 106, 107; Osborne's
        Look Back in Anger, 2;
        Phaedra's Love, 71, 73, 75, 106
    conversations: Ashfield, 163–6,
        167; Evans, 168; Kenyon, 144,
        145–7; Macdonald, 121–2,
        126; McQuarrie, 184; Nagy,
        155, 156, 157, 158, 160–1;
        Tabert, 134, 135–6, 137–8,
        139–40
    critical response, viii, 3–4, 9–12,
        23–5, 37–8, 40–1, 46, 53, 54,
        66: Germany, 134–6; Kenyon
        on, 146–7; Tinker, 11n., 96
    humour, 147
    illustration, 85
    imagery, 63–4, 160–1: baby, 66–7;
        compromises over, 126;
        disease, 43; door, 56–8; rain,
        17, 20, 22
    impact, 4, 5, 69–70, 117, 188–9:
        New Brutalism, 8
    influences on, ix, 54–70, 93:
        Barker, 155; Beckett's Waiting

        for Godot, 54–5, 56, 58, 59, 68;
        Bosnian war, 20, 26, 27–8,
        38–9, 41, 48, 53, 94, 122, 126,
        147; Jacobeanism, 19;
        Shakespeare's King Lear, 54,
        58–63, 67–8
Jacobeanism, 20–1, 23, 25
minimalism, 44, 50
morality, 27, 28
non-realism, 88, 121, 158
productions: Birmingham, 33,
    39, 42, 45, 46–7, 52, 57–8, 69,
    145; Brussels, 67, 137;
    Düsseldorf, 135; Hamburg, 26,
    33, 122, 134, 136, 138, 166;
    Vienna, 136
rehearsals, 42, 50, 63–4, 164, 166
and Seneca's tragedies, 72
setting, 49, 115
stage set and effects, 41–2
structure, 40–51
themes, 69: death, 47; gender
    issues, 30, 31, 32–3, 74;
    honesty, 33; love, 92, 125;
    nationalism, 51–4; rape, 45,
    46–8, 77, 157; religion, 22–3,
    60, 64, 78, 166; sex, 31, 77, 138,
    166; suicide, 59; violence, 9,
    19–20, 23–8, 44–8, 89, 122, 138
translation, 139–40
writing of, 44, 147
Cleansed, 86–99
    acting role of Kane, 13, 88, 161,
        177
    audience, 145, 152, 159, 186
    comparisons with other works:
        4.48 Psychosis, 88, 113; Blasted,
        106; Crave, 88, 106; Phaedra's
        Love, 81, 88, 99, 106;
        Shakespeare's The Taming of
        the Shrew, 182
    conversations: Evans, 168, 169,
        170–1, 172, 174, 177, 178;
        Kenyon, 145, 148, 151–2;
        Macdonald, 121–3, 126;
        McQuarrie, 180–7; Nagy, 156,

157, 159; Tabert, 134, 135, 136,
    138–41, 142
costume, 183
critical response, 12, 88–9, 90,
    102, 135, 186
Duke of York's Theatre, 145
imagery, 16, 20, 88–90, 122, 152:
    norms, 94–5; ring, 97–8
influences on, ix, 87, 141, 169:
    Büchner's *Woyzeck*, 87, 141,
    170, 178; Holocaust, 93–4,
    126; Orwell's *Nineteen Eighty-
    Four*, 96–7, 170; Shakespeare's
    Twelfth Night, 95, 96, 169, 178;
    Strindberg's *The Ghost Sonata*,
    94, 99
Jacobeanism, 19, 20, 21, 90–1, 96,
    97
minimalism, 88, 171, 180
non-realism, 8, 87, 88, 121, 123
rehearsals, 169, 170–1, 178,
    180–1, 185, 186
setting, 87, 94, 115, 152, 183
theatrical medium, 13–14, 87:
    stage set and effects, 86,
    115–16, 124, 141, 160, 170,
    171, 181, 185–6
themes: gender issues, 30, 31;
    honesty, 33–4; love, 33–4,
    92–3, 96–9, 108, 148, 173, 185;
    sex, 31; violence, 88–90, 92,
    122–3, 180–1
translation, 139–40
writing of, 101, 151, 170–1, 178
Zadek's production, 134, 136,
    141, 170
Crave, 99, 100–8
acting role of Kane, 13, 161, 187
audience, 158–9
comparisons with other works:
    4.48 Psychosis, 108, 111–12,
    113, 114, 115, 131, 133;
    Beckett's *Waiting for Godot*,
    106–7, 132; *Blasted*, 105–6;
    Life, 111, 132, 174; *Phaedra's
    Love*, 81

conversations: Evans, 174, 176,
    177–8; Featherstone, 128–31;
    Kenyon, 148–9; Nagy, 155,
    158–60, 162; Tabert, 135, 137,
    142
critical response, 102
German productions, 135, 137
illustration, 85
imagery, 160
influences on, 104–5: Eliot's *The
    Waste Land*, 102–4, 105,
    107–8, 129–30, 155
minimalism, 107
New Brutalism, 7, 8
non-realism, 12, 102, 121
rehearsals, 129, 130, 133, 174
rhythm, 101–2, 106–7, 129,
    130–1, 133
setting, 132–3, 158
theatrical medium, 17, 106,
    131–2
themes: gender issues, 30, 31, 32;
    love, 107, 108; violence,
    absence of, 108, 135
writing of, 101–2, 127, 128–9,
    149, 178
critical practice, 11–12, 46
death, ix, 135, 153, 189, 190, 191
depression, 73, 91
directing, 152
    Büchner's *Woyzeck*, 13, 88, 152,
        161
    Phaedra's Love, 13, 71, 80, 152–3,
        161
education, 39
gender issues, 29–34
honesty, 148, 182
humour, 125
illustrations, iii, 82–3
imagery, 16, 46, 50, 126, 143, 160–1
influence of, viii, 117, 126, 138,
    143–4
Jacobeanism and Calvinism, ix,
    18–23, 173
love, 92, 125, 148, 156–7
monologues, 149n., 150

morality, 23–9
New Brutalism, 7–8
non-realism, 8–12, 121, 137
Phaedra's Love, 71–81
  audience, 80–1
  comparisons with other works:
    4.48 Psychosis, 81; *Blasted*, 71,
    73, 75, 106; *Cleansed*, 81, 88,
    99, 106; *Crave*, 81, 106
  conversations: Evans, 170;
    Kenyon, 143, 144, 149, 152–3;
    Macdonald, 122; McQuarrie,
    184; Nagy, 160, 161; Tabert,
    136, 138, 139
  critical response, 78
  directing role of Kane, 13, 71, 80,
    152–3, 161
  Gate Theatre, 13, 71, 72, 84, 149
  German production, 136
  humour, 78, 81
  illustrations, 84
  imagery, 20
  Jacobeanism, 21, 80
  non-realism, 88
  theatrical medium, 17: stage set
    and effects, 160, 170
  themes, 72–3: death, 77–8, 81;
    depression, 73, 78; gender
    issues, 30, 31, 33, 74–5;
    honesty, 33, 73–4, 76, 77,
    79–80; love, 76, 173; rape, 77,
    78; religion, 78–9; sex, 31,
    74–7; violence, 80
  translation, 139
poetry, 155
religious faith, 22–3, 174
reputation, viii, 134–5, 136
Romanticism, 64
Skin, x, 13, 88, 110, 150, 176
suicide, ix, 135, 153, 189, 190, 191
theatrical medium, 12–18, 150, 161
  audience, 17, 18, 144–5, 161
unfinished projects, 150–1
violence, 23–9, 135
writing process, 1, 147
Kane, Simon, 104, 130, 145, 171, 179

Keats, John, 64
Kelly, Sam, 146
Kelvedon, Marie (Kane's pseudonym),
  102, 129, 148–9
Kenyon, Mel, 143–53
  Kane's *4.48 Psychosis*, 110, 117,
    142n.
  Kane's *Blasted*, 39, 40
Kott, Jan, 59
Kretzmer, Herbert, 24

Ladyboys of Bangkok, The, 17
Langridge, Natasha, 29
Lappin, Lou, 61
Laurens, Joanna, *The Three Birds*, 143
Lepage, Robert, 175
Lesser, Wendy, 2–3
Letts, Tracy, *Killer Joe*, 11
Lewis, C. S., *The Silver Chair*, 178

Macdonald, James
  Grosso's *Peaches*, 163
  Kane's work
    4.48 Psychosis, 121, 123–5, 126–7,
     153, 174, 175
    association with, 144, 162
    Blasted, 3, 121–2: Ashfield on,
     163; Kenyon on, 146; rain, 50;
     religion, 166n.; reputation, 4
    Cleansed, 121–2: imagery, 88;
     love, 92; non-realism, 8–9,
     170; rehearsals, 169; violence,
     89
  on Kane, 22, 117, 121–7
  Shepard's *Simpatico*, 3
Major, John, 85
Mamet, David, 29–30
Mandela, Nelson, 170
Marlowe, Christopher, *Edward II*, 90
Marlowe, Sam, 19n.
Maudesley Hospital, 172
McInnes, Jo, 173, 174
McQuarrie, Stuart, 169, 180–7
Middleton, Thomas, 20
Molière, 190
  Misanthrope, 189

Morley, Sheridan, 88n.
Morris, Tom, 5
Morrison, Richard, 2, 11n.
Motton, Gregory, 25
Muir, Kenneth, 58

Nagy, Phyllis, 154–62
  Disappeared, 161
  Never Land, 161
  The Strip, 10
Nasa Theatre, 17
National Theatre, 160
Natural Born Killers, 23
Naturalism, 41, 42
Neilson, Anthony, *Penetrator*, 5
New Brutalism, 4–8, 23, 166
New Dramatists, 101
New Jacobeans, 19
Nightingale, Benedict, 1–2, 5–6, 7, 18

Oakes, Meredith, 25
O'Connell, Vincent, 149n.
Orton, Joe, 164
Orwell, George, *Nineteen Eighty-Four*,
    30–1, 87, 92, 96–7, 141, 170
Osborne, John, 1, 2
  Look Back in Anger, 51
    critical response, 9, 10
    impact, 1, 2, 3, 4, 69, 117
  The Entertainer, 51
Ostermeier, Thomas, 137
Owen, Wilfred, 64

Paines Plough, 13, 100, 128, 149
  Crave, 102, 148–9
  illustration, 85
Penhall, Joe, 4, 146, 173
  Pale Horse, 5
Peter, John, 23, 38, 90–1
Philippou, Nick, 142n.
Pinter, Harold, 2
  Kane compared to, 7, 54, 56
  Kane's *Blasted*, 25, 54, 56
  The Birthday Party, 10
  The Dumb Waiter, 56
  The Room, 57

Plath, Sylvia
  Edge, 110
  The Bell Jar, 178
Plessen, Elisabeth, 139
Potter, Dennis, 14
Potter, Madeleine, 174, 177
Presley, Elvis, 74
Prichard, Rebecca, viii, 10, 129, 157
  gender issues, 29–30
  New Brutalism, 4
Priestley, J. B., *An Inspector Calls*, 2
pseudonym (Marie Kelvedon), 102,
    129, 148–9
Pulp Fiction, 23

Racine, Jean, 55, 189, 191
  Phèdre, 72, 75
radio, 150
Radley, Virginia, 65
Ravenhill, Mark, viii, 157, 173
  gender issues, 29, 34
  influence of, 138
  Kane's *Blasted*, 55
  New Brutalism, 4
  on Kane, 19
  Paines Plough, 149
  Shopping and Fucking, 4, 5, 8, 166
Rebellato, Dan, 98, 112
religion and drama, connections
    between, 190
Reservoir Dogs, 23
Rickson, Ian, 3, 152
Ridley, Philip, *Ghost from a Perfect
    Place*, 5
Riviere, Jacques, 123
Rodenburg, Patsy, 177
Royal Court Theatre
  Bond's *Saved*, 24
  Butterworth's *Mojo*, 7
  Daldry, 2–3
  Kane's works, 12, 13, 149, 150
    4.48 Psychosis, 113, 114, 116
    Blasted, viii, 2, 3, 39, 69: Ashfield
      on, 165–6; audience response,
      14; compromises, 126; critical
      response, 9, 11; death and

resurrection of Ian, 63–4;
impact, 5; Kenyon on, 145–6;
rehearsals, 50; reputation, 4
Cleansed, 86, 91, 145, 151–2, 171,
182, 185, 186
Crave, 100
season, 144n.
Macdonald, *see* Macdonald, James
non-realism, 9
playwright's evening, 173
Prichard, 129
Ravenhill's *Shopping and Fucking*, 4
violence, 23
Royal Shakespeare Company (RSC),
151
Rylance, Mark, 6

Saatchi *Sensation* exhibition, 28
Saville, Jenny, 6
Schauspiel, Bonn, 136
Schmidt, Leah, 146
Schreidman, Edwin, *The Suicidal
Mind*, 178
Seneca
Phaedra, 21, 71, 72–4, 75–8, 80
Thyestes, 72
Shakespeare, William, 154, 155, 190,
191
As You Like It, 97
A Winter's Tale, 10, 160
Kane's *Blasted*, 19–20, 21, 54, 58–62,
67–8
Kane's *Cleansed*, 20, 87, 95, 96, 169,
178
King Lear, ix, 21, 54, 58–63, 66,
67–8, 161
Macbeth, 6
Merchant of Venice, 97
Much Ado About Nothing, 97
Romeo and Juliet, 173
The Taming of the Shrew, 182
Titus Andronicus, 89, 90
Twelfth Night, 86, 87, 95, 96, 169,
178
Shannon, Michael, 82, 166
Shepard, Sam, *Simpatico*, 3

Sierz, Aleks, 5, 7, 8, 34
Kane's *Blasted*, 4, 63
Sion, Georgina, 132
Smith, Janette, 91
Sore Throats Theatre Company, 149n.
Sphinx Theatre, 151
Stafford-Clarke, Max, 161
Stephenson, Heidi, 29
Stoppard, Tom, 2
Strindberg, August, 95, 182
The Ghost Sonata, 87, 94, 99, 141
Sylvester, Suzan, 13, 88

Tabert, Nils, 118, 134–42
Tarantino, Quentin, 25–6, 138
Taylor, John Russell, 19
Taylor, Paul, 3, 23, 30, 92, 146
television, 14, 150–1, 189, 191
Terfel, Bryn, 6
Theatre Museum, 123
Theatre of Ennui, 34
Tinker, Jack, 11n., 37, 96
total theatre, 16, 123
Trainspotting, viii, 8
Traverse Theatre, 100
Tynan, Kenneth, 9

Upton, Judy, 146
Ashes and Sand, 4

violence
New Brutalism, 4–8, 23
New Jacobeans, 19

Watson, Robert, 21
Webster, John, 20, 21, 154
The Duchess of Malfi, 20, 21, 97
Weller, Jeremy, *Mad*, 18
Wesker, Arnold, 4, 51, 161
The Kitchen, 2
Whiteread, Rachel, 6
Wigglesworth, Mark, 6
Williams, Alan, 85
Williams, Phillipa, 84
Wolpert, Louis, 172
Anatomy of Despair, 179

Wright, Nicholas, viii

Wurtzel, Elizabeth
   Prozac Nation, 179

Wynne, Michael, 4

Zadek, Peter, 134, 136, 139, 141